W9-CSP-667

Sport and Society

Series Editors
Benjamin G. Rader
Randy Roberts

*A list of books in the series appears
at the end of this volume.*

SANDLOT SEASONS

Sport in Black Pittsburgh

Rob Ruck

SANDLOT SEASONS

Sport in Black Pittsburgh

University of Illinois Press

Urbana and Chicago

For Carl and Elaine

Illini Books edition, 1993
© 1987, 1993 by the Board of Trustees of the University of Illinois
Manufactured in the United States of America
P 5 4 3 2 1
This book is printed on acid-free paper.

Library of Congress Cataloging-in-Publication Data

Ruck, Rob, 1950–
Sandlot seasons : sport in black Pittsburgh / Rob Ruck.—Illini
Books ed.

(Sport and society)
Originally published: Urbana : University of Illinois Press, 1987.
Includes bibliographical references (p.   ) and index.
ISBN 0-252-06342-2
1. Sports—Pennsylvania—Pittsburgh—History.
2. Afro-American athletes—Pennsylvania—Pittsburgh—History.
3. Afro-American baseball players—Pennsylvania—Pittsburgh—
History.   I. Title.   II. Series.
[GV584.5.P57R83   1993]
796'.09748—dc20   92-46304
                                                                          CIP

Contents

Preface to the Paperback Edition

"I loved the game. I played it with all my heart," the Rev. Harold Tinker recalls with a faint smile as he sits in the sanctuary of Central Baptist Church in Pittsburgh. "I ran over hills, I ran into fences, I dove into pigpens. I'll never forget that. OOOOHHH! I can smell it now."[1]

It's been almost seventy years since Harold Tinker plunged headfirst into a pigpen on the outskirts of Coraopolis as captain of the Pittsburgh Crawfords. Yet few days go by for the now eighty-eight-year-old preacher without some reminder of those seasons when the Crawfords were on their way to becoming the best Negro League ball club ever assembled and Pittsburgh was the center of black baseball in the Americas.

The threads of Harold Tinker's sporting past are woven into the fabric of the Hill, the black Pittsburgh neighborhood in which he has resided since migrating from Birmingham as a boy. In the last few years, many others have joined him in recalling a once overlooked part of our nation's past.

For over half a century baseball in the United States was divided by race. But on one side of the color line drawn by segregation, black America built a baseball world of its own. From the 1920s through the 1940s the Negro Leagues flourished as teams like the Kansas City Monarchs, the Newark Eagles, and the Chicago American Giants barnstormed their way into baseball history. "When you talk about the Negro Leagues," explains Homestead native Mal Goode, the first African-American ever to work as a national television news correspondent, "you want to remember that, first, you saw skilled baseball way ahead of its times—fellows who should have been in the major leagues, you saw that. . . . You have to recall some of those plays! You have to see that ball hit by Josh Gibson over Greenlee Field and the ball falling down on the boulevard, probably striking somebody's car. . . . You have to see Satchel Paige say to a fellow, 'I'm gonna strike you out, boy,' and strike him out."[2]

With Cool Papa Bell flying around the base paths, Josh Gibson drawing accolades as the black Babe Ruth, and Satchel Paige walking the bases loaded, telling his fielders to sit down, and then striking out the side, black baseball's reputation spread across the nation and into the Caribbean, where the best Negro Leaguers competed each winter. Paige and Gibson became mythic figures, heroes who could beat white America at its own game. As the black press and word-of-mouth told and retold tales of their exploits, baseball became much more than a game to black America.

In black baseball, the writer John Edgar Wideman observes, the best black athletes not only "put on a good show" competing against each other but "beat the stuffing" out of their white contemporaries. Even when a black team didn't, it could "produce, in the folk, stories that are better than winning, in which the exploits get exaggerated and fabled." According to Wideman, "All that was very important, particularly at a time in America when race relations were at their nadir."[3] And no town better captured the athletic brilliance and social import of black baseball than Pittsburgh, headquarters of the Negro National League and home to the Pittsburgh Crawfords and the Homestead Grays. Seven of the eleven Negro Leaguers elected to the Hall of Fame played for one or both of these two franchises, which combined for over a dozen league championships.

Black Pittsburgh, like black America, looked to itself for sport in the early twentieth century. Racial reaction in the 1890s had driven off the field the score of African-Americans playing integrated professional ball. So the black community looked mostly to the sandlots, where teams like the Grays and the Crawfords began before evolving into professional ball clubs with national constituencies. During the 1930s and 1940s, these clubs were a part of the Negro National League, founded by Hall of Famer Rube Foster in 1920. What the Grays and the Crawfords meant to Pittsburgh, the Monarchs signified to Kansas City, the Eagles to Newark, the Elite Giants to Baltimore, and a dozen other black teams to their respective cities. Collectively, these clubs and their sandlot counterparts contributed a sense of cohesion to black communities after the disruptive impact of the World War I–era northward migrations. They helped define the consciousness of a people and offered a bridge to white America at a time when the major leagues and much else in society were still off-limits.

"Sport was segregated in those days," Mal Goode recalls, "but when you found blacks were playing white teams, our pride was showing. It had to be. There was so much negative living that we had to do, over which we had no control." Pointing out that few blacks held any authority until the civil rights movement, Goode concludes, "Anything that we could hang onto from the standpoint of pride, it was there, and it showed."[4]

John Edgar Wideman, who grew up in Homewood, a mostly black Pittsburgh neighborhood about which he has written a trio of novels, found sport was central to his youth, as it had been for Goode forty years earlier. "Sports in the '20s and '30s and '40s was probably most simply a manhood rite. It was an area in which black men could exert some control," Wideman offers. "When I grew up, all the talk was about sports. Nobody ever said, 'Here, now, we're going to discuss the possibilities of manhood and realizing ourselves in this culture,' but that was the subtheme, that was the hidden agenda all the time." Wideman listened to his elders in the barbershops and on the street corners. "What they talked about was not deals on the market or jobs or selling cars—they talked about hitting a home run or stealing a base. That was entree. You had to have that sports knowledge or sports ability to prove yourself. So behind every black man was the archetypal athlete."[5]

Wideman's contemporary, the playwright August Wilson, made that archetypal athlete into Troy Maxson, the central protagonist in *Fences*, Wilson's Pulitzer Prize–winning play set on Pittsburgh's Hill in the 1950s. Maxson, a former Negro League star now working as a garbageman, remains bitter about never having had the chance to play in the major leagues. "Troy Maxson is a composite," Wilson explains one spring afternoon in a mostly deserted Pittsburgh Public Theatre. "He stands for all of the guys, whether they were baseball players or not, who were denied opportunity . . . and what that does to people. It was an opportunity to show how the deprivation of possibility has an effect on a person's life and how they deal with their family."[6]

But exclusion, Wilson argues, was the impetus for African-

Americans to create their own community: "If you are all together standing outside the doors of white American society and
you cannot participate in this society, then there is a certain
strengthening in who you are as a people." He continues, "If
you take black baseball, the owners of the teams were black, the
community had something to do on a Saturday or Sunday afternoon. . . . You see all these economic things belonging to the
people. More importantly, though, you had your own thing and
it gave you a sense of belonging."[7] That sense of belonging occurred wherever black neighborhoods fielded local teams. On a
citywide basis, it happened when teams representing different
cities clashed in Negro League contests. For black America, it
took place whenever black teams played white teams, whether
on the sandlots, during postseason barnstorming tours of Negro
and major leaguers, or in the Caribbean.

Black Pittsburgh was unique in that it had two Negro League
teams, both owned by African-Americans. During the 1930s,
the Pittsburgh Crawfords boasted a lineup with five future Hall
of Famers and the finest black-owned stadium in the country,
while their crosstown rivals, the Homestead Grays, created a
dynasty that won nine consecutive pennants. "Coming to Pittsburgh was a big thrill," Hall of Famer Monte Irvin recounts as
he dines at a restaurant that had been the train station where the
former Newark Eagle star and his teammates disembarked
when they came to the city in earlier years. "If you had a four-
game series, the fact that you could win one game was really
something! You were lucky. You see, the Pittsburgh Crawfords
and the Homestead Grays, they dominated baseball at that
time."[8]

Irvin considers the 1930s Crawfords black baseball's answer
to the 1927 Yankees of Ruth and Gehrig. The baseball historian
John Holway weighs in for the Homestead Grays. "Oh! They
had a Hall of Fame team," Holway exclaims. "They had Oscar
Charleston, perhaps the greatest black player of all time, who'd
been a terrific centerfielder, compared to Tris Speaker in the
field. Some people called him the black Ty Cobb and others said
'No-no! Cobb is the white Oscar Charleston." Holway also
notes, "They had Smokey Joe Williams—a great ballplayer. He
was half black, half Indian, six foot three or so, and he had an

amazing record against white major league stars of twenty-one victories and seven defeats. Of course, they played each other frequently in October. He's beaten Walter Johnson 1–0. He's beaten Grover Alexander. He beat Chief Bender, Rube Marquard, Waite Hoyt, all of whom are in the Hall of Fame. Smokey Joe is not yet a Hall of Famer and he very well ought to be."[9]

Clarence Bruce, who played for the Grays during the 1940s, points out, "We didn't just play and think we were inferior. We thought we were great ballplayers and I think we walked with that air. When we walked into a town, we held our heads high. We knew we were great players. And the fans knew it. I think the white fans knew it."[10] Certainly the fans and the players in Pittsburgh and in Washington, D.C., where the Grays played three times a week at Griffith Stadium, knew it.

The Grays first baseman, Buck Leonard, recounts how Washington Senators owner Clark Griffith invited him and Josh Gibson into his office after a Negro League game in 1938 and asked if they would like to play major league baseball. "We said, 'We like it fine.' 'Do you think you can play major league baseball?' We said, 'We will try.' 'Do you think you could hit major league pitchers?' 'Well, we could hit some of them and some of them we couldn't.' 'Well,' he said now, 'the reason why we haven't got you colored baseball players on the team, the time hasn't come for you fellas to get on the team. The time hasn't come for you to be integrated.'"[11]

But in the wake of World War II, the time did come. In October 1945, Brooklyn Dodger president Branch Rickey made baseball history when he signed Kansas City Monarch shortstop Jack Roosevelt Robinson to a contract with the Dodgers' Montreal farmclub. All eyes turned to Robinson, who played a season in the minors before debuting with the Dodgers in April 1947.

"I wanted to be like Jackie Robinson—as good as Jackie Robinson." Pittsburgh city councilman Jake Milliones laughs as he described his youth. "You know, Jackie Robinson was pigeon-toed, and I can remember as a kid running pigeon-toed, although I wasn't. But you wanted to be Jackie Robinson so you ran pigeon-toed."[12] Massachusetts judge Norris Coleman, with whom I began this study in the late 1970s, remembers his mother encouraging her children to "be a Jackie Robinson."[13]

Robinson also was a cause for some concern. "Jackie Robinson was a vexed figure for me," John Edgar Wideman admits. "One thing you were taught is not to put your behind out there too visibly. That was a no-no. You understood that you could get in trouble by having attention called to yourself. So someone like Jackie Robinson was potentially a troublemaker and that was scary. . . . In my heart and soul I was rooting for him, but he was worrisome as well as a hero, as well as somebody who was opening up vistas and possibilities."[14]

Baseball's great experiment, as Jules Tygiel titled his wonderful account of Robinson crossing the color line, was a resounding success. Jackie Robinson, Roy Campanella, Monte Irvin, Willie Mays, and the other blacks in the vanguard of integration proved their worth on the field. Their presence was felt off the field, too, opening other possibilities for black America. But that success, long overdue and welcome as it was, proved costly. Although some Negro Leaguers found themselves in the major leagues, for most of them integration came too late. Harold Tinker shakes his head at the fate of Josh Gibson, considered black baseball's best by Monte Irvin and others. "Josh never got that opportunity," Tinker says, before contrasting Gibson with Baltimore Elite Giant and later Brooklyn Dodger catcher Roy Campanella, who set the standard for excellence at his position in the National League during the 1950s. "Campanella couldn't have held Josh's glove, and we went crazy over Campanella. Campanella used to sit on his haunches and throw 'em out, but he couldn't throw 'em out like Josh could. And I know Campanella hit home runs, but he never hit home runs like Josh. And all he needed was the chance to do it in the majors. He would have been something. I believe that." With a glance at the church around him, Tinker concludes, "And I'm sitting on holy ground right now and I sure wouldn't say it if I didn't believe it."[15]

Integration destroyed the Negro Leagues within a matter of years as the majors took the best young black players, the attention of the black press, and the paying black customers. "The real significance of the Jackie Robinson revolution," argues John Holway, "was that it got the black owners and the black fans out. Now the great black players played for white owners. Now the great black players played for white fans. They entertained whites. They used to entertain blacks. Now if you go to the game, you very rarely see a black in the grandstand."[16]

Mal Goode compares baseball's integration to the integration of the public schools. The baseball owners could see that the game's integration "was going into other areas of life. . . . We gained something, but we lost something too. But what we gained was the greater. We got our self-respect, and you have to be black to understand what that meant."[17]

John Edgar Wideman also draws comparisons between baseball's integration and that of other parts of society. "I think a lot was lost when the Negro Leagues went belly up," Wideman reasons. "I think a lot was lost when the black colleges began to lose students and funds. After all, this is supposed to be a culture, a society of diversity. And losing institutions that have that long a life and play that crucial a role in the community . . . it's very worrisome. That is some measure of what was lost. What was contained in those institutions was not simply a black version of what white people were doing, but the game was played differently. . . . Those schools had their own character . . . reflective of long-lasting, deep-seated parts of Afro-American culture. And so rather than having those institutions change the total picture, change what we all do, we lost them, and that to me continues to be a great loss. That's not what integration is supposed to be about."[18]

Like Wideman, August Wilson stresses the significance of the community defining and controlling its sporting life. "This was our thing and I think it's important. If you transfer that over into the community, we have our everything—until integration—and then we don't have our nothing."[19] Monte Irvin also acknowledges some loss. "It didn't hit me until later on that we were living in a special era. In other words, we had provided a form of entertainment for a group of people who were downtrodden, who had no hope, who didn't get much encouragement. But then on a Saturday or a Sunday or a Tuesday night,

they could come out to the ballpark and see some guy that could
play baseball very well and that would give them hope. And say,
well, at least somebody is making it."[20]

* * *

I began the study of sport in black Pittsburgh when I was a
doctoral student in history at the University of Pittsburgh. My
investigations led to this book, first published in 1987. Before its
completion, I began what became a four-year effort to persuade
the Pittsburgh Pirates to honor these men and their teams while
some of them were still alive to appreciate it.

After the Pirates were bought by a unique city-corporate
coalition in 1986, the club became receptive to remembering
black baseball's legacy in Pittsburgh. In September 1988, the
Pirates celebrated the fortieth anniversary of the 1948 Negro
League World Series, the last ever played, which was won by the
Homestead Grays. The *New York Times* and the *Wall Street
Journal* covered the night, as the Pirates presented a plaque honoring the teams to the city (other major league clubs held similar
events in subsequent years). Then commissioner of baseball
A. Bartlett Giamatti told my friend and former college room-
mate Doron Levin, who was covering the event for the *Times*,
"We must never lose sight of our history, insofar as it is ugly,
never to repeat it, and insofar as it is glorious, to cherish it."[21]

As survivors from the Grays and the Crawfords stood in the
infield that balmy September evening, I had a sense of completion. I could never have written this book without the efforts of
these men and women and many more like them. While several
of those I had interviewed did not live to witness the tribute, at
least—and at last—their sporting legacy was acknowledged. I
felt as if I had paid off my debts.

I plunged into research for a book about baseball in the Caribbean, which led me to San Pedro de Macoris, the sport's
mecca in the Dominican Republic, and a score of other Caribbean and Central American baseball venues. I found that the
roles that sport played in the Caribbean bore many similarities
to those it played in black Pittsburgh. I also learned more about

the Caribbean's role as the first international and interracial setting for the game.

The sense of closure over the end of the Negro League project did not last for long. The following summer, I was assisting Kazuo Sayama, a friend and colleague, who had led a Japanese television crew to Pittsburgh to make a documentary about the Negro Leagues and their effect on Japanese baseball. They were interviewing Harold Tinker and Fuzzy Walton at Ammon Field on the Hill when some young boys asked me what the Japanese were doing in Pittsburgh's principal ghetto on a hot August afternoon. When I responded that they were asking about the old Negro League teams, about Josh Gibson and Cool Papa Bell, the boys did not recognize the names. When I said that Gibson and Bell had played baseball before Jackie Robinson, they asked, "Who's Jackie Robinson?"

I can't say that I was surprised. But the incident drove home the reality that if the memory and meaning of sport in black America prior to integration were to be preserved, it was going to take something more than a book. I had already seen that a set of baseball cards written for the Pirates' celebration reached more people than my scholarly efforts. I decided to see if I could make a television documentary about these teams and what they meant.

I have spent most of the four years since that decision working with Molly Youngling on *Kings on the Hill: Baseball's Forgotten Men* (San Pedro Productions, Ltd.). The project afforded me the chance to revisit some of those who had made this book possible and to meet others. That's how I came to talk with Mal Goode, John Edgar Wideman, August Wilson, Clarence Bruce, Monte Irvin, and John Holway, and to continue my friendship with Harold Tinker. I only wish I could have had their insights to guide me when I was first tackling this subject.

The Negro Leagues are much more a part of the historical landscape these days than when I began my research in the late 1970s. A legion of scholars, writers, and memorabilia-makers ensures that they are no longer baseball's forgotten men. If I may offer a benediction to this paperback edition, allow me to quote Harold Tinker: "We really were the kings on the Hill—no one like them. God bless them. God rest. But you know, it brings back a lot of glorious memories to think the way we came up from nothing to be somebody, respected by both white and black."[22]

Notes

1. Interview with Harold Tinker, 8/31/90, Pittsburgh.
2. Interview with Mal Goode, 2/23/91, Pittsburgh.
3. Interview with John Edgar Wideman, 5/9/91, Pittsburgh.
4. Interview with Mal Goode, 2/23/91.
5. Interview with John Edgar Wideman, 5/9/91.
6. Interview with August Wilson, 3/19/91, Pittsburgh.
7. Ibid.
8. Interview with Monte Irvin, 11/4/91, Pittsburgh.
9. Interview with John Holway, 9/2/90, Pittsburgh.
10. Interview with Clarence Bruce, 8/8/89, Pittsburgh.
11. Interview with Buck Leonard, 11/16/91, Rocky Mount, N.C.
12. Interview with Jake Milliones, 11/18/91, Pittsburgh.
13. Interview with Norris Coleman, 11/18/91, Pittsburgh.
14. Interview with John Edgar Wideman, 5/9/91.
15. Interview with Harold Tinker, 8/31/90.
16. Interview with John Holway, 9/2/90.
17. Interview with Mal Goode, 2/23/91.
18. Interview with John Edgar Wideman, 5/9/91.
19. Interview with August Wilson, 3/19/91.
20. Interview with Monte Irvin, 11/4/91.
21. Doron P. Levin, "Pittsburgh Recalls a Neglected Title," *New York Times,* 9/12/88.
22. Interview with Harold Tinker, 8/31/90.

Acknowledgments

The genesis of this piece came on a late summer's run with Norris Coleman in 1978. At a bend in the Schenley Park trail that overlooks a now-abandoned steel mill along the Mononga-hela River, Norris began wondering aloud about Pittsburgh's old black baseball clubs, a subject about which we both knew very little. A stop at the library later revealed that the historical record was just as scanty, and we decided to see if we could add to it. We approached David Montgomery, a historian at the University of Pittsburgh, to co-sponsor a grant application to the National Endowment for the Humanities. He agreed and the NEH did, too, enabling us to conduct interviews with men and women who remembered not only the Homestead Grays and the Pittsburgh Crawfords but the sandlots on which these teams emerged.

Norris soon left Pittsburgh to study labor relations and then the law, but this project never would have begun without him. David Montgomery left, too, for Yale. I am grateful for his early guidance on this project and even more for the chance to learn from him during his tenure at Pitt. I was lucky to find another able adviser in Richard Smethurst, a scholar who wields a graceful editorial scalpel. He and the other members of my dissertation committee, Richard Blackett, Larry Glasco, Van Beck Hall, and Dick Oestreicher, went over several drafts of my work, exposing contradictions and encouraging me to write with greater clarity.

Rollo Turner, Robert Colodny, Bill Trimble, Ben Rader, Doug McCormick, Randy Roberts, Art Smith, Larry Malley, Jules Tygiel, and Jim Barrett (my collaborator from earlier days), read all or parts of this manuscript and offered comments and sup-port. Fred Hetzel read these pages, too, and continually advised me on publishing matters.

Mark Cohen, with whom I discussed this project on a number of journeys, gave these pages their stiffest reading—until Terry Sears at the University of Illinois Press got hold of them. Nora

Faires taught me the ways of word-processing and did her best to make a historian out of me. The camaraderie of Mark and Nora, and that of Dave Madison and Lester Guest, who shared with me their intimate knowledge of the black community, made the going smoother.

A special thanks to Faye Schneider, Gerrie Katz, Millie Baer, and Marge Yeager, who kept the university's bureaucracy off my back, and to Jonathan Levine, a wizard at grantsmanship, who helped with the initial grant proposal.

My deepest appreciation goes to the following men and women who shared their thoughts with me in the course of researching this book. Many of their recollections are part of the records of the Archives of an Industrial Society, at the Hillman Library, University of Pittsburgh.

Cleveland Bailey	Charlie Hughes
Gertrude Barranti	Walt Hughes
Joe Barranti	Ray Irvin
Gene Benson	Benny Jackson
Eleanor Benswanger	Helen Jackson
Cos Blount	Ray Kemp
Chet Brewer	Chuck Klausing
Billy Caye	Ralph Koger
Bus Christian	Carl Kohlman
Clarence Clark	Charles Kramer
Fred Clark	Buck Leonard
John Crunkleton	Archie Litman
George Cupples	Effa Manley
Ray Dandridge	Doug McCormick
James Dorsey, Jr.	Ralph Mellix
Zerbie Dorsey	Willis Moody
Andrew Dugo	Euthumm Napier
Ed Fleming	Bill Nunn, Jr.
Larnell Goodman	Jack Parker
Gil Gordon	Ted Page
Charles Greenlee, M.D.	Gabe Patterson
Bill Harris	Catherine Phillips
Teenie Harris	Vernon Phillips
Jack Hopkins	Nick Raddick

Walter Rainey
Hernando Rivera Fixa
Bill ("Pigmeat") Robinson
Jimmy Joe Robinson
Art Rooney
James Rooney
Sam Solomon
Jaspar Stevens
James Stewart, M.D.

Sam Streeter
Ocey Swain
Harold Tinker
C. Rollo Turner
Wyatt Turner
Everett Utterback
Joe Ware
Russell Weiskircher
Henry Yandell

My last debt is one I can never hope to repay—to my buddy, colleague, and wife, Maggie Patterson. Her scholarly and personal counsel and the excitement in her voice every time Willie Stargell came to bat have meant more to me than she will ever know. She also brought Alex onto the roster along the way.

SANDLOT SEASONS
Sport in Black Pittsburgh

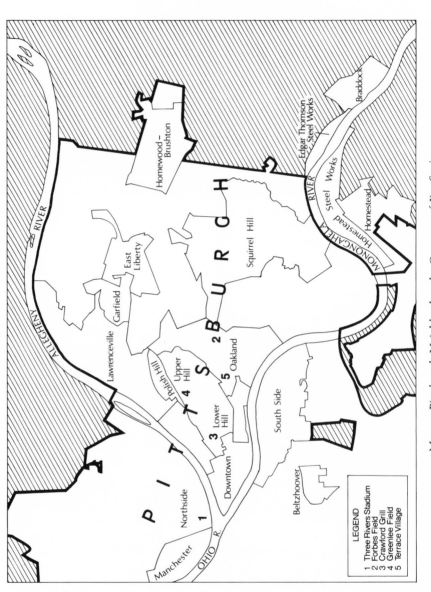

Map 1. Pittsburgh Neighborhoods. Courtesy of Jim Senior.

Introduction

In the first half of the twentieth century, sport in black Pittsburgh, as in most of black America, remained hidden beyond a racial boundary that few blacks could cross. But on the other side of that pale, a sporting life that centered on the sandlots and the Negro Leagues flourished. That sporting life held an array of different meanings for black Pittsburgh, not just the often illusory offer of a ticket out.

Sport helped bring forth black Pittsburgh's potential for self-organization, creativity, and expression in these years. It played a supportive role in the coalescence of a black community both during and after the migrations of the early twentieth century. Through identification with teams and players, sport fostered a sense of pride in black Pittsburgh that often transcended divisions between migrant and Pittsburgh-born blacks and among those of different social classes.

Sport served an important social function, too, one that was vital to team members' self-esteem and to neighborhood identity. It provided black Pittsburgh with a pleasant cultural counterpoint to the often grim experiences encountered at work and in the neighborhood. On the gridirons and diamonds, at least, blacks in Pittsburgh could experience a sense of their own competence and revel in their athletic grace and prowess.

Finally, sport was a forum for symbolic political assertion and an arena for real political struggle. Through competition with whites in a variety of contests, sport provided the black community, in Pittsburgh and nationwide, with its most visible heroes and its most tangible elements of a new self-esteem. It energized black consciousness during the 1930s and 1940s in ways that went unmatched by other aspects of black life.

The meaning of sport to black Pittsburgh changed over the years, depending not only on who organized and controlled black sport but also on its relation to white sport. Despite the seemingly spontaneous nature of organized play and sport, these aspects of leisure-time activity are consciously organized by someone or some institution. The identity of the organizers, who ranged from settlement agencies and local industries to black entrepreneurs and racketeers, indicates where sport was centered and who was trying to influence and control it at a particular time.

Moreover, black sport, although frequently obscured from white society by segregation, did not develop in a vacuum. Despite its growth and autonomy within a larger commercialized system, black sport was nonetheless subject to that system's economic and political pressures. By the late 1950s, that sporting system had killed independent black professional sport and crippled the sandlots, leading to a redefinition of the role of sport in black Pittsburgh and elsewhere. Now success meant making it in the commercial sports world.

There were three overlapping periods of development in black sport in Pittsburgh. The greatest control over black sporting life was attained in the middle phase, from the late 1920s through the 1940s. This control was evident in the way the community's sporting life increasingly came to be organized: forces outside black Pittsburgh gave way to those within the city. The rise of the black sandlots and their most illustrious teams, the Homestead Grays and the Pittsburgh Crawfords, also pointed to this change.

Sport in black Pittsburgh became the domain of black Pittsburghers, not of forces external to the community. The sandlots set the tone, and on them blacks ran their own affairs. The Homestead Grays, the Pittsburgh Crawfords, the Garfield Eagles, and the 18th Ward, among others, were self-organized teams whose destinies, both on and off the field, were largely of their own making. These teams prospered within a black community that supported them with cheers and spare change and looked to them for recreation and a source of identity. While they garnered the backing of local businessmen and ward politicians, and were subject to the commercial pressures attendant on their semiprofessional status, they remained autonomous black institutions embedded in their respective neighborhoods.

The sandlots were also the foundation for the emergence of black professional baseball in Pittsburgh. The Grays and the Crawfords both originated and matured on the sandlots before becoming professional enterprises. Their transition from one to the other demonstrates the close relationship between sandlot and professional sport.

Pittsburgh was the center of black professional baseball from the late 1920s until its demise, following the integration of the major leagues in the late 1940s. Its pro clubs, unlike those in many other cities, were black-owned and black-operated. Each was ascendant within black baseball, the Crawfords for a brief span during the mid-1930s and the Grays during the late 1920s and once again in the 1940s. Their owners, Cumberland Posey of the Grays and Gus Greenlee of the Crawfords, shaped black sport in Pittsburgh and nationally during the 1930s and 1940s. Each club also relied on revenue from the numbers racket, a dependency that underscored both the precarious economic existence of black professional sport and the critical role of the numbers in the black community.

The money generated by the numbers allowed black baseball to reach its highest levels of athletic and financial success. Black talent developed to the point where it could more than hold its own once the color line was crossed. The success of the Grays and the Crawfords also boosted their owners' political clout and, indirectly, that of black Pittsburgh. Moreover, their spectacular play lent a sense of accomplishment and power to the black community off the field. The Grays and the Crawfords were situated on a sporting continuum, however, that extended from the black sandlots to the white professional leagues: they began on the former but aspired to the economic viability of the latter. Ultimately, white pro sport limited their potential growth prior to integration and drained their lifeblood afterward.

Sport in black Pittsburgh was neither well developed nor completely autonomous during its early years, before the expansion of the sandlots and the resurrection of Negro League baseball in the late 1920s and 1930s. During these early decades, forces outside the black community, including local industry, the city, settlement agencies, the YMCA, and the organized play movement, invested money and manpower to organize black Pittsburgh's sporting network. Their goals ranged from helping migrant blacks adjust to urban-industrial life to winning the hearts and minds of black workers. While these groups' aims and the extent of their involvement differed, their legacy was an improved physical infrastructure of pools, playing fields, and gymnasiums, and a core of sports activists committed to sport and recreation in black Pittsburgh.

There was a sporting life in turn-of-the-century black Pittsburgh, but it and black Pittsburgh changed dramatically in the early twentieth century as migration both swelled and re-formed the black community. Sport played a part in this re-formation by providing migrants and Pittsburgh-born blacks with teams and athletes that both groups could identify with. Just as experiences at work and in the community shaped black Pittsburgh's consciousness of itself, so too did its sporting life. The black sporting network that evolved was clearly less bothered by questions of race, social class, and place of birth than were other aspects of black community life, although this informal coalition with outside groups dissolved with the advent of economic depression. The field was left to the sandlot and Negro League clubs which typified black team sport from the late 1920s through the 1940s.

Black sandlot and professional sport reached its zenith during World War II but began to fade soon afterward. During the 1950s black sandlot ball and the Negro Leagues disintegrated. Part of an overall decline of community-based sport, their rapid demise was the result of the integration of the previously all-white professional leagues that had begun in the late 1940s. Integration in major league baseball robbed the Negro Leagues of their best players, their paying customers, and even the attention of the black press. Black sandlot ball, along with white sandlot ball, fell victim to a new emphasis on televised commercial sport, a change that ushered in a new era for the black athlete and heightened the perception of sport as an economic passport for black youth. But the cost was high: the black community lost control over its sporting destiny. In the 1960s sport for black Pittsburgh entered a new phase in which integrated schools, colleges, and pro leagues replaced the sandlots and the Negro Leagues. The once-segregated sporting life was largely history.

Despite its mixed blessings for black Pittsburgh, sport's grip on the fancy of black youth and the attention of their elders is not likely to slip in the near future. Nor is the post–World War II perception that sport is an effective ladder of social mobility about to crumble. This focus on sport at the expense of the pursuit of other educational, cultural, and vocational opportunities has had tragic implications for blacks and has dramatically distorted the meaning of sport in the black community. Perhaps a sense of what sport once meant to black Pittsburgh can contribute to a more realistic perspective on what sport offers and what it could offer black America.

1 Sport and Black Pittsburgh, 1900–1930

One can still feel a sense of neighborhood in Pittsburgh, of its ethnic pockets and groupings. Pierogies and kielbasas lend their fragrance to the Southside, and Italian remains the native tongue for many in Bloomfield and East Liberty. The Northside retains a faint Germanic ambience, and on Polish Hill a plaque marks the 1969 visit of Karol Wojtyla, now Pope John Paul II.

Pittsburgh's rivers, ravines, bluffs, and hollows divide the city into dozens of smaller communities, just as they have for almost two centuries. These formidable natural barriers were reinforced by the historic clustering of the different ethnic and racial groups that migrated to Pittsburgh in the course of the city's rise as the nation's iron and steel workshop. The Irish and Germans who came in the nineteenth century soon were followed by Italians and Poles, Serbo-Croatians and Russians, and blacks from the American South. By the turn of the century they made Pittsburgh and its satellite mill towns into a multiethnic metropolis of over half a million people, many of whom labored to produce 40 percent of the country's steel.

Each ethnic group that came to Pittsburgh tended to settle in a particular neighborhood where nationality dictated which church one attended and where one drank. But ethnicity was not an absolute factor: one did not need an ethnic passport to move to the Hill, which loomed over the city's downtown, or to reside in Braddock, Homestead, or any of the other mill towns along the banks of the Monongahela and Allegheny rivers. These neighborhoods may have become ghettos, but they were multiethnic ones. Polish, Italian, Yiddish, and Croatian were spoken on the street and in the stores, intermingled with English and the dialect of migrants from the Black Belt.

It was in this multiethnic, industrial city that a black community began to form in the nineteenth century. Unlike the city's white immigrant neighborhoods, where the residential and occupational gains of the first generation were bequeathed to the second, black Pittsburghers found it harder to lay the foundation for community growth. White ethnic neighborhoods became increasingly stable and cohesive during the twentieth century as a result of a strong social infrastructure of churches and neighborhood associations, residential persistence, and greater workplace security. Moreover, by the 1930s the steady stream of European immigrants had slowed to a trickle. The sons and daughters of the earlier migrants built on the efforts of their parents, especially at work and in becoming homeowners in tightly knit ethnic enclaves.[1] Blacks were not so fortunate.

The efforts of black Pittsburghers to achieve second-generation status were hampered by continuing waves of black immigrants and emigrants well into the 1950s. An estimated two-thirds of all blacks living in Pittsburgh in 1910 left the city by 1920, to be replaced a decade later by relative newcomers. Although blacks attained slightly greater occupational and residential stability in the 1930s, a second wave of migration during and after World War II soon recast black Pittsburgh yet again.[2]

Those blacks who came to Pittsburgh after the 1920s discovered a city that was already past its economic prime. The earlier competitive advantage held by Pittsburgh in heavy industrial production faded after World War I, resulting in long-term economic decline. Nonetheless, blacks poured into the city in unprecedented numbers between 1930 and 1960, as the black population increased from about 55,000 to over 100,000. These newcomers faced both dwindling economic opportunities and a black community that had yet to completely shed its first-generation urban status.[3]

The Making of a Black Community

By 1900 there were over 20,000 blacks in Pittsburgh, the majority living on the Hill. Black Pittsburgh was a community in the making in the early twentieth century, but it was one beset by forces pulling it apart. Against a backdrop of discrimination in the workplace and the neighborhood, black Pittsburgh's already inadequate facilities were soon overwhelmed by a swelling tide of southern migrants. In the early stages of this migration, the

black community appeared to divide along the lines of Pittsburgh-born versus migrant, with some parallels to the social
class and occupations of the two groups. It was not until the
1920s and later that black Pittsburgh came to terms with itself
and emerged with a new sense of identity as both a community
and a part of an emerging national black consciousness.

In the early twentieth century black Pittsburgh grew along
with the city's expanding industrial base. When World War I
shut off the flow of southern and eastern European immigrants
to area mines and mills, blacks from the American South stepped
in to fill the void. The number of blacks in the city more than
doubled between 1910 and 1930, exceeding 50,000 and giving
Pittsburgh the fifth largest black population in the country.
Simultaneously, the percentage of blacks among the total city
population rose from 4.8 to 8.2.[4] Drawn by the prospects of
better work and improved social conditions, alternatives that the
South seemed unlikely to offer, increasing numbers of blacks
trekked northward to the Steel City from Virginia, Georgia,
Alabama, and elsewhere. By 1930 less than a third of Pittsburgh's black population had been born in Pennsylvania.[5]

Migration affected both the demographics and the geography
of black Pittsburgh. Men were more likely than women to make
the trip north to look for work; hence the black community soon
found a disproportionate number of black southern males on its
streets and in its boardinghouses. While the migrants settled in
mill towns up and down the rivers, most found their way to the
district known as the Hill. A traditional gathering point for
migrants of all backgrounds, the Hill had supported a black
population since before the Civil War, when it was popularly
known as Little Hayti.[6] About half of Pittsburgh's black population lived there in the 1930s, with the remainder clustered in
smaller groups in the eastern portion of the city.[7] Over time,
black enclaves developed in the Manchester and Beltzhoover
sections as well. The Hill, like most of Pittsburgh and the nearby
mill towns, was composed of a heavily foreign-born or second-
generation population, with large numbers of Irish, Italians,
Jews, and Syrians living alongside blacks. While blacks and
whites sometimes shared the same building and often lived side

by side, there was a marked tendency toward racial and ethnic clustering within the distrct.[8]

There was a definite clustering, too, of migrants and old-stock blacks. Pittsburgh-born blacks were generally better off economically than the more recent migrants, especially those from the Deep South.[9] There was even a local black elite with middle-class aspirations, referred to as "OPs," or Old Pittsburghers. These class differences were compounded by a residential separation of most migrants from the northerners. In the nearby steel town of Homestead, across the river from Pittsburgh, skilled black workers, professionals, and shopkeepers lived in the "Hilltop" neighborhood while the migrants who labored on work gangs in the steel mills lived in crowded boardinghouses in the "Ward" along the river.[10] They went to different churches on Sunday and returned to different neighborhoods afterward, one a fairly pleasant residential section and the other a district with a.reputation for prostitution and gambling.[11] This geographic separation held for Pittsburgh, too, as the more economically secure Pittsburgh-born blacks moved into particular parts of the Hill and into Beltzhoover and Homewood, away from the newcomers.[12]

Southern migrants and northern blacks also encountered different experiences at work. The migrants were more likely to join the industrial work force, sometimes introduced to break strikes but more often to make up for a diminishing supply of southern and eastern European labor. By contrast, Pittsburgh-born blacks could be found in domestic, clerical, or service positions. When both worked in the mills, the locals were more likely to hold the few skilled jobs allotted to black workers.[13]

This southern influx aggravated the growing class divisions and led to two nearly separate black communities in Pittsburgh based on place of birth and occupation. The two groups lived apart, worked apart, and played apart. OPs formed their own fraternal and literary societies in reaction to the migration, while many of the migrants in turn brought their native community organizations with them.[14] The migrants, observers noted, kept to themselves, while the older families remained aloof, believing themselves to be socially superior because of long residence in a northern city with its advantages of higher literacy rates, a broader culture, greater economic security, and a higher standard of living.[15]

Another reason the black community divided was that increased numbers of newcomers taxed scanty housing and social services and heightened competition for work. Interviews conducted with residents of the Soho neighborhood in 1941, for example, indicated that blacks there believed that migration had led to greater racial animosity. Prejudice, they argued, grew as more and more people moved into the neighborhood. The black middle classes especially saw the migrants as a threat to their own public image of respectability.[16]

Black Pittsburgh's internal problems were compounded by the fact that migration was not simply a one-way movement from south to north. Many migrants, because of family ties, holidays, and the need to help out on the farm, made seasonal pilgrimages back home. With frequent returns south, these migrants were less likely to establish roots and meld with the northern-born population. The two-way flow was a common experience, at least between World War I and the early 1930s.[17] For other migrants Pittsburgh was just a temporary layover in an often frustrated quest for a better life that took them from city to city.[18]

This sense of unease over its own makeup was deepened by the material conditions facing the black community in Pittsburgh. Life was harsh for most early-twentieth-century migrants, but its realities were particularly grim for blacks. The 1907 *Pittsburgh Survey* found that housing was already a serious problem for black and immigrant Pittsburghers, and conditions would only deteriorate as the number of residents climbed during the next two decades. Housing accommodations were taxed well beyond their limits as families doubled and tripled up and often took on boarders as well to meet rent payments. Black homeownership remained at less than 4 percent on the Hill during the 1920s, and rental properties were scarce. Blacks moved in to virtually any space with a roof over it, crowding into abandoned boxcars, cellars, and shacks. As the black population increased, so did the tendency for blacks to live in segregated communities as whites sought to prevent them from moving to certain parts of town. Small black communities coalesced in Beltzhoover, East Liberty, and Homewood, their founders often having fled the deteriorating Hill neighborhood. It was not until 1925 that black-owned housing began to increase in Pittsburgh.[19]

The Hill, as a consequence of its population density and low per capita income, suffered from the greatest incidence of disease and public health problems in the city. Death rates in the Third and Fifth wards were among the highest in the city, with the Third Ward having the highest death rate due to transmissible diseases in Pittsburgh. Infant mortality and deaths due to all causes were higher for blacks than whites.[20]

Nor did the world of work offer any respite. The opportunity for a better job had induced many blacks to migrate in the first place. A black beachhead in industrial work was established during the relatively labor-scarce 1920s, especially in local steel mills, on the railroads, and in the mines.[21] Black women labored as domestics, cleaners, and laundresses, while the men were primarily engaged as porters, janitors, and laborers in the mills and on construction sites; and only a small percentage escaped low-paying, unskilled labor to practice a more skilled, rewarding occupation. However, when the Great Depression hit the iron and steel industry, black employment plummeted, and the gains of the 1920s were all but wiped out as black unemployment and underemployment in Allegheny County totaled 69 percent in 1934.[22] The upshot was that work was neither particularly steady, financially remunerative, nor likely to instill a sense of competence. Like conditions in the black community, the world of work was found severely lacking.

Another factor fragmenting black Pittsburgh was its geographic dispersal. In Chicago, New York, and Philadelphia, the black community formed one contiguous area. In Pittsburgh, however, the black populace was splintered into one fairly large enclave on the Hill and smaller neighborhoods on the Southside and in East Liberty, Homewood, Manchester, Woods Run, and Beltzhoover.[23] This absence of a consolidated black community undercut black business and electoral strength. "The economic basis upon which rests the social, political and cultural life in [black] Pittsburgh is weaker and more shifting than that of any other group," social commentator J. Ernest Wright argued in 1940. "Because of such variability and the existence of several communities rather than one concentrated settlement such as Harlem or South Chicago, the group mood and outlook has not stabilized or coalesced. The group unity has remained weak."24

The Evolution of a Black Sporting Life

Black Pittsburghers took to the streets in jubilation after Jack Johnson knocked out Jim Jeffries in their racially charged 1910 championship bout, and they followed Joe Louis's career with a fascination approaching reverence. But sport for them carried more subtle political meanings, too. Through its pantheon of sandlot and national heroes, the struggles over the desegregation of recreation and play, and its role in everyday life, sport played a central role in the coalescence of black Pittsburgh after the disruptive migrations of the World War I years. In the 1920s, 1930s, and 1940s, sport offered black Pittsburgh a cultural counterpoint to its collective lot, one that promoted internal cohesion and brought together both the Pittsburgh-born residents and the southern migrants in the context of a changing black consciousness. Moreover, sport helped the scattered black Pittsburgh community to gain a sense of itself as part of a national black community.

Just as experiences at work and in the community shaped black Pittsburgh's consciousness of itself, so too did its sporting life. Sport in black Pittsburgh during the early twentieth century was not solely the creation of black Pittsburghers, however. While it lent a sense of cohesion to black Pittsburgh, it did so at a time when various groups and institutions external to the community sought to organize black sporting life. They ranged from local industry and city government to settlement agencies and the organized play movement, and the context for their work was a black community in flux as migration reshaped it and allowed a greater latitude for outside influence. While this loosely knit coalition contributed to the development of black Pittsburgh sport, it eventually faded from the sporting arena during the late 1920s, and in subsequent years black Pittsburgh was more fully in control of its own sporting life.

A fairly wide spectrum of sport already existed in the black community, ranging from a vibrant street life to the more restricted facilities of private clubs. In the middle, both in terms of scope and accessibility by all classes in the black community, were the sandlots, neighborhood gyms, and recreation centers. But these facilities were never that abundant, and black Pittsburghers, like white immigrant and industrial workers, resorted to the streets and the materials of everyday life for their sport and recreation.[25]

Street Life and Sport

At the beginning of the twentieth century the Hill was without a single municipal playground. Almost four decades later, a three-year study of the city and county concluded that with the exception of a few parks, "no form of recreational facility is available in proportions even approximating recognized standards. . . . If the Negro population has less access to leisure time activities than has the general population, they must be limited indeed."[26] But the streets and empty lots were available, even if public and private recreational opportunities were not. Street culture has long been a part of black community life, and in Pittsburgh it took the form of endless pick-up games played amid the daily interactions of neighbors and community residents on the stoop and sidewalk, in the pool hall and the barbershop. The street scene included a yearly carnival and musicians performing on street corners on the Hill, an informally organized outdoor dance hall with a phonograph and jitterbugging on Shetland Street in East Liberty, and nightly congregations along Wylie and Frankstown avenues.[27]

The street scene flourished in Pittsburgh because blacks were denied access to a wider range of recreational facilities. In some cases the streets and the rivers along which black mill-town populations lived were the only available recreational resources. In others, the facilities existed but black youths had to look elsewhere, because public recreation centers like the Warrington Center and Highland Park pool were segregated on a de facto basis. Many thus gravitated to the streets and played ball there. For a brief span during the 1930s, the Works Progress Administration (WPA) pumped money and 1,500 WPA workers from the Division of Community Service into the playgrounds and recreation centers of Allegheny County. But World War II brought an end to the program. As one columnist for Pittsburgh's black weekly, the *Pittsburgh Courier,* saw it, "There will be little else for the local children to do but return to the dusty, traffic-filled streets and alleys from which this project was intended to rescue them."[28]

Building a Sporting Network from the Outside

The street scene was largely spontaneous, filling in the gaps of social life without a formal organizing center. However, a fairly wide spectrum of forces consciously began to organize the sporting and recreational life of the black community. Capitalizing on a growing enthusiasm for organized team sport, these forces sought to channel that energy to meet their own particular goals. Outside influences ranged from local government, social agencies, and area industry, to private social clubs and sports promoters. The general trend was toward the latter, the sports entrepreneur, who operated in conjunction with an ever stronger impulse toward self-organization by the players themselves. The increasing influence of commercial pressures on sport also was evident as the locus of organization moved within the black community.

The making of an organized sporting life in black Pittsburgh involved both the building of a physical infrastructure and the sponsorship of teams, clubs, and leagues. The first required the construction of gymnasiums, pools, playing fields, and recreation centers, facilities that were scarce for black Pittsburghers before the twentieth century. The second built on a history of organized team and club sport extending back to the late nineteenth century. The efforts of a loosely knit coalition of the city, social agencies, and local industry combined with the energies of sports promoters, social clubs, and self-organized teams to build a fairly substantial sporting network in the black community by the 1920s. The backbone of this growing structure was the sandlot and community teams playing on local fields and in neighborhood gyms and centers. Yet black Pittsburgh's sporting banner was already being carried by barnstorming baseball and basketball clubs and a contingent of track and field athletes representing not only their community but their country in both national and Olympic competition. As dramatic an improvement as this sporting life was, it nevertheless was inadequate and marred by racial and class discrimination.

The City and the Organized Play Movement

The city government's role in the recreational and sporting life of Pittsburgh, both black and white, historically had been a limited one and was rarely supplemented by other levels of government. City hall did add considerably to Pittsburgh's sporting facilities in the early years of the twentieth century as it acted in concert with a growing organized play movement then campaigning in urban areas across the country. This organized play movement, with its supervised playgrounds and recreation centers, was in conscious opposition to the world of street life and the sort of sport it fostered. Cary Goodman, a scholar of the movement, argues that the alternatives supported by this national play movement were intended not only to lure children away from the streets but to socialize the offspring of the immigrant population to a particular system of class-bred values and behavior.[29] The city was induced by the Pittsburgh Playground Association (PPA), the local arm of the organized play movement, to take a more activist role in promoting sport and recreation among its residents. It turned Washington Park, on the lower Hill, over to the PPA in 1903, and the group proceeded to erect a wood-frame recreational center on what had once been a dumping grounds. An athletic field and bleachers were built, and in 1908 a more modern center was constructed. The first fully equipped playground and athletic field in the city, Washington Park became a center for baseball, boxing, basketball, and football for the next forty-odd years. Its name still evokes fond memories in many parts of the city.

By 1929 Pittsburgh's Bureau of Recreation was running seventy-eight recreational centers, eight of which were located on the Hill. There was an assortment of playgrounds, swimming pools, athletic fields, and recreation centers, with an emphasis on summer sport and recreation. Of the eight facilities on the Hill, two were all-year recreation centers—the Crawford Bath House and Washington Park—one was a swimming pool, and the others were a mix of summer playgrounds and athletic fields.

The recreation centers and the athletic fields were more of a focus for organized sport than the playgrounds, where younger children gathered. The Crawford Bath House, named for its Crawford Street address, was a combination bathhouse and club center for sport.[30] But sport was only part of its more widely designed program to help migrant blacks adjust to urban-industrial life. This program included a kindergarten as well as classes for adults. Lacking an athletic field, the Crawford Bath House served as a center for both girls' and boys' basketball teams and housed a boxing ring where some of Pittsburgh's finest pugilists trained, including Jackie Wilson and Charles Burley, contenders who worked out there in the 1930s and 1940s. And in 1926 the bathhouse sponsored and lent its name to a ragtag group of black youths who would become one of the best baseball teams in the western hemisphere, the Pittsburgh Crawfords.

The Crawford Bath House, with an all-black staff in 1929, catered mainly to blacks. The racial mix was greater at Washington Park, where only about one-third of the participants on any given day were likely to be black. The playgrounds were usually either predominantly black or predominantly white. While the city's general policy was not ostensibly segregationist, there were strong tendencies toward a de facto segregation of certain centers and facilities. In some cases swimming pool hours were divvied up along racial lines; in others a pattern of friction and sometimes physical violence persuaded blacks not to use the pool or center.[31] The Urban League surveyed social conditions in 1930 and concluded, "There seems to be a feeling that they would not be welcomed and they just do not apply for admission."[32] On the other hand, where both blacks and whites used the same facilities there seems to have been a high degree of interaction.

Most of the city-run centers catering to blacks were on the Hill, where the largest concentration of blacks in the city lived. Blacks in other parts of the city frequently traveled there if they wanted to use the city's recreation centers because of subtle and not-so-subtle discouragement from using centers located elsewhere. The city's services, which were criticized repeatedly for their inadequacies, were augmented by the work of various social agencies and settlement houses.

Social Agencies and Settlement Houses

The Soho and Morgan community houses, the YMCA and YWCA, the Urban League, the Kay Club, and the black churches all directed some energy into the sporting life of black Pittsburgh. The sum total of their efforts was an additon to both physical plant and the sponsorship of teams and leagues.[33]

The YMCA became the cornerstone of this social agency work in sport, but its impact in the black community was severely circumscribed by its racial and class biases. In the first place, YMCAs generally were found in communities where there was a combination of strong Protestant influence and some affluence.[34] By serving an economically favored strata, the YMCAs discouraged black participation. Moreover, certain local branches, such as the ones in McKeesport, Sewickley, and Coraopolis, simply excluded blacks. The racial compromise was to build a YMCA on the Hill, designated the "colored" branch among the fourteen local facilities operating in 1928. This was standard operating procedure for the YMCA nationally in those years. While concentrating its energies among the most ghettoized of the black populace, the YMCA's policy of segregation left blacks in other parts of the city outside its program.[35]

Black Pittsburgh's YMCA was built at the heart of the Hill, across Centre Avenue from the building that housed the *Pittsburgh Courier*. The *Courier*'s editor, Robert L. Vann, chaired the fundraising efforts for the new building, which relied heavily on the contributions of the Rosenwald Fund. Julius Rosenwald, a Chicago mail-order magnate, contributed to the construction of this and more than a score of YMCAs in other black communities. Completed in 1923, the Centre Avenue Y rapidly emerged as a key social and political center for black Pittsburgh. Its rooms and auditoriums were used for community meetings and served as a gathering point during political campaigns. With classrooms and club rooms, a dormitory, a pool, and a gymnasium, the YMCA had its hands in a variety of activities ranging from industrial work and health education to sport and recreation.

The YMCA provided sports facilities and sponsored teams

and league activity. Blacks participated in tennis, volleyball, track and field, and swimming, as well as basketball, the most widely played sport among the YMCA's programs. As of 1930, the YMCA had the only basketball court consistently available to blacks in the city. In the spring of 1929, eighteen different black teams played here. Although it did not sponsor baseball or football directly, the YMCA participated in a mushball (softball) league and helped coordinate a black industrial workers' baseball league. The black churches worked through the YMCA in establishing a church athletic league, as did the Urban League and local industry.

YMCA-sponsored teams competed within all-black leagues in addition to entering tournaments and leagues hosted by the American Athletic Union, the *Pittsburgh Press,* and regional and state YMCA organizing bodies. Participation in the latter often meant breaching racial barriers. When the Centre Avenue Y's lightweight team won the state basketball title in 1924, it was the first black team to have played in the state YMCA tournament. Its teams also integrated volleyball and swimming meets, as well as the Keystone Softball League in 1945. In track and field, which was probably the most racially mixed amateur sport, the Centre Avenue squad won the *Press,* YMCA, and AAU meets on a regular basis.

Nonetheless, the YMCA was criticized for reaching only a relatively small part of the black community. The Urban League estimated that of over 20,000 black males between the ages of ten and fifty who lived in the city during the 1920s, the YMCA served only about 1.5 percent of them. It argued for programs that would include the "underprivileged Negro boy" and urged that additional funds and personnel be allocated to supplement the work being done. However, interviews conducted with some sixty participants in Pittsburgh's sporting past, as well as newspaper accounts of the YMCA's activities, indicate that at least its sport program reached a fairly wide cross section of the black community. Its teams included such men as sportswriters Wendell Smith and Chester Washington from the *Pittsburgh Courier;* former collegiate athletes Everett Utterback, Max Thompson, and Woody Harris; black professional athletes Ted Page and Josh

Gibson; sandlot stars Gabe Patterson and Ralph Mellix; and a host of young boys and men from working-class backgrounds.[36]

Sport in the black community was heavily biased toward males and females were often excluded. As the YMCA was severely restricted in its activities due to a lack of suitable physical facilities, what sport and recreational work it sponsored was usually done through the facilities of local high schools.[37] YMCA sport afforded black youth a chance to play and to compete on an organized basis, and in later years it also was a possible stepping-stone to a collegiate career. Some blacks made the YMCA their primary sporting outlet and spent their entire athletic lives competing for its teams and in its leagues.

The settlement house movement also added to the recreational life of black Pittsburgh by sponsoring several teams. Yet settlement work was for the most part a transitory phenomenon hindered by its own racial practices. Settlements were traditionally oriented toward meeting the needs of poor, frequently immigrant communities, and black Pittsburgh met both these qualifications. There were, however, but a few settlement houses that either worked within black communities or opened their facilities to blacks.[38] Moreover, these settlements were hampered by scarce funding.

Three different settlements served the Hill in the migration years; two of them closed their doors by 1928. The Soho Community House, founded in 1907 in an integrated working-class neighborhood near the Hill, provided limited play and sporting facilities to its members, about 15 percent of whom were black. The Bryant Community Center and the Morgan Community House were church-supported centers for blacks on the Hill. The lack of steady funding brought both to an end in the 1920s. The Morgan Community House, despite its short life span between 1919 and 1924, nonetheless hosted a unique sporting aggregation.[39]

In 1919 the racially mixed but predominantly black Scholastic Club of Pittsburgh sponsored a track and field squad coached by Hunter Johnson, then trainer for the football team at the University of Pittsburgh and former head of the Century Athletic Club in New York. Johnson actively recruited blacks to come to

Pittsburgh to run for the Scholastic Club. He persuaded Earl
Johnson from Baltimore, Charley West from Washington and
Jefferson College, and DeHart Hubbard from his redcap stand
at Pittsburgh's Union Station to move to town and train under
him. The following year, 1920, Johnson became trainer and
manager of the Morgan Community Athletic Club (MCAC),
and Earl Johnson, Charley West, and DeHart Hubbard went
with him. The MCAC sponsored baseball, basketball, and boxing in addition to track, and such players as Vic Harris and
Pappy Williams developed on their squads. But the club's forte
was track, and three of its members—Johnson, Hubbard, and
West—represented the United States at the 1924 Olympic Games
in Paris. Hubbard, a long jumper, was the first black American
to win an Olympic championship. Johnson, who became a
fixture in black Pittsburgh's sporting world, placed third in the
10,000-meter race behind Paavo Nurmi, the Flying Finn, and his
compatriot, Willie Ritola. However, the MCAC, which had had
no money to send candidates to the 1920 Olympic tryouts, soon
disbanded as the settlement house closed due to lack of funds.[40]

There were other settlement-type centers, such as the Kay
Boys' Club and the Rankin Christian Center, involved in sport
and recreation, yet these centers were always hampered by insuf-
ficent financing. The black churches, which provided some financial support and sponsored leagues and teams through the
YMCA, and the Urban League, which acted similarly, had virtually no independent sports programs.[41] These organizations
took a conscious interest in sport and recreation, however, and
cooperated with the YMCA and local industry in a variety of
ventures.

The churches and social agencies were undoubtedly driven by
a great deal of sincere concern for the plight of black Pittsburghers. But they also had a political and social agenda for the
black community that reflected the economic realities of Pittsburgh in the 1920s. The region's growing economic base and the
restriction of European immigration had created unprecedented
opportunities for blacks. The YMCA, the Urban League, and
many black ministers and settlement leaders wanted to make
sure that blacks took advantage of the situation. Sport and
recreation were inducements to boys and young men to take part

in the larger programs, which, in the organizers' own words, were bent on "improving the morale, efficiency and consciousness of Negro workers."[42] They facilitated the adjustment of blacks, especially those from the South, to the routines and demands of area industry. Acting as labor recruiters for industry, they also helped black laborers to make their work habits more acceptable to white society. Sport teams and recreational facilities were but a part of this larger program; the direct link was more concrete in these agencies' cooperation with local industry in the field of industrial sport and recreation.

Industrial Sport and Recreation

The capitalist world system was shaken to its very foundations in the first two decades of the twentieth century. A world war, the Russian Revolution, and a labor upsurge of almost unprecedented proportions combined to pose a direct challenge to managerial authority.[43] When adverse economic conditions undercut the labor movement's organizational strength in the early 1920s, however, American manufacturers counterattacked and launched a broad set of changes in industrial life to ensure that the upsurge would not be repeated.

This American plan was perceived as an alternative to both Bolshevism and unionism. It stressed the open (i.e., nonunion) shop and introduced employee representation plans as a company-sanctioned organizational forum from which workers might communicate their grievances, thus defusing potential shop-floor dissent. The plan revamped production processes as the precepts of scientific management forced a reevaluation with the goals of managerial control over production and greater productivity. For the more skilled workers, management was willing to try to guarantee some semblance of employment security. Finally, the American plan made use of new plant professionals, the personnel managers, who introduced a variety of workplace welfare measures including lunchrooms, company newspapers, and clean washrooms. As a *Time* magazine advertisement extolling the virtues of Scot Tissue Towels put it, "Is your washroom breeding Bolsheviks?"[44] Foremost among these schemes was a focus on athletic teams and recreation.

The immediate tasks were to solve the problem of turnover

that plagued American industry and to devise more effective hiring procedures and a means of shaping the attitudes of the work force. Long concerned with the supply of labor, American industry always has gone to great lengths to ensure that it would be both adequate in size and willing to work. In the early twentieth century the labor supply fluctuated dramatically with the strength of the economy and as waves of migrants flooded American cities only to retreat when war struck Europe in August 1914. When the demand for labor was high, workers commonly left one job for a better deal somewhere else. It was not unusual for a worker to accept a half-dozen or more job offers in a single day, then report only to the one offering the highest wages and best working conditions. Annual turnover rates were as high as 1,600 to 2,000 percent in a single factory during World War I.[45]

While industry was addressing its concerns over astronomical turnover rates and labor turbulence, it also had to consider another changing aspect of work, that of shorter workdays. The second decade of the twentieth century was the critical period in the struggle for the eight-hour workday. During that time, those who worked forty-eight hours per week or less increased from 8 to 48 percent of the work force; those working more than fifty-four hours per week dropped from almost 70 percent to less than 26 percent.[46] Even the steel industry, where the norm was a twelve-hour day and alternate six- and seven-day workweeks with a full twenty-four-hour turnabout shift every other week, went to an eight-hour workday by the end of 1923. This decline in the number of hours worked was a vital precondition for greater participation by workers in sport and recreation. It raised questions in the minds of personnel managers as to who would direct and influence the nature of working-class leisure time.

The United States was the world's leading industrial manufacturer during the 1920s, producing a higher percentage of the world's manufactured goods than it ever had before or would afterward. The nation's manufacturers did not reach this pinnacle by ignoring the attitudes and aspirations of their workers, however; on the contrary, American industry sought to take advantage of them. The writings of L. C. Gardner, the superintendent of the Homestead Works of Carnegie-Illinois Steel Company (later United States Steel), are indicative of the thinking of American industry.[47] Carnegie-Illinois sponsored a wide range of athletic teams and recreational facilities at its Monongahela River Valley plants, not only for its workers but the surrounding communities too.

Gardner's essay on "Community Athletic Recreation for Employees and Their Families" begins with the assumption that practical managers will "see to it that the lot of their employees is as pleasant as possible because it is good business." Gardner suggested, "The matter of recreation is one that may promise to be a cure-all. It is attractive, it looks easy to handle and a certain element of [the work force] is outspoken for it. . . . A sane, moderate program of recreation that aims to give everybody something to do in his leisure time is one way the employer can insure his workers coming to work refreshed and alert and in a happy frame of mind."

The superintendent also urged his fellow plant managers to look beyond the confines of their factory. "Good will is not a sentiment that trickles down from above. It comes into existence at the bottom of the social structure. The place to cultivate good will is where it grows naturally—in the community, in the neighborhood, where people meet as folks." Consequently, industrial plants should foster sport in the community in addition to the plant. Gardner went on to list twenty-eight activities, ranging from sport teams to playgrounds and festivals, for an industrial firm to consider.

Gardner justified these commitments for a number of reasons, beginning with the matter of labor: "The best and most logical supply of labor is in the immediate community of a plant. Every resident, man, woman, boy or girl is a potential employee." Second, he noted that community recreation "helps to make good will. And the good will of a community is a real asset." Third, the program would help the workers develop "strong bodies and alert minds"; children "grow into better specimens of manhood and the adults will keep in better physical condition." Gardner also suggested that recreation would instill a certain sense of organization and ideology: "It trains leaders to work with the company and does so in non-controversial subjects, so that these leaders are likely to be anchors to windward when outside leaders attempt to gather a following." Moreover, recreation would act as a powerful force in "preaching the gospel of clean living" and would allow youngsters to find an outlet in games so that there would be "less desire or inclination to violate laws and destroy property." Gardner concluded, "The industrial firm that takes a long look ahead, and invests in Community Recreation can expect as a dividend, loyal, healthy, clean living and team working employees drawn from its immediate neighborhoods."

Company sport became a national phenomenon as a majority of the larger firms sponsored some sort of recreational program during the 1920s.[48] One big automaker sponsored twenty-seven uniformed teams which belonged either to intercity or local twilight leagues. Another company, with twenty-six teams, built a steel and concrete stadium with a seating capacity of 4,000 in 1925. Most of the firms donated uniforms and equipment, paid the umpires and traveling costs, and provided some sort of reward or banquet for the players. Teams ranged from intramural departmental outfits, to an auto company soccer team with a national reputation, to an iron and steel company team which toured Europe each year, with all expenses being paid by the company. Some of the squads eventually turned professional: for examples, the Chicago Bears, one of America's oldest professional football teams, had its beginnings as the A. E. Staley company team in Decatur, Illinois.[49]

In addition to football, basketball, and volleyball teams, many companies also provided tennis courts, baseball diamonds, and golf courses, and they even sponsored employee athletic associations. A midwestern company with 17,000 employees built an athletic field with a grandstand seating 10,000, complete with locker rooms, showers, six tennis courts, four baseball diamonds, horseshoe courts, a cinder running track, and a playground for the workers' children. The official stance was, "Given a square-deal management, industrial amateur athletics organized on a businesslike basis will promote plant morale quicker than any other single method."[50]

Many firms worked with the local branch of the childrens' playground movement and cooperated with the YMCA, the YWCA, and the settlement houses; at times, local industries also worked with each other. In Newark, New Jersey, some forty of the largest local companies financed the Ironbound Community and Industrial Service in the predominantly immigrant Ironbound district. It provided health and sanitation services along with gymnasiums, athletic leagues, and playgrounds. Similar industrial athletic associations could be found in nearby Paterson as well as in Baltimore, Cleveland, and Johnstown, Pennsylvania.

Pittsburgh's working men and women were at the forefront of the labor upsurge. They engaged in violent confrontations at the Pressed Steel Car Company in McKees Rocks, and the Westinghouse complex in East Pittsburgh, and joined the 1919 steel strike and a score of other strikes. When the dust of battle had settled, industry responded with a variety of welfare provisions. The steel and electrical industries, which dominated Pittsburgh's river valleys, set the tone for community recreation and company sport. During the relatively prosperous Coolidge years of the 1920s, they built playgrounds, nurseries, and community centers near many of their mills. Andrew Carnegie, the titan of the American iron and steel industry, endowed combined libraries and athletic clubs in Munhall, Braddock, Duquesne, and Carnegie and contributed to the construction of Schwab Vocational High School in Homestead and Renziehausen Park in McKeesport. Westinghouse Electric and Manufacturing Company (WEMCO) and Spang-Chalfant built and maintained recreation centers in Turtle Creek and Etna. The railroads and the coal companies also sponsored teams and leagues for their workers.[51]

The Homestead Works of Carnegie-Illinois Steel conducted what was probably the most extensive sport and recreation program in the area. The Homestead Library Athletic Club (HLAC), an appendage of the Carnegie-financed Munhall Carnegie Library, could trace its athletic heritage to the late nineteenth century. In the 1890s their football team, composed of former collegians from the Ivy League, was recognized as one of the top semipro squads in the nation and its semipro baseball team, with the eminently eccentric Hall of Famer Rube Waddell on the mound, played before large and enthusiastic crowds. Throughout the early twentieth century the HLAC was a mecca for local children, who used its swimming pool, bowling alleys, and gymnasium. Concerts and plays competed for space with wrestling, water polo, swimming, and team sports. HLAC teams won national amateur championships in wrestling and in track and field and also sent members of its women's swim team to the 1932 and the 1936 Olympics.

Shortly before the United States entered World War I, Carnegie-Illinois Steel expanded its community program, building two playgrounds in Munhall and two in Homestead. The company showed outdoor movies once a week and employed playground directors to supervise both young children and team sports. Older children played soccer, mushball, field hockey, basketball, or baseball, while their mothers took advantage of the well-baby clinic and brought their toddlers to the wading pool. The entire program was directed by the superintendent of the Homestead Works' employee welfare department.

This same department also sponsored baseball and basketball teams for company workers, and games were held almost every night of the week at nearby West Field. The best players from the Homestead Works often tangled with teams from other mills in exhibition and industrial league matches.[52]

Much of this company welfare was off-limits to the black community, however. What was not strictly proscribed was segregated by race. In Homestead and Duquesne, the Carnegie Library clubs, with their swimming pools, gymnasiums, and books, were open to any club member who could afford the dues, but membership was closed to blacks. In the plant, blacks could play ball but only on all-black teams. As one historian of the black migration to Pittsburgh noted, blacks might have shopped and dined with whites in Homestead's commercial district and worked alongside them in the mill, but when it came to the company's recreational program, Jim Crow was the rule.[53]

The sum total of industry's involvement in sport in the black community was nonetheless rather impressive. Many of the larger companies employed "Negro welfare workers" during the migration, men who supervised black teams and recreation during the 1920s.[54] Earl Johnson of the Edgar Thomson Steel Works in Braddock, Cyrus T. Green of Westinghouse, Charles Deevers and J. D. Barr of Pennsylvania Railways Company,

William ("Pimp") Young of Lockhart Iron and Steel, Charles Betts of Homestead Steel Works, and W. R. Johnson of the Philadelphia Company constituted a group of company welfare and community workers who aligned themselves with their counterparts at the YMCA, the Urban League, and the settlement houses. Together they promoted not only teams and athletic clubs at their respective workplaces but leagues made up of company, community, and YMCA squads.[55]

Earl Johnson, an Olympic medalist and feature writer for the *Pittsburgh Courier*'s sports pages, directed the diverse activities of the black Edgar Thomson Steel Works Club.[56] Johnson also ran for the club in national and local track and field meets. In the American Athletic Union national five-mile championship in Chicago in the fall of 1923, he defeated Willie Ritola, the Finnish marathoner who would edge him out for the silver medal the following summer at the 1924 Olympic Games in Paris.

The Edgar Thomson Works, commonly referred to as ET, fielded baseball, track and field, basketball, and boxing teams. The baseball roster included youths who would go on to play Negro League ball as well as men in the twilight of their playing careers who had previously been with the Homestead Grays or the Pittsburgh Crawfords. While the ET ball club was formed to meet the recreational needs of black steelworkers, its players were frequently offered jobs and money by the company to play ball. When John Herron, financial backer and manager of the Pittsburgh Monarchs, was forced to disband his black sandlot team in 1926, a number of the players wound up at ET. Harold Tinker, one of the Monarchs making the switch, recalled that the ET team "wasn't doing too well, but Earl Johnson was a very progressive guy and he went out and looked for ballplayers. He took the nucleus of the Monarchs."[57] Charlie Hughes, Ormsby Roy, Neal Harris, Claude Johnson, William Kimbo, and Tinker had grown up playing ball with each other, and when the Monarchs folded they decided to stick together. An offer of employment made moving en masse to the ET squad an easy decision. Hughes recalled getting a job at the mill in order to play on the team: "It was an easy job, steady daylight and they gave you time off to play and everything."[58] His brother Walt indicated that while the team had company support and most of the players got jobs in the mills, some simply played for the team on a semi-professional basis, receiving payment for each game played.[59] Such arrangements were fairly common on company teams. Willis Moody, a sandlot and Negro League star for a score of seasons, went to work for the Homestead plant of Carnegie-Illinois Steel and wound up managing their black ball club. He was able to get men jobs so they could play on the team and also was allowed to include on the roster five players who had nothing to do with the mill. How they were remunerated was "none of my concern," he explained.[60]

The ET baseball team graced area sandlots for the better part of two decades, from 1923 through World War II. The steel company's financial support apparently tailed off in the 1930s, however, and community groups like the Oak Leaf Club and the Young Men's Business Club picked up the slack. Still headed by Earl Johnson, the ball club passed the hat at games and hosted a series of entertainment features to raise money. In the late 1930s Rufus ("Sonnyman") Jackson, co-owner of the Homestead Grays and a prominent numbers banker in Homestead, was rumored to be lending a hand. ET teams were crowned the "mythical sandlot champs" of western Pennsylvania in 1937 and 1938 after winning the honors in Pittsburgh's top sandlot circuit, the Greater Pittsburgh League.[61] Playing not only other black mill teams but white sandlot clubs as well, the ET squad often took the field for as many as sixty or seventy games a season. In 1938, for example, the team won fifty-six, lost four, and had five games end in ties. Over the years, men like Lefty Williams, Joe Strong, Bus Clarkson, Pete Watson, Fuzzy Walton, and Dodo Baden played for the team. Some made their mark in the black professional leagues while others acquired reputations on the local sandlots. Still more played simply to take part in the game of baseball and compete on one of the area's more highly regarded squads.

Westinghouse (WEMCO), Homestead Steel, Pittsburgh Railways, Gimbel Brothers, the Philadelphia Company, Carnegie Steel, Pittsburgh Screw and Bolt, and probably another dozen or so companies sponsored baseball and basketball teams for their black workers. Some of them, like Gimbels and the Philadelphia Company, ran entire leagues; others, like WEMCO, sponsored individual clubs. Organized in 1922, with 150 members, the WEMCO Club was open to black employees of Westinghouse and a handful of honorary white members. Pursuing "civic, social and industrial" ends with the aim of promoting good will and better relationships among the employees, the WEMCO Club sponsored basketball teams and an annual field day.[62] These field days regularly drew 1,500 to 2,000 fans to Wildin Field in Wilmerding, in the Turtle Creek Valley. Music, stunts, and races vied with prizes for the children, a grand drawing, and an enormous barbecue. Boxing matches and a doubleheader featuring the WEMCO team highlighted the day.[63]

The WEMCO field day was typical of activities sponsored by sanctioned company workers' associations. The Philadelphia Company Colored Employees Association held similar affairs at Olympia Park, in McKeesport, for the workers, their families, and friends of the Philadelphia Company and its affiliated corporations, Duquesne Light, Pittsburgh Railways, and Equitable Gas.[64]

Industry also helped their black company teams align themselves with neighborhood clubs and organized leagues. Beyond the pale of organized baseball and informally barred from the top local semipro and sandlot circuits during the 1920s, 1930s, and 1940s, black ball clubs for the most part played independent ball. Teams arranged games with each other on an ad hoc basis. The sports pages of the *Courier* issued periodic calls for a black baseball league comprising the better sandlot outfits, and local companies, through their employee welfare agents, backed these ventures. It was one thing to play independent ball, booking separate engagements with other teams; it was quite another proposition to organize a league, providing for structure and leadership, ticket distribution, press contacts, a regular schedule, and championships. Besides the internal departmental leagues of the Philadelphia Company and Gimbel Brothers, there were at least four other workplace-based leagues in Pittsburgh during the 1920s.

The Negro Industrial Baseball League was the earliest, operating in 1922 and 1923. It stipulated that team rosters should be filled with amateurs, the majority of whom were industrial workmen connected with the same plant. Most of the teams were from steel mills like Fort Pitt, Carnegie, Lockhart, Woodlawn, and Coraopolis. Its first president, John T. Clark, who was also secretary of the Urban League, resigned during the 1923 season in protest over the dilution of this amateur-only policy. Leadership devolved to Cyrus T. Green, league secretary and a welfare worker for Westinghouse. A second effort, the Colored Industrial and Community Basketball League, appeared a few seasons later and was the centerpiece of local amateur basketball in 1926 and 1927. Teams from Edgar Thomson and the Duquesne Steel Works, the Philadelphia Company, and the WEMCO Club represented the industrial side of the league, while the Paramount and the Holy Cross athletic clubs and the North Side Scholastics and the Vandals represented the neighborhoods. The league's leadership included the tireless Earl Johnson, Max Bond, who was the physical director of the Centre Avenue branch of the YMCA and a former athlete at Chicago University, W. R. Johnson, who was the physical activities director of the Philadelphia Company, and Cyrus T. Green. Playing their games at the ET gym and the Centre Avenue Y, the Colored Industrial and Community Basketball League attempted to bar all the "so-called and recognized professional colored floor stars," an indication of encroaching commerical influence.[65]

Two other baseball leagues came together in the late 1920s and pitted industrial and community teams in regular competition. The Mon-Yough League was made up of teams from workplaces along the Monongahela and Youghiogheny rivers. Donora, Duquesne, Clairton, Wilmerding, Hays, and Christie Park were its mainstays. The Colored Industrial loop was a mix of community and mill teams, with WEMCO, Carnegie Steel, and the Philadelphia Company joining the East Liberty Greys and the Mendor, Hemlock, Bidwell, and fledgling Crawford athletic clubs.[66]

Scanning the list of team and league organizers reveals that a core of black sport activists, representing the YMCA, the Urban League, city recreation centers, settlement houses, and local industry, was behind most of the league activity. Some of them went back and forth between the private and public sector but retained their commitment to recreation. Charles Betts is one such example. Betts moved to Homestead in 1911 at the age of ten and found work in his teens at Westinghouse. From 1921 to 1928 he was the assistant director of welfare there, and during that time he played for the Loendi Reserves and the Homestead Athletic Association basketball, football, and baseball teams. The Great Depression cost him his job, but he was eventually hired by the Works Progress Administration for a local project to renovate an abandoned building and turn it into the McClure Community Center. The Carnegie Steel Works Colored Club wired the building and paid for the electricity, and the Homestead Council was petitioned to pay the rent and water bills. Betts later became director of the Ammon Recreation Center on the Hill, a post he held for twenty-four years. During that time he coached the Ammon Track Club, whose ranks included Herb Douglas, an Olympic medalist in 1948. Betts also helped form the Uptown Little League in 1952. His employers changed regularly but his involvement in black sport was a constant. Leagues and organized competition were thus an arena where men like Betts cooperated in building sport and recreation in black Pittsburgh. They saw their goals as common ones.[67]

Backing Off: The Decline of External Influence

Between the efforts of social agencies and settlement houses, companies and the city, a greatly enlarged sporting network took shape in the first thirty years of the twentieth century. But this coalition dissipated with the advent of economic depression. While the need for recreational facilities and sporting opportunities was greater than ever during hard times, when enforced idleness left many with time on their hands and little else, the physical plant and sport programs sponsored by this coalition did not grow to fill the void. Indeed, company, city, and social agency commitment to sport shrunk at a rate almost proportional to the declining economy.

City and community recreational programs would have been insufficient during the 1930s even if they had been maintained at their maximum level of funding from the 1920s. But when tax revenues from depressed industries fell, social and civic programs were cut back or terminated. Police, fire, and medical care suffered throughout the Monongahela River Valley, and with these essential services in trouble, it is no surprise that recreational programs received little backing. Clairton, a steel town on the Monongahela River north of Pittsburgh, had appropriated $2,500 to childrens' playgrounds in 1929; six years later it surrendered the program to the small recreation committee of the Citizen's League, which could muster less than $200 to maintain the playgrounds. Things were no different in places like Homestead, Duquesne, and McKeesport.[68]

The decline of city and community support was compounded by the almost total withdrawal of industry commitment in the early 1930s. With financial retrenchment came a drive to cut back unnecessary expenses, and the subsidies for company sport and recreation were among the first to go. Suddenly, the tremendous amount of money pumped into area sport by companies whose coffers had overflowed from profits garnered during World War I and the 1920s was reduced to a trickle and then cut off completely. Recreation centers like those maintained by WEMCO in Turtle Creek and Spang-Chalfant in Etna were boarded up. The athletic facilities of the Carnegie Library were closed. Playground equipment bought by the companies during the early 1920s and in need of upkeep and replacement in the 1930s simply deteriorated. Fewer teams and leagues could depend on company financing and support in terms of getting players hired and letting them off from work for practice and games.[69]

Most of the settlement houses had closed of their own volition by the 1930s, and with the depression, the YMCA and other social agencies were forced to restrict their services as well. As their financial support declined, they had to make cuts in staff, and in some cases even close down their centers. The membership fees at some of the endowed Carnegie Libraries were reduced, but even this lower rate was often too high to keep or to attract members.[70]

The demise of this informal coalition undercut sport and recreation in black Pittsburgh, but the blow was hardly a lethal one. Nor was it the end to the role that social agencies, city and community departments, and local companies would play in sport, as all of these forces either continued to maintain some level of commitment or returned to the field when economic conditions improved.[71] Yet none of these groups were ever again as much a factor in the sporting life of black Pittsburgh as they were during the years prior to the depression.

It is difficult to assess how successful these forces were in meeting their goals because sport and recreation were usually only part of a larger program. Moreover, ascribing political aims to particular sports ventures often tortures the connections between them. Yet it is a fact that the settlement houses, agencies like the YMCA and the Urban League, the city, and local companies were pursuing these undertakings for their own reasons, which can be broken down into three sets.

The first set represents the goals of the national organized play movement and partly explains the involvement of the settlement houses, the social agencies, and the city in sport. Emphasizing supervised play, the movement sought to employ recreation as a means of socializing children to the values of an industrializing American society. It saw itself in opposition to the street culture of immigrant communities, both white and black.

The second set of motives overlapped with the first. The key question was how to help black migrants adjust to urban-industrial life. The YMCA and YWCA, the Urban League, and the settlement houses confronted this problem through a variety of measures, sport being one of them. A team, a league, a gymnasium, and a bathhouse were means by which these agencies reached the migrants and sought to influence them.

The third set was less ambiguous than the first two and much more ambitious. The sporting and recreational agenda of industry was perceived as a potential tonic for industrial peace, worker productivity, and a steady flow of labor from surrounding communities. The dividends of sport, to recall L. C. Gardner's advice, would be "loyal, healthy, clean-living and team working employees" who would be "anchors to windward" when the ubiquitous outside agitators appeared.[72]

How effective were the programs and efforts of these forces in meeting these ends? The values of the organized play movement certainly took root, and many of the truisms about the meaning of sport and its role in reducing juvenile delinquency and fostering clean-living youth are still potent. Such sentiments were encountered repeatedly in my discussions with members of the black community in recent years, especially among those with a long history of commitment to either youth or sport. The organized play movement, while probably an effective means of socialization, hardly slew the enemy, street life. Nevertheless, contemporary community-based sport projects among black Pittsburghers echo the rhetoric about the role of sport for black youth.[73]

The black migration to Pittsburgh ebbed with hard times but picked up considerably when World War II refueled the economy. The efforts of the Urban League, the Y's, and the settlement houses to help migrants adjust to an urban-industrial environment and advance in terms of education and employment were partly successful, but underlying economic forces loomed large here. The role these agencies played in sport and recreation certainly enhanced their image in the black community and probably made their other programs more effective. The leaders of these agencies were often considered by the *Pittsburgh Courier* and the black community as black Pittsburgh's leadership, and their association with sport did them no harm.

The 1920s were relatively free of labor problems, and the black community proved to be a steady supplier of labor wherever industry would hire black workers. From a vantage point of fifty or more years, many of the black recipients of the various companies' largess in sport gave industry credit for their recreational activity at the same time that they acknowledged an understanding of why the companies were involved. Few seemed to think that the programs had a major impact on the thinking of black workers or suggested that it deterred anyone from later participating in the labor movement when it returned in force to Pittsburgh in the 1930s. Yet area firms still employ black athletes in public relations roles and hire them to advertise their products. If sport was not an antidote to labor organizing then, it at least temporarily improved the image of certain companies. By reverting to a policy of nonsupport during hard times and unionization, much of that goodwill was lost. A company or social agency could sponsor a team, but it took a sport activist or core group of players to really organize it, thus reducing the ideological impact of the sponsoring agency on the players who saw themselves or men like Earl Johnson or Sam Alexander, not Edgar Thomson Steel Works or WEMCO, as the driving force.

Even in the black press, it was Earl Johnson's squad more than Edgar Thomson's, and the industrial leagues were the work of a handful of sport activists, not of industry.

The sum total of these efforts in sport was not so much to create a fair and decent set of recreational opportunities for black Pittsburgh as to foster a sense that black Pittsburgh had a shared sporting life with enough dazzle and competence to be a source of self-esteem. The legacy was that of a core of sport activists, a cadre committed to sport and recreation for black Pittsburgh with goals and values which transcended the particular funding interests employing them. It left, too, a minimal number of playgrounds and fields, gyms and swimming pools, which, while never enough, were better than nothing. This coalition of forces pumped money into team and league sport and supported them in other ways as well. In a sense, these forces legitimized sport in the black community by involving members of the black elite.

At the same time, sport began to emerge as a source of cohesion for the community, transcending the divisions of class and place of birth. Many blacks were exposed to sport, especially sports other than baseball and basketball, because of these efforts. There was such an interest in sport that *Courier* writer Wendell Smith would claim not long afterward that he was "absolutely sure that no other section of the city is more sports conscious than this neglected, deprived civic orphan," the Hill.[74]

Another part of this legacy was a reinforcement of color lines in sport. The settlement houses, the social agencies, the city, and the companies all contributed in some way to either the erection or maintenance of these barriers. Integrated teams and recreational opportunities existed, but they were neither guaranteed nor the norm. Ironically, the very street scene that the organized play movement wanted to eradicate was more integrated and less bothered by racial differences than the settlement houses and supervised playgrounds.[75]

This history of exclusion and the curtailment of programs sponsored by local companies, settlement houses, and social agencies left black Pittsburgh on its own in the 1930s and 1940s. Exclusion meant that black sport would have to be built by the black community, not forces external to it. The economic realities implied that black sport would require a greater degree of self-reliance. The field was increasingly left to black social clubs, sports entrepreneurs, and the players themselves. They expanded rapidly to fill whatever void was left by the disappearance of company sport and the decline of city and social agency efforts. During the 1930s and 1940s, black Pittsburgh was to sport what Harlem was to the cultural and intellectual renaissance of the 1920s. Nowhere was this more striking than on the sandlots.

2 Sandlot Ball

Sandlot had its season, until its fragile ecology gave way before the incessant pounding of forces beyond its control. Now, the sandlots are more a memory than anything else. Their disappearance represents the contrast between contemporary sport and sport in the first half of the century. The sandlots belonged to an epoch in sport history when a different scale of economics applied and self-organized, independent ball clubs thrived in almost every neighborhood in and around cities like Pittsburgh, Brooklyn, Chicago, and Detroit. As community-oriented sport, the sandlots presented a counterpoint to the more heavily commercialized system of professional sport that reigned in the twentieth century. Yet in their prime, Pittsburgh's sandlot teams collectively drew more fans and meant more to people on a day-to-day basis than any of the city's professional franchises. Their decline after World War II profoundly affected the subsequent development of sport and community throughout America.

The sandlots link baseball and football, as traditional community recreations, with the late twentieth century's corporate money-ball. At first, *sandlot* simply referred to the field of play, but in the early decades of this century it came to be identified with independent ball, specifically baseball, that was not part of the professional major leagues and their minor league appendages. As baseball evolved from rounders and such games as "one old cat" on the town greens of eighteenth-century New England, young men began to organize teams and to adopt increasingly standardized rules to make competition possible. In New York City alone there were some fifty organized ball clubs by the late 1850s. Teams of doctors, lawyers, and bankers were soon matched by teams of artisans, firemen, and laborers, as the costs of playing did not bar admission to working men who often manufactured their own equipment and used vacant lots as their diamonds.

The portion of this chapter on the Pittsburgh Crawfords orginally appeared as "Black Sandlot Baseball: The Pittsburgh Crawfords," *Western Pennsylvania Historical Magazine* 66 (no. 1, Jan. 1983): 49–68.

While a professional component to baseball developed in the
1870s following the creation in 1869 of the first fully professional team, the Cincinnati Red Stockings, the nation's most
popular sport was still overwhelmingly a community recreation
by the late nineteenth century. However, organized baseball, as
the professional league and its affiliates became known in later
years, soon took on more of the aspects of the business world—
for example, teams banded together to form a league, with
assigned markets and labor practices designed to restrict player
movement.[1] By the turn of the century, baseball was a fairly
substantial business wedded to the press, a sporting goods industry, and a score of owners with ties to local breweries, trac-
tion companies, and politics.

Alongside this industry-in-the-making, nonprofessional teams
were formed wherever the expanding population warranted such
action. Virtually every town and urban neighborhood had its
own ball club. While commercial sponsorship was common,
these teams were not playing to make a profit but rather to give
local boys and men a chance to play and the community a
chance to cheer.

Scores of essentially amateur teams were organized in the
Ohio River Valley and western Pennsylvania during baseball's
post–Civil War expansion. The first local professional club, the
Alleghenies, made its debut in Pittsburgh in 1876 but folded
after one season. Pro ball did not reappear in the area until 1887,
when Pittsburgh was awarded a franchise in the National
League. Even with a pro team in their midst, Pittsburghers still
went in greater numbers to the games of such local squads as the
East Liberty Stars, the East End Gymns, and the black Keystones.[2] These sandlot rivalries generated more interest and filled
more of a social and community role than the struggling professionals did.

In the early twentieth century, the professional game of baseball grew in strength, as did sandlot baseball. The term *sandlot*
acquired a set of common if sometimes contradictory meanings.
Baseball mythology has it that a sandy lot traditionally used as a
ball field in Oakland, California, became known as The Sandlot,
a name that stuck and was used for any appropriate playing field.
Sandlot ball meant baseball, and later football, independent of

the professional game, yet in fact it co-mingled amateur and semiprofessional elements. Sandlot players could frequently expect payment, in some cases equal to or more than the amounts given to players in the pro leagues, but for most sandlot players the money was in addition to, not a substitute for, a regular paycheck; more often than not, the amount was not enough to support a man and his family. Simon-pure sport, as amateur ball was often described, was more honored in the breach. The designation "amateur" has long been an ambiguous category haphazardly applied to American athletes. If a group of young baseball players passed the hat at a game and split the proceeds, they technically jeopardized their amateur status. However, if such a standard had been uniformly applied, amateur ball would have been left almost exclusively to the economic elites early in the century.

The difference between sandlot and organized ball, then, was not that one welcomed commercial interests and the other did not, but the relative level of capitalization and commercialism. In many cases sandlot players shared their equipment, with everyone chipping in to buy a team ball, and so on; but in some cases there were sandlot players, especially during the 1950s, who earned $300–400 a month. Many of the players who helped establish the professional game started out on the sandlots. And more than a few returned there when their professional careers were at an end.[3]

Honus Wagner, the Pirate's incomparable Flying Dutchman, was born outside of Pittsburgh in a small coal-mining community. As a boy, Wagner worked in the mines, loading a ton of coal for seventy cents. He and his four brothers formed a basketball quintet and the better half of the Wagner Brothers baseball club. From local sandlots, Wagner played through a half-dozen minor leagues before signing on with the Louisville club in the National League in 1897. Twenty-one years later he retired, but not before joining the select 3,000-hit club and establishing a reputation on the field that would earn him a spot in Cooperstown and a statue outside of Forbes Field.[4] Even while a Pirate, Wagner could often be found playing ball with the kids in his neighborhood. When he left professional baseball after the 1917 season, he returned to the sandlots and played first base for the Green Cab semipros and the Carnegie Elks, in Pittsburgh, for another eight seasons, until the age of fifty-one.[5]

Wagner's career from the sandlots through the big leagues and back to the sandlots was typical of the sporting life cycle of many ballplayers, from the late nineteenth century through the 1950s. The majority of sandlotters never left their locales, however. A boy could learn how to play on the sandlots of Pittsburgh, mature and reach his peak as a ballplayer there, and then hang on with a local team even as his playing capacities diminished. While on the sandlots that player could compete with future and former big leaguers like Paul Waner, Lou Gehrig, Satchel Paige, or Dizzy Dean. The sandlots linked the game of baseball as kids played it with the pro game. By providing intermediate levels of ball, the sandlots prevented the development of a large gap in terms of levels of skill, personalities, and money between the different ranks of baseball. Consequently, the game of baseball as played by the pros was much closer to nonprofessional ball, and players and spectators went back and forth between the two.

Sandlot ball reached its zenith during the years between the two world wars. World War I, as do most wars, had a radicalizing effect on various aspects of society.[6] Secretary of War Newton Baker's "work or fight" order was not intended to spur the growth of sandlot ball, but it did just that. While over half of the ballplayers in the National and American leagues entered the armed services, many others sought war jobs at steel mills, munitions factories, and shipyards. Just as many of the armed forces enlistees wound up playing ball on base or unit teams, so too did many who joined the work force, supplementing their earnings with ball and bat. Certain industries, particularly steel and shipbuilding, already sponsored teams, and they intensified these athletic programs during the war. Industry agents contacted players and induced them to join their work force, where they seldom worked but often played. Although baseball owners objected and their workmates wondered where they were, many major and minor leaguers spent the war years playing ball.[7]

In Pittsburgh, Baker's decree and industry's desire to promote sport prompted the formation of a number of strong sandlot teams, including the Westinghouse Munitions and the Allegheny Steel and Aluminum nine.[8] Industry's involvement was so intense that many observers were worried that amateur sandlot ball would perish. One sportswriter claimed: "The amateurs were almost wrecked in the years just following the war by the semi-pro invasion. . . . The sport became over-inflated and over-emphasized . . . almost crowding the little amateur sandlotters out of the picture."[9] The semiprofessional aspect of the game indeed grew, but the sandlots were not about to perish.

The armed services stimulated sandlot's postwar development by serving as a sports training grounds for the four to five million men in uniform. *Scientific American* observed that "Uncle Sam has created not only an army of soldiers, but an army of athletes."[10] The journal asserted that never before had so many men participated in athletics, nor had physical welfare received such a boost, as during the war. The enlisted men regularly played sports designed to physically prepare them for combat and to keep their morale up during lulls in the fighting. Football and especially boxing gained new adherents, and their increasing popularity in the 1920s was due in no small part to the exposure to these sports which hundreds of thousands of men received in military training camps. The most widely played sport of all in these army and navy camps, however, was baseball.

While the war served as a catalyst, the postwar sports boom that swept the country provided a supportive context for the expansion of sandlot ball. Professional boxing and baseball and collegiate football welcomed this "golden age of sport" with open ledgers. There were more players than ever before on the sandlots. Industry's involvement in promoting sport during the 1920s expanded with its American plan for employee welfare schemes and the open shop. And the American people, after years of a frequently divisive war, were ready to play.[11] Even nature was compelled to lend a hand. The nation experimented briefly with a plan to advance the clocks one hour from late March through October, thus forestalling darkness. Although opposition from farmers led to a repeal of the law on a national basis, many municipalities and a few states adopted their own ordinances. Daylight savings time was a boon to twilight ball games, and players were quick to take advantage of it.

Between the wars, at least 200–500 clubs played on Pittsburgh area sandlots each season. A 1926 directory of baseball clubs, printed in the *Pittsburgh Press* to facilitate contact between team managers, listed 223 clubs, including 11 black ones.[12] The "Sandlotters' Baseball Guide," issued in booklet form by the *Pittsburgh Post* a year later, noted that 53 fields were available for local sandlotters. Its listings for 124 teams in 19 leagues, like those in the *Pittsburgh Press,* covered only a portion of sandlot activity, mainly among the tri-state region's leading teams.[13] A 1931 *Press* feature on sandlot ball estimated that more than 400 clubs and 50 leagues operated annually during the late 1920s.[14] The leagues' organizational structures varied immensely; some were basically company affairs while others had newspaper and municipal sponsorship. Sporting goods firms also had a stake in league activity and were active promoters. Certain leagues and teams held membership in the National Baseball Federation, a body which tried to control amateur baseball. Others, especially black teams, paid the federation little mind.

When the Great Depression hit area industry and many teams found their subsidies terminated, some teams folded while others simply adopted a more autonomous, self-funding approach. Some clubs actually formed in response to the depression, as many young men found themselves with a surplus of enforced leisure time. Although economic hard times affected gate receipts and lowered financial contributions from community backers, sandlot ball refused to fold. Baseball and sandlot football both prospered in the 1920s and 1930s. Local papers covered the games as the gridiron alternated with the diamond for the fans' allegiance. For many, football and then club basketball were simply the natural responses to the changing seasons. At least a hundred different elevens took to the field each fall.

Black Pittsburgh was swept along in the postwar expansion in sport, its teams multiplying in number and improving in ability. At one time black sport in Pittsburgh mostly meant basketball, and its cagemen were among the best in the nation. The Monticellos and the Loendi Club vied for national honors in the years prior to World War I, but in the postwar decades black baseball and football took center stage.

From the late 1920s through the 1940s, black Pittsburgh defined its own sporting life on the sandlots. The community never controlled its sport as much before or afterward. The teams were originally products of black Pittsburgh's different neighborhoods, and their players and fans reflected these origins. Clubs like the 18th Ward, the Garfield Eagles, and the Crawfords helped bind their neighborhoods around teams that excelled in one of the few fields equally open to blacks and whites. As commercial pressures increased, these teams shifted from neighborhood-based clubs to those representing the larger black community, which pledged them their allegiance, taking heart from the victories of favorite sons.

Black Pittsburgh looked to itself for sport in the early twentieth century largely because of the class and racial dynamics of white professional and major college sport. Its sandlots and gymnasiums, and those of neighboring communities, were particularly important because much of professional and collegiate sport was still beyond the racial boundary until the late 1940s.

In the early decades of this century there were clear class and racial differences between sandlot ball and the pro game. The cost of admission, the absence of Sunday ball in Pennsylvania until 1933, and the early afternoon starting time all discouraged working-class attendance at Pirate games. Blacks, along with many immigrant and industrial workers, were much more likely to watch or play on the sandlots of their own or a neighboring community, where admission was a contribution to the passing hat, games were played in the twilight or on weekends, and players were neighbors, workmates, and kin.[15]

Nor was the black professional game much of an alternative to sandlot and community ball in the 1920s. Pittsburgh had no representation in the various national black baseball leagues of those years, and there never was a national black football league. Black professional sport, then, was akin to semiprofessional sport, with the players as often as not relying on other jobs to support themselves during the off-season or to supplement their meager professional incomes. While the Homestead Grays and some basketball clubs played on a semiprofessional basis in Pittsburgh during the 1920s, the locus of black sport activity was clearly noncommercial and nonprofessional.

If there were only a handful of black sandlot clubs in Pittsburgh before the war, the 1920s witnessed the creation of scores of black sandlot nines. And none left a more indelible mark on sport than the Crawfords.

Kings on the Hill: The Crawfords

What in time became known as one of the greatest baseball clubs in the world began as a group of black and white Pittsburgh youths playing ball on the sandlots of the Hill. Organized baseball might have been lily-white in the 1920s, but race didn't count that much on the Hill when it came time to choose up sides for a game. Blacks and whites played together, ate meals at each other's homes, and often were whipped by both black and white mamas when they got into trouble. The Hill was a racial and ethnic smorgasbord, and pick-up games reflected that variety. As street play became increasingly organized into team competition, however, a sorting out by race occurred. Consequently, sandlot clubs were rarely composed of both black and white players, even though their members might have grown up playing ball together. The Crawfords came out of this interracial mix but became an all-black squad as they moved further away from the streets.

The roots of the Crawfords were in the South and the subsequent migration northward. Bill Harris was born on Christmas day 1909 in Calhoun, Alabama. His parents had met while working as cooks at the local public school, but neither a piece of land nor a job inspecting cars for the railroad was sufficient inducement to resist the lures of the North. The Harrises' oldest son, Earl, was the first to leave. He moved to Pittsburgh and worked construction jobs. When Earl wrote home that the money was good, the Harris family soon joined him. His father worked construction, too, beginning as a laborer and eventually becoming a pusher, or gang leader. The five Harris brothers held a variety of jobs but became better known for their feats on the diamond, first in Pittsburgh and then across black America.[16]

Bill Harris had his first taste of ball in the South, where the sport revolved around a multitude of small-town teams and a few big-city clubs like the Birmingham Black Barons and the Memphis Red Sox. But he really learned the game on the streets

and school lots of the Hill. By the time Bill was in the eighth grade at McKelvey School, he had left the pitcher's mound for a position in the infield and had become the de facto leader of the grade-school team. "It was just a playground bunch but the guys wanted to play ball," he told me. There were four blacks on the McKelvey team in 1925; "the rest were Jewish boys and Italians and white boys," about thirteen to fifteen years old. They played rival school or street teams in games Harris and the other team leaders arranged. One opponent was the team from Watt School.[17] McKelvey's black enrollment was slightly over 28 percent of the student body in the mid-1920s, while Watt's was the highest on the Hill at 88 percent. The Watt team consisted of seven black and two white players.[18]

Teenie Harris managed the Watt team, and while no relation to Bill, the two considered themselves "pretty close." It was simply a matter of time before they arranged a contest. Some sixty-five years later, Bill Harris recalled that when "I told our guys that we were going to play Watt School they said, 'Oh no! We're not going to play them cause they fight. If you beat Watt School you got to outrun them, too.' They didn't want to play so I said, 'Look, fellas. Teenie's got those fellas under control the same way I got you fellows. We're going to play them.'"[19] Winning over his teammates, Bill booked the game for a nearby playground.

When that first game ended with Watt on top of a one-to-nothing score, the McKelvey players, who may have been youngsters but were still mature enough ballplayers to appreciate a close, well-played game, approached Bill Harris. "Bill, they no argue, they no fight. They got a good team. Book 'em again." Three weeks later the two teams tangled in a rematch, and Watt once more emerged victorious, this time by three runs to two. Afterward, Bill and Teenie hashed over the game. "Look at this," Bill argued. "Two games going down like this and your eight or nine black dudes playing pretty good ball. We have four of us here and each one of us plays a different position. Let's get a ball team together." Teenie agreed. The black youngsters from the two school teams thus became one squad and started playing and practicing down at Washington Park. The white players from both teams fell by the wayside. Bill Harris thought they were less proficient than the black players, but perhaps more important than this remembered difference in playing abilities was the reality that organized competition on the sandlots of Pittsburgh was usually between squads made up of players with the same skin color. A black team frequently played a white squad, but a team with both black and white players was the exception.

For the rest of that summer the as-yet-unnamed team played games arranged by Bill and Teenie, picking up a player here or there. The following season, 1926, saw most of the players back on the field ready to see just how good they were. They entered the city's recreation league as the representative of the Crawford Bath House and became known as the Crawfords. A combination bathhouse and recreation center catering primarily to blacks on the Hill, the Crawford Street club distributed food baskets at Christmas and had the support of both black and white merchants, professionals, and sportsmen on the Lower Hill.[20]

The Crawford Bath House was never totally segregated, but in the early 1920s the director of the Bureau of Recreation had put up signs there announcing that the center was for blacks. The black *Pittsburgh American* warned that the director seemed "very anxious to herd certain citizens off to themselves to keep down 'clashes,'" and after a spirited resistance by the black community the signs came down.[21] Several years later, John Clark was encouraged to report in his "Wylie Avenue" column in the *Pittsburgh Courier* that white clubs were competing in the sport programs at the bathhouse and that a mixed team had been entered in the Press Meet, an annual track and field competition. The Bath House boys won the May Day meet with a squad of thirty-seven, including thirty-two blacks, three Jews, and two Italians.[22] In his column lauding the victory of this mixed entry, Clark compared them to Hunter Johnson's Scholastic Club and praised the work of the director, Harry Hall.

A partisan of the sporting life, Clark issued a plea for his readers to back the team.

Crawford Center must have a baseball team. Avenue patrons want to see their boys active on the diamond under able direction. Twilight games played by youngsters furnish a thrill to parents that is absent in the professional exhibitions. The participants are closer to us. We are interested in their every movement—they are ours.

The Column is begging. There is no appropriation from the city for uniforms. So the Column requests that every one of its readers donate one dime (ten cents) to Harry Hall, care of Crawford Recreation Center, Wylie Avenue and Crawford Street, Pittsburgh, Pa.

As you know, the Column is not in the habit of begging, and this request is made in the interests of the boys who cannot reach you. Incidentally, it will give the Column an idea of how widely its efforts are appreciated.

A week later Clark lamented his apparent lack of readers with spare change, but he found some solace in the contributions the Crawfords began to receive from Wylie Avenue businessmen and patrons. Both Bill Harris and Teenie Harris recall that the key donation came from Gus Greenlee, the proprietor of an avenue nightspot.[23]

The Crawfords won the 1926 pennant of the city's recreation league and posed in their new uniforms on the steps of the Carnegie Library on Wylie Avenue on the Hill. Thirteen youths appear in the photograph, most of whom had been with the Crawfords from their Watt and McKelvey school beginnings in 1925. They were a serious, unsmiling group, clad in pinstripes and spiked shoes.[24]

The Crawfords retained their affiliation with the bathhouse and recreation center for the next two seasons, although they were essentially a self-organized, self-directed team. Bill Harris and Harry Beale booked the games and called most of the shots on the field, while Jim Dorsey, Sr., from the center, served as their nominal coach. Players came and went but the Crawfords continued to improve, with streaks of twenty-five or more consecutive victories. Soon writers for the *Courier* were calling them the most promising team in the Colored Industrial Baseball League, the "fastest and cleverest outfit . . . to perform on a local diamond in the first-class division in many seasons." Perhaps the highest praise came for the Bath House boys when they were referred to as the "Little Homestead Grays," after the area's top black professional club, which was itself attracting considerable national attention in the late 1920s.[25]

In the fall of 1927 the nucleus of the Crawfords joined forces with five Jewish boys from the Hill to represent the McKelvey playgrounds in the Senior Inter-Playground League Championship. Outclassing their opponents, this rare integrated nine swept through the tourney and won a large silver trophy depicting a catcher crouching atop a baseball mounted on a base. The *Courier* hailed it as a major victory, the first time in the history of the city that such a large number of "race lads" had taken part in summer playground activities. The trophy was exhibited at the Centre Avenue YMCA and in other parts of the city where blacks could view it.[26]

During the 1927 and 1928 seasons the Crawfords played their way to the top ranks of black sandlot baseball in Pittsburgh. At first the young team had trouble getting the other black clubs, made up of men in their twenties, thirties, and forties, to play them. But the Crawfords were fast becoming one of the best draws in town, and when the Hill's favorite team played, crowds from several hundred to a few thousand were guaranteed.[27] They took on the area's top black clubs, and as they beat them, they recruited some of their vanquished opponents.

When the Crawfords played the Pittsburgh Black Sox at Washington Park, they repeatedly bunted their way on base. Relying on speed, the Crawfords won, and when the "Dark Hose" demanded a rematch, the Crawfords beat them again. After the second victory, four members of the Black Sox jumped to the Crawfords: Harry and Roy Williams, and Eddie and Willie Bryant, two pairs of brothers. Bill Harris explained the transition as a simple one: "The fellows that were with us playing those positions—they just fell out. No questions asked. They just quit." In the meantime, Teenie Harris had left the club to help his brother Woogie in a new venture—the popularization of the numbers racket in Pittsburgh.

Next, the Crawfords beat the Clark Athletic Club and the Garfield ABCs, picking up an infielder and two pitchers in addition to their victories. Finally, the young Crawfords tangled with the Edgar Thomson ball club in Braddock. The ET club, coached by former Olympian Earl Johnson, had been built around a nucleus of young ballplayers who had joined the steel mill's club when John Herron had disbanded his Pittsburgh Monarchs in 1924. Harold Tinker, Neal Harris, Charlie Hughes, Ormsby Roy, Claude Johnson, and William Kimbo were still with the ET team four seasons later when they met the

Crawfords. As Tinker recalled it: "Those kids came to play Edgar Thomson and we were amazed that we could only beat them two to one or something like that. Those kids were really hustlers. Now, Neal Harris's brother, Bill Harris, . . . he played third base for the kids and that had something to do with us coming from Edgar Thomson, because he insisted to his brother, Neal, 'Why don't you come down and we'll make this a real ball team?' So we quit Edgar Thomson and went down to play with these kids at Washington Park."[28] With the acquisition of the ET players, the Crawfords were far and away the best black sandlot club in town. Their high percentage of victories over white sandlotters indicates that they were likely the best sandlot club, black or white, in all of western Pennsylvania.[29]

By the fall of 1928, Bill Harris and Johnny Moore had been picked up by Cumberland Posey's Homestead Grays. Both Harris and Moore, in addition to their baseball feats, were all-city basketball players in high school, Harris at Fifth Avenue and Moore at Schenley. Johnny Moore also quarterbacked the Crawfords' counterparts in sandlot football, the Garfield Eagles. Their absence was more than compensated for by Tinker, Hughes, and the other recruits. Among the latter was a husky youth from the Northside, Joshua Gibson, who would become the premier slugger of black baseball.

Harold Tinker was born in Birmingham in 1905 and came to Pittsburgh with his family in 1917. His father found work at Horne's Department Store and also as a barber. Tinker grew up playing baseball and soccer on the Hill and running track for Hunter Johnson's Scholastics. He briefly took the field for the Keystone Juniors, along with Bill Harris's brother, Neal. "I didn't play baseball just because it was a pastime," Tinker recollected. "I played it because I loved it. If my mother wanted to find me, she didn't have to worry. She'd say, 'Go down to the ball field and tell Harry to come home.' I lived on that ball field." A kid with an uncanny ability to judge and track down a fly ball did not go unnoticed, and at the age of fifteen Tinker was recruited by the WEMCO ball club.

I'll never forget the first game I played. I made a couple of sensational catches—they were sensational partly because of my inexperience. I was running for the Schenley High track team and played baseball in my track shoes. I came in for a line drive, first line drive I'd ever fielded in a sandlot game and the ball was over my head after I started in. I had misjudged it. I tried to put on the brakes, you know, with my heels, and you know how trackshoes are. I stood up on my heels and my feet went up and my hand flew up and I caught that ball. They thought I was a sensation. And I chased one of the balls that day very much off of the playing field and rounded it up. They wouldn't let me go. They said, "Play."[30]

From WEMCO to the Pittsburgh Monarchs and then to the Edgar Thomson club, Tinker matured as a player and found his natural position in center field. Along the way he picked up the nickname "Hooks," for his pronounced bow-leggedness. He made a few dollars playing for the Monarchs and received some small remuneration from ET, which played virtually every night of the week. The money alone was not enough to live on, so Tinker began working for RKO pictures in downtown Pittsburgh, first as a janitor and then as head of the shipping department. He would leave work and catch a street car to the ET field every night, not getting home until late in the evening. Holding down a job during the day did not impair his capacity to play in the twilight, however. Tinker acquired a local reputation as a black Tris Speaker, after the brilliant defensive center fielder and Hall of Famer for the Boston Red Sox and the Cleveland Indians.[31] Tinker chuckled when reminded of these accolades during an interview in his Hill district home more than a half-century later, and he modestly credited his success to watching the ball "from the time it left the pitcher's hand until it left the bat. I was ready to move."

Charlie Hughes's father became a molder in Chattanooga and worked at his trade in McKeesport after moving to Pittsburgh. Charlie grew up in the predominantly white working-class section of Lawrenceville in the company of immigrant families from southern and eastern Europe. He played pick-up games with Polish boys on Herron Hill before joining the Pittsburgh Blue Sox, a sandlot team from the Lawrenceville and Herron Hill black communities. He met Tinker, who was playing for the Monarchs, and both made the switch to the Edgar Thomson team. It has often been said that for a baseball team to be good, it has to be strong up the middle, that is, the catcher, shortstop, second baseman, and center fielder must be good defensive players. With Tinker in center and Hughes at short, their clubs always had that potential. Hughes was induced to join the ET team with the offer of a job, one he returned to whenever he was unable to play professional ball full-time. With breaks for ball and a stint in the army during World War II, Hughes still managed to accumulate thirty-two years of service at ET before retiring. Despite a stroke that left him half-paralyzed, when I finally tracked him down at his sister's apartment in the Garfield Towers housing project, his eyes danced as he quietly traced his development into one of Pittsburgh's premier ballplayers.[32]

Recently, while going over the roster of the Crawfords, Harold Tinker stopped and smiled when he got to Charlie Hughes's name.

The greatest ground-ball man I've ever seen in my life. As much as we cared for that field up there [Ammon Field], there would be a gutter that ran across second base every time it rained. And Hughes would be digging it out, and scraping it and raking it but it would be right back. Balls would get to that gutter and jump right up in his face. You know what he'd do with it? He'd come up with it on his ear [laughs]. You know, I watched this kid make miraculous catches so many times. One day, I said, "Charlie, how do you catch those balls that make that bounce right into your face?" and he said, "I'll tell you something. I watch the ball until it goes into the glove." This boy was marvelous. I never saw him make the wrong throw.[33]

Tinker was responsible for recruiting Josh Gibson to the Crawfords. Gibson's father had left Buena Vista, Georgia, in 1921 to work for Carnegie-Illinois Steel in Pittsburgh. Three years later, Mark Gibson was able to send for his wife and three kids. Josh was not quite thirteen when the family moved to the Pleasant Valley section on the Northside. He left school after the ninth grade and worked for Westinghouse Airbrake, a steel mill, and Gimbel Brothers Department Store before finding his calling on the ball field. A strong, solidly built young man—he weighed 190 pounds and stood six feet tall by the time he was eighteen— Gibson played for the Pleasant Valley Red Sox and then the Gimbel Brothers Athletic Club.[34] "Hooks" Tinker, who had been playing ball for a team on the Northside, recalled: "I went over there to play with them one day and this boy was playing third base. There were gullies and everything there but this guy was digging balls out and he amazed me by the way he played, not by his hitting. And then I saw him hit a ball up on top of that hill and I said, 'Josh, don't you want to play with a real team?' And he said, 'Yes, sir, I guess so.' I said, 'Well, I'll tell you what. When we play on Tuesday, you come up.' "[35]

The Crawfords already had a fine defensive catcher in Wyatt Turner. According to Tinker, "He was a smart catcher, but he wasn't an excellent hitter—not then he wasn't. We suggested when we saw the way Josh could throw that we would let him catch." Josh had done some catching before, and from his first game with the Crawfords he was behind the plate. "He became a tremendous success. He hit balls out on Bedford Avenue and up in that hospital [a powerful blast from Ammon Field]. He was actually the most tremendous hitter I've ever come across in baseball—I'm barring none."[36] Wyatt Turner, who found himself on the bench when the awesome young slugger and future Hall of Famer took his place, accepted his demotion in good spirits. Decades later, while recounting some of Josh's feats, Turner summed up his thoughts: "If he put his bat down, I'd be ashamed to pick it up."[37]

Gibson stories around Pittsburgh are legion. They often begin with the narrator commenting that it was "the longest hit ball I ever saw." Tinker's favorite involved a game the Crawfords were playing against a white ball club from Port Vue, up the river from McKeesport.

> That team got ahead of us some kind of way and they stayed there until about the 6th inning. They were two runs ahead and I was the first man up and I got on base. The next man up hit an infield single and moved me over to second. Josh was due up. He was the clean-up batter. Quite naturally, you know, you walk a man when you got an open base. They didn't have no open base, but they knew Josh. So the man threw two pitch-outs, Josh called time and he called over to me. I met him there on the infield grass and he said, "Can I hit the ball?"
>
> I said, "What do you mean, Josh? The man is giving you the intentional walk and we need two runs to tie."
>
> "I don't know. The man is pitching out too close to the plate."
>
> "Josh, you mean to tell me you could reach out and hit the ball where he's throwing it?"

Josh smiled and said, "I can hit it."

"Well, Josh, if you feel you can hit it, you go ahead and hit it." I walked back to second base and the next pitch-out that boy threw him was a pitch-out on the outside, way out, and Josh didn't hit that ball over the right field fence—he hit that ball over the centerfield fence. The people went crazy. I couldn't believe it . . . the ball was really out there.

Josh was built like metal. There was no fat on him. If you ran into him, it was just like you run into a wall. Yes, sir, that's the way he was built. Man, he was hard. He was a powerful boy.[38]

As young men like Gibson, Tinker, and Hughes replaced players from the Watt and McKelvey playgrounds, the Crawfords underwent a transition from a neighborhood team to one of the best sandlot teams in black Pittsburgh. The internal workings of the team also changed as the institutional affiliation with the Crawford Bath House was a thing of the past by the 1929 season. Even during their years as the center's team, the Crawfords were basically a self-managed operation, with Bill Harris and Teenie Harris handling most of the bookings and making the managerial decisions in the early years. When Teenie left the club to work for his brother, Harry Beale took on some of the work and emerged as the real organizer of the Crawfords off the field, especially after Bill Harris signed with the Homestead Grays.

Beale was both a manager and a public relations man, setting up games and handling the finances. Highly respected by his teammates, he was regarded as an intelligent, level-headed guy. "If Harry said it," Tinker reminisced, "we did it." Beale had been a pitcher, but as the general calibre of the Crawfords improved, "he realized he didn't have the ability for the kind of ball we were playing. He knew where his ability would help us best and that's what he did."[39] Thus, Beale left the mound for the bench and put his energies into promoting the Crawfords and arranging their games. He also began writing a column about sandlot ball for the *Pittsburgh Courier*. Field decisions were increasingly being made by Tinker, team captain and co-manager with Beale during the 1929 season. Tinker called the shots from the bench, determining when to bunt, steal, or hit and run; the men coached each other, sharing their knowledge of the game and passing on their skills.

The Crawfords began preparations for the 1929 season at a meeting in February at the Centre Avenue YMCA. Beale and Tinker were reelected co-managers, and the team acquired a financial backer,[40] J. W. King, a Democratic ward heeler who worked as a policeman in Soho. King lived on the Hill, where he also had a coal and ice delivery service. He backed the team financially, not out of a desire to make money, but simply out of his fondness for the players and the game and the publicity which accrued from his support. He bought uniforms and equipment and emptied the ice out of his truck to transport the team to away games. King attended all of the Crawfords' games but kept in the background. "Without him," Harold Tinker argued, "I don't think we would have made it. He was a grand old man who just wanted to help out." According to Charlie Hughes, King "wasn't making a quarter" on the team but nonetheless contributed heavily to its upkeep. During the season, Steve Cox, from the Spalding-Spiegal Sporting Goods store and a force in area sandlot ball, began booking games for them, too. Cox had contacts with the top white sandlot clubs and was willing to arrange games for the Crawfords without taking a percentage of the gate for himself.

By the middle of the 1929 season, the Crawfords were drawing over 3,000 fans to their Tuesday, Friday, and Saturday home games at Ammon Field. To boost attendance and reciprocate community support, the Crawfords frequently staged benefit games for such institutions as the Coleman Home or the Livingston Memorial Hospital, thus guaranteeing substantial ticket sales. The *Courier* trumpeted these games, playing up both the charity angle and the actual contest.[41] When the team traveled, a good-sized contingent of Hill residents went with them. Bill Harris remembered a doubleheader in Vandergrift, some thirty miles from Pittsburgh, for which the Crawfords' fans arrived so early and in such numbers that when the hometown crowd arrived they had no place to sit. The size of the crowd did not necessarily mean that the Crawfords were a money-making organization, however.

Outside Pittsburgh ball fields were commonly fenced off and spectators had to pay their way in. The city, however, prohibited sandlot teams from charging admission at city fields. Teams and promoters got around this ban by passing the hat among the crowd. Unfortunately, many fans failed to make a contribution, and crowds of several thousand sometimes wound up contributing only fifty or sixty dollars. The cost of baseballs and umpires used up most of that; and the visiting team usually got a flat fee or, when not in the city, a cut of the gate. Tinker recalled that there was a "mob of people" at the first game he played as a Crawford but donations amounted to less than ten dollars.

In 1928 the city was about to open a new ball field on Bedford Avenue, and Harry Beale suggested that the Crawfords apply for a permit to play there. Ammon Field thus became their home grounds, and the Crawfords played there first one and then two and three nights a week. At Ammon, they took on the best teams the area had to offer and usually beat them, teams like Book-Shoe, W.O.W., J. L. Thomas, and Dormont. The latter, one of the top semipro teams in the area, often employed former major leaguers and gave the Homestead Grays a hard time, but they could not top the Crawfords. The take from the passing hat at Ammon doubled, but it was still meager. Away games were usually more lucrative, sometimes bringing in a few hundred dollars. After a string of several such games, Beale and Tinker began to divvy up the profits among the players. The most Tinker ever took home in his pay envelope was twelve dollars, and that held true more or less for everybody. The Crawfords became such a good drawing card in some small white outlying communities, and Harry Beale such an adept negotiator, that the team sometimes got rain guarantees, meaning that the Crawfords received a flat fee even if the game was cancelled due to rain. The Homestead Grays "wouldn't go anywhere without a rain guarantee," but it was rare for a sandlot club to comand such a commitment.[42]

During an elimination series for a tournament in the 1929 season, Cumberland Posey's brother See approached the Crawfords and asked them to let him run a game for them at Ammon Field. "I'm going to show you kids what you're missing," Bill Harris recalled him saying.[43] The red-hot Crawfords, with a late August record of sixty-five wins and eleven losses, were already attracting large crowds.[44] See Posey blocked off the upper part of the field and stationed two policemen there. Everybody had to get in through one gate, and while there was no set admission, each spectator had to contribute something to get by Posey. After the ball game, Posey spread the take out on a table— over $2,000, as Bill Harris remembered it. The startled players indeed began to wonder what they might be missing.

By the late 1920s, the Crawfords had captured the attention of baseball fans because of their youthfulness and their exceptional play. They were the Hill's team even when the roster expanded to include more and more players from other parts of the city. Furthermore, they were perceived as black Pittsburgh's team, and most blacks felt a proprietary interest in them much the way the citizens of a city today feel that a professional sports team is theirs. The Crawfords belonged to black Pittsburgh in a way the Homestead Grays did not, for each member of the Crawfords in the 1920s was either Pittsburgh-born or had moved there with his family; none had come to Pittsburgh simply to play ball. While the Grays had begun in a similar fashion, by the 1920s they were an amalgam of the best black ballplayers in the nation. The fans responded to the hometown character of the Crawfords by filling the grandstands and lining the baselines whenever they played. The strongest support came from the black population of the Hill, but local whites and blacks elsewhere were among their most ardent backers. After several matches with the Immaculate Heart team from Lawrenceville, a contingent of white Lawrenceville fans also started showing up regularly at Ammon Field, where they mingled with Hill residents and blacks from Homewood, East Liberty, and Beltzhoover. The crowds for home games were predominantly black, with anywhere from 15 to 30 percent of the audience made up of whites. On the road, especially outside the city, the crowds were often overwhelmingly white. At times, the Crawfords played in small towns outside Pittsburgh where they were the only blacks around.

The Crawfords were a hot topic for conversation on street corners and in barbershops, and the *Pittsburgh Courier* followed their ascension on the sandlots with enthusiasm and pride. Many of the Crawfords' black supporters also began to place bets directly with fans of the rival squads; those who bet on the Crawfords were more often than not the winners. Most fans simply came to enjoy the game, however, witnessing baseball being played with a style and skill few blacks or working-class whites were accustomed to seeing. Some knew the players as neighbors, schoolmates, or workmates; most recognized them as young men who, except for their athletic talent, were very much like themselves. By supporting the Crawfords, they seemed to affirm not only the players' abilities but their own sense of self-competence—and for some, their racial identity.

Games were an occasion for socializing and entertainment. What better or cheaper attraction could be found on a warm summer night in a migrant ghetto. Baseball provided the sort of entertainment that could transcend the social setting. Spectacular feats on the diamond or even a close, well-played game could temporarily transport the players and fans from the racial and economic realities of Pittsburgh to a place where what was happening before their eyes was all that mattered. While these moments of transcendence might have been relatively few, they were powerful enough to keep the fans coming back in hopes of recapturing that sensation.

This enthusiasm for the team did not translate into economic support, however. A crowd of 6,000 at a Memorial Day game in 1930 contributed less than eighty dollars. After paying the umpires twenty-four dollars and the visiting team fifty, the Crawfords had less than six dollars left, which they put toward the cost (fifteen dollars) of the dozen balls used that day. Wendell Smith and other *Courier* writers took the fans to task for their failure to contribute more to the passing hat. In his weekly column Smith proclaimed:

One of the most disgusting things the writer has ever witnessed has been the "poor sportsmanship" of some of our people at Ammon Field, where the Crawfords, an up and coming young team, hold forth about twice a week.

Here is a young team with all the earmarks of future greatness. They play the game for all that it is worth. Playing for love of the sport, they give their followers thrills that one seldom sees in this age of "machine baseball."

They're popular and that's a fact. Any time they play a game on their home field, crowds estimated at from 3,500 to 5,000 people pack and jam their way into the park. And right now, they're playing to larger crowds daily, than ANY team in this section.

But here is the irony of the situation. Mr. King, who backs the team, and Harry Beale, the young, wide awake, hustling and resourceful "kid boss," inform us that it is a rare thing when more than $50 is taken up at the gate.

These youngsters have the opposing team to pay, baseballs to buy (and they need plenty at $2.50 each), their uniforms to pay for and numerous other sundry expenses co-incident with running a ball club. A nickel a person would see the youngsters on top.

But, no! Out of every ten people who pass through, nine of them have "iron-clad" alibis. We say "iron-clad" because very seldom does one hear the clink of silver. Copper pennies rattle in the box from the fingers of "dressed-up" sheiks, who cleverly hide their contributions.

Mr. Hendel, owner and manager of the Roosevelt Theatre, imbued with community spirit, is offering valuable assistance, but we feel that "cheapsports," the greatest dredge mankind has ever known, should take heed.

Be a real sport. Pay for what you see. Surely to see these games is worth at least a dime a head. Let's vindicate our inherent faith in humanity. It'll be appreciated.[45]

While a pay envelope with ten or fifteen dollars in it was a welcome addition to a young man's income, few Crawfords depended on occasional remunerations from baseball as their sole source of money. Most of the players held down regular jobs or had not yet entered the work force. Lefty Burton, a pitcher who had jumped to the Crawfords from the Garfield ABCs, was a mailman. Harold Tinker was a janitor and Charlie Hughes, Bill and Neal Harris, and Bucky Williams all labored in area mills and factories. Wyatt Turner chauffeured and Bus Christian collected rubbish for the city. Certainly, the prospects of becoming a full-time, paid professional ballplayer were enticing, but the chances for a black youth making it to the pros were slim, especially when compared to a white boy, who would have a much larger professional apparatus to shoot for. The rewards, too, reflected the economic disparities between white and black America.

Some members of the Crawfords pursued youthful fantasies of playing pro ball, but most of them were motivated chiefly by a simple desire to play. They had grown up playing ball, often with each other, and that camaraderie was a valuable and treasured aspect of their lives. When Harold Tinker was asked if there was a fear that any of the Crawford players would be lured away by other teams, he responded emphatically, "No. They loved each other. Now, you talk about a family. They thought of each other as one. They thought that our left fielder was the best left fielder in baseball, that our pitchers and our catcher was the best. You couldn't argue with them about each other. You couldn't bring anything up about each other. I think that was the thing that held us together."[46]

Some of the players had families of their own and most of them came to the games along with assorted parents, brothers, and sisters. Afterward, players and their families went off together, while many of the single players socialized with each other. As Bill Harris remembers it, the only division on the team was one that came naturally between the older and younger players; the former "were getting the girls, I guess." Perhaps the best indication of how players felt about each other is the closeness and respect many say they still have for each other more than fifty years later.

The 1930 Crawfords were ready to take on the Grays, who were fast becoming the best team in black America, and for some of the players it was about time. "I had an ambition," Harold Tinker explained, "and I said to myself, when I fulfill that ambition, I'll be ready to quit." He wanted to beat the Homestead Grays. Tinker related: "I sat down there in Forbes Field [home of the Pirates during most of this century and a frequent playing field for the Grays] as a kid and I watched them play. I told myself, 'Boy, one day I'm gonna be on a team that will beat these Homestead Grays.' That was my life's desire—to develop a team to beat the Grays."[47] But getting a date to play the Grays was not that simple. Cumberland Posey, the Grays' owner and manager, put the Crawfords off until the newspapers and fans clamored for a match and he knew the game would draw a huge crowd.

Ironically, as the Crawfords geared up for their impending showdown with the Homestead Grays, they began a transition that was more significant than their evolution from a schoolyard nine to a citywide team. The Crawfords would soon shed their sandlot character and become a professional outfit, relinquishing their self-organized internal structure to accept salaried positions on a club they no longer owned themselves.

The Crawfords and the Grays first met at Forbes Field in the summer of 1930, with Oscar Owens on the mound for the Grays against the Crawfords' Harry Kincannon. Owens pitched no-hit ball through five innings, then Tinker broke the ice in the sixth and four consecutive batters connected safely to drive in two runs. But the Crawfords went into the ninth inning trailing by a run and lost the game when Bill Harris's brother Vic made a running catch of a line drive off Charlie Hughes's bat with two out and two men on base. The two teams did not meet again until the following summer, and by then the Crawfords were about to leave the sandlots behind.

Sandlot's Longest Act: The 18th Ward Club

The Crawfords were born on the sandlots but remained there only a few seasons before commercial pressures and their own prowess pushed them up the professional ladder. Other black teams stayed on the sandlots for decades, subject more to the economic difficulties of maintaining a squad than to the commercial temptations of pro ball. These teams might occasionally embark on a barnstorming tour or supply a Negro League team with extra players, but their field of play was basically twilight and weekend ball before a neighborhood crowd. Over a score of black teams in Pittsburgh followed this pattern from the 1920s through the 1950s. One squad, the 18th Ward, played during the entire period.

The 18th Ward team took its name from the political unit encompassing the Beltzhoover community. Situated south of the Monongahela River, Beltzhoover extends from the heights of Mount Washington southward toward the seventy-two-acre McKinley Park where the ball club played its home games. The black population of Beltzhoover numbered only a few hundred on the eve of World War I but more than tripled during the 1920s to about 1,500. Many of them were the more economically secure black families that had moved to Beltzhoover when economic and social conditions deteriorated on the Hill during the southern migrations. Over the years, Beltzhoover's black population had grown steadily, both in absolute numbers and as a percentage of the neighborhood's total population. By 1960, when blacks represented over 43 percent of the 18th Ward's population, the neighborhood had achieved a reputation as the top predominantly black neighborhood in the city.[48] But even then, black Beltzhoover had only a little over 3,000 residents. In fact, for most of the thirty-plus years the 18th Ward ball club existed the black community numbered less than 2,000.

From its beginnings in 1922, the Beltzhoover-based team answered the call of spring for thirty-three consecutive seasons, making it the longest-running act in black sandlot baseball.[49] While the community and widespread enthusiasm for baseball in Pittsburgh provided a supportive context for the 18th Ward, the team's body and soul came from the friendship of two men, Willis Moody and Ralph Mellix. They began the 18th Ward ball club and worked to hold it together for over thirty years.

Both Moody and Mellix had moved to the hilly Beltzhoover community with the intent "to do something for the kids" as well as to provide themselves with still another outlet for playing ball.[50] Although they continued to play for other teams, they found the energy to launch a new club. Looking back, Moody explained, "I started to get the kids over there together and it turned out better than I thought it would, because it turned out to be a pretty good ball club." Indeed, it was good enough to last well into the 1950s.

It would be difficult to find two men whose styles on the diamond were more in contrast. Moody was quiet understatement while Mellix projected a Dizzy Gillespie sort of exuberance, wit, and joviality. They shared not only a close friendship but a deep appreciation for the game, matched only by their own ability to play it.

Born in the late 1890s in Clarksburg, West Virginia, about 100 miles south of Pittsburgh, Willis Moody came to the Steel City to play ball. His athletic skills determined where he lived even as a high school student. Clarksburg "didn't have a team that amounted to anything," so Moody traveled across three counties to play football for Sumner High in Parkersburg.[51] When "they snuck me over there to play, it caused quite a stir,"

Moody confessed, but the move resulted in a black state championship for Sumner High. After high school, Moody returned to Clarksburg to play baseball for local teams. Black semipro Pittsburgh clubs, like Sellers Hall's Pittsburgh Giants and Cumberland Posey's Homestead Grays, frequently barnstormed through Ohio and West Virginia, stopping in Clarksburg for a game. Sell Hall watched young Moody play a few times and persuaded him to move to Pittsburgh and join his squad. At the time, Moody remembered, "I just wanted to play ball," and Hall's offer of playing for pay was irresistible. It was on Sell Hall's ball club that Moody first met and played with a young, lanky first baseman and sometimes pitcher named Ralph Mellix.

Sellers McKee Hall ran a shoeshine parlor on the Hill, and was a key figure in local sandlot and semipro baseball. He not only managed and promoted the Pittsburgh Giants, he pitched for them, too.[52] In Moody's mind, "Hall had everything. He was a big tall fella and he could *pitch.*" One thing he couldn't do, however, was hold on to Moody. Cumberland Posey, Hall's chief rival, was ever on the lookout for baseball talent, and the young ball-hawking outfielder of the Pittsburgh Giants caught his eye. As Moody describes it, "The Grays were getting so they had a little bit of money." While Cum Posey could offer his players neither sizable nor a particularly steady income, it was enough to lure Moody away from Sell Hall. Once in a Grays' uniform, Moody established himself as one of the finest ballplayers on the best team in western Pennsylvania. No comprehensive records exist for those seasons, and the uneven calibre of the opposition would, in any case, call into question the picture they might paint. It can be said, however, that Moody was usually good for two or three base hits a game and nearly flawless play on the field.[53]

Willis Moody first settled in the East Liberty section of Pittsburgh. In the off-season he played football for a local sandlot team that Hunter Johnson, the trainer at the University of Pittsburgh, provided with cast-off equipment. More important, Moody found employment at Carnegie-Illinois Steel's Homestead Works. The management, more impressed by his reputation as a ballplayer than his possible contributions to a labor gang, made him the manager of their black company ball team.

There was no fundamental contradiction in Moody's continuing to play for the Grays; it was basically a matter of scheduling. Oscar Owens, who also played for the Grays, was the mill team's ace hurler. Moody eventually left the mill for an office job at United States Steel's downtown building. There, he worked with twelve or fifteen other black men in a reception pool, running errands and attending to clerical matters.

The conflict between holding down a steady office job and the Gray's barnstorming led to Moody's decision to leave the team. Years later, Bill Nunn, Jr., a columnist for the *Pittsburgh Courier,* succinctly assessed Moody's career: "In those days a tan star's future in baseball was limited to how far he could climb in the Negro Leagues. Moody had reached the top so he was ready to call it a day."[54] But Moody was not about to retire from baseball altogether; he was simply unwilling to go on the road and make baseball his sole source of income. He captained the Donora A's in the Mon-Yough League and frequently offered his services to various teams on a game-by-game basis. After moving to Beltzhoover and joining forces with his friend Ralph Mellix, he also had the 18th Ward ball club to fall back on.

Mellix could perhaps best be considered a local Satchel Paige. Paige, one of the greatest pitchers in the history of both the Negro Leagues and the Caribbean baseball circuit (in which blacks figured prominently before the integration of baseball in 1947), was undoubtedly the best known black ballplayer of his times. Remembered for his flamboyance as well as his mastery of the mound, Paige probably pitched in front of more fans than any other player, black or white. His longevity as a pitcher and the incredible number of appearances he made in games may never be equaled. What statistics have survived reflect a more than impressive career record. Like Paige, Mellix was appreciated as much for his style as his ability. The latter he possessed in abundance, and his record on the Pittsburgh sandlots is possibly the best any pitcher ever compiled.

Twelve years after his birth in Atlantic City in 1896, Ralph Mellix appeared in his first sandlot game. His father, who had moved to Pittsburgh shortly after the turn of the century, ran a semipro club called the Mellix Stars. Ralph played ball in his East Liberty neighborhood with other youths and was the mascot for his father's team. One day the Stars came up a player short as they assembled at Union Station to catch a southbound train to Uniontown for a game. Rather than forfeit the game, for which a contract had been signed, they decided "to put the kid on first." From that summer day in 1908, Ralph Mellix was to stay in the line-up for one club or another for the next forty-three seasons. Several years later, when playing for the Grays, Sell Hall was in need of a pitcher and sent Mellix to the mound for an afternoon game. Mellix won not only that game but another twenty-five over the course of the season, losing only one.[55]

Before his career ended, Mellix pitched in over 1,500 games, tossing nine no-hitters, six one-hitters, and once striking out thirteen men in a row without a single ball being called. Mellix estimates that he won well over 600 games against local sandlot, semipro, and pro teams, and he has the newspaper clippings to back up his claims. "Lefty" Mellix was known as "the Stopper," for when he started a game he usually finished it, and when he came off the bench or moved from first base to the pitcher's mound in a close game, he more often than not stopped the other team cold. Mellix was one of the top draws in local sandlot ball, not only because he was a good pitcher, but because he was fun to watch. The crowds clamored for him, mostly because he obviously enjoyed playing.

The fans, the opposing team, and even his own teammates never knew what Mellix was likely to do next. In his early years he had played for a team known as the Cuban X Giants, allegedly composed of Cuban ballplayers. The team actually was the Donora A's from the Mon-Yough League, which Sell Hall had taken over. There were two or three Cubans on the squad, but the remainder were American-born blacks like Mellix who masqueraded as Cubans. Under the name of Mellico, Ralph, who "didn't know a word of Spanish," jabbered away in what he hoped would pass for the language but which only drew quizzical looks from the real Cubans on the team. That sense of humor stuck with him over the years.

As a pitcher, Mellix knew he was the center of attention and held his audience with a mixture of grimaces, one-liners, and fine pitching. A lanky southpaw, Mellix's windmill wind-up and delivery concealed his wide repertoire of pitches. More of a control and finesse thrower than a power pitcher, he relied on a curve, a drop-ball, and a "sneaky-fastball." Studying opposing batters for their strengths and weaknesses, he threw to the latter. On the mound, Mellix was as likely to indulge in some sort of antics as to pitch. He might take a pair of dice out of his pocket and pretend to shoot craps behind the pitching rubber or engage in a soliloquy about some aspect of the game. His catcher over the years, Wyatt Turner, put it simply enough: "He was weird on the mound, pretending to spit on the ball or when he was up at bat, pretending he was going lame when he ran down to first base and then stealing second on the next pitch." Once, Turner recalls, "Josh [Gibson] was at bat and I wanted a low inside fast ball. Ralph wanted a curve. I said, 'Don't throw him that! He can see it.' But Ralph insisted. I yelled back, 'This is your idea.'" For all his antics, Mellix was, in the words of a contemporary, "one hellacious pitcher."[56]

Mellix held a steady job with the city and then the county from the early 1920s on, yet he was more successful than most players in also earning a good income from sandlot ball. At times, he played for such Negro League clubs as the Grays or the Newark Eagles, but for the most part he either played for his sandlot team, the 18th Ward, or hired himself out to various semipro teams in need of pitching help. His "Have Arm, Will Travel" approach led *Courier* sportswriter Wendell Smith to title a 1945 feature article on Mellix, "The $35,000 Sandlot Pitcher."[57] Pitching for anywhere from $50 to $150 a game, Mellix conservatively estimated that he never made less than $1,000 for each of the thirty-five seasons he played up until then; and on some occasions he made as much as several hundred dollars in one night. Smith wrote that "old R.M." could show youth "a pot o' gold can be obtained by staying right on the sandlots."

Like Satchel Paige, Mellix had a hard time retiring from baseball. He was still pitching well into his fifties, and he even made an appearance in a Canadian baseball game at the age of seventy-four. A perennial autumn story in the *Pittsburgh Courier* was the Ralph Mellix retirement story. Bill Nunn, Jr., now director of player development for the Pittsburgh Steelers and then a writer for the *Courier,* asked Mellix in 1951 when he was going to end his astonishing career. " 'This is it,' [Mellix] replied in apparent seriousness. 'After this season, I am going to take it easy. Instead of going out there and pitchin' my heart out, me and the Madam are going to go to the ball games and just be spectators.' " "While he was announcing his retirement," Nunn commented, "Mellix didn't seem to be aware of the fact that he was retelling the same story he had come up with last year," and the year before that, and the year before that. Mellix reckoned he called it quits at least ten times, yet every spring he answered the crack of a ball off a bat and returned for another season as the "Grandaddy of the Sandlots."[58] He would often cap his retirement announcements by passing around a water bucket for the fans to place contributions in between innings. With $300 or more in the bucket, he carried it to the mound with him each time he went out to pitch, explaining, "If I left it on the bench, I wouldn't have had no money when I got back."

The integration of the major leagues came too late for Ralph Mellix, although he had an offer to join a minor league team in Titusville when he was in his late forties. Rather than give up his seniority at his county job, however, he turned down the offer, reckoning that it would have taken five seasons before he was eligible for a baseball pension. He lasted more than another five years in and around Pittsburgh, though. Mellix remained the center of any crowd, creating a vortex of anecdotes, remembrances, and laughter, until his death in the spring of 1985, only a few weeks before his eighty-ninth birthday.

There were four critical factors to the 18th Ward's success: community support, financial backers, the inclination of team members to play ball, and the irrepressible tandem of Mellix and Moody. The latter not only played and managed the team but set up the schedule, recruited players and financial supporters, and masterminded promotional and fundraising efforts.

Mellix and Moody began their fundraising with a splash in 1922: they threw "a big party, shaking girls and everything, right there in Beltzhoover."[59] They rented Weil's Hall on Climax Street, and after printing tickets and securing a supply of liquor, they set out to recruit some entertainment. "Mellix and I went over in the Hill and we sneaked around. We didn't know where to get dancing girls but we asked around." They finally tracked down one stripper, who in turn secured the services of two others. Ticket sales were slow at first, but on the night of the event, Weil's Hall was filled to capacity with an all-male crowd that found the whiskey and the floor show to its liking. "We was married," Moody explains, "but pshaw, we was making money for the ball team." In fact, they made enough to buy a set of uniforms for the squad.

Although they never brought the "shaking girls" back for a return engagement, Mellix and Moody repeated their social coup at Weil's Hall every year with a fundraising smoker or an awards banquet. In later years, Mellix lamented: "The dumbest thing that we done—he wanted to sell us the place for $10,000. They had four floors in the place—three apartments and the fourth floor was just a great big hall. All we had to do was just put $1,000 down. At that time Negroes didn't have no halls to go to. We had to go over to town to have any kind of affair. If we had got that hall there, we'd have had something for the people to go to."[60] The Jewish real estate agent who owned the hall donated its use, and by charging a buck or two at the door, the club often cleared $500–600 from such an affair. At the smokers, city councilmen, state representatives, and ward politicos like David B. Roberts, city prothonotary and Fifth Ward boss, vied with black attorneys and notables in addressing the audience. Several hundred boosters, local businessmen, and sandlot fans mingled with ballplayers and other local athletes, the roster at these annual fetes reading like a "who's who" of black Pittsburgh sports. The gatherings were always celebrated in the black press.[61]

In addition to these annual fundraisers, the club garnered support from three other sources. The first, a standard device among well-organized sandlot teams, was a club program.[62] Filled with advertisements from the local baker, grocer, funeral director, and beer distributor, as well as citywide black establishments and an occasional corporation like United States Steel, the program proved to be a financial success. Advertising space was sold for anywhere from $5 to $100, and three score or more individuals donated $2, $5, or $10 to be listed as team boosters. Mellix and Moody hustled the advertising spots and then contracted with a printer to turn out several thousand copies each season. At important ball games, team members would circulate throughout the crowd, handing out the programs.

The second source of funding was two brothers, George and Pete Armstrong. The Armstrongs represented the rare black entrepreneur of the time. Owners of the Montooth Hotel, in Beltzhoover, and the Corner Tavern, on Wylie Avenue on the Hill, they were well known in the black community; their chief source of capital, however, was a coal mine in Lewiston, Pennsylvania. Both men had played ball and enjoyed reputations as sportsmen, a rather ambiguous category covering those who made the scene at local sporting events. The Armstrong brothers provided money for uniforms, bats, and travel expenses and received in turn a certain amount of publicity and personal satisfaction. In later years, they backed the Brooklyn Brown Dodgers franchise in the United States League.[63]

The third and largest source of funds was the Beltzhoover community and spectators at the 18th Ward's games. Lotteries and raffles were held several times during a season, and each game the team played also brought in money. When the Homestead Grays or the Newark Eagles appeared at McKinley Park, the crowd numbered in the thousands and the take was fairly high. Much of that, however, went to the visiting professional team. The 18th Ward played a regular schedule of forty-eight games each season in the South Hills League, of which it was a founding member and the sole black team in the 1930s. A notch below the Greater Pittsburgh League, the city's top sandlot circuit, teams in the South Hills League split the gate 60–40, with the home team receiving the larger share. The size of the gate, according to Mellix and Moody, was basically a reflection of playing location and economic backgrounds: it might total twenty or thirty dollars, or it might be a couple of thousand dollars courtesy of the well-heeled fans at a crucial game in Mount Lebanon, a prosperous suburb.

The 18th Ward, like many well-rooted sandlot clubs, enjoyed the support of working people from Beltzhoover as well as the backing of the community's businessmen and political leaders. It is unlikely that local merchants and politicians would have patronized the team if not for the larger community's sense that the 18th Ward was their club. The Beltzhoover business establishments that took out ads in the yearly programs depended on local consumers—the very people who saw their ads—and elected officials depended on their votes. It would not have been good politics or good business to acquire a reputation as someone who spurned the 18th Ward team.

People from Beltzhoover backed the team because they felt it was theirs. Mellix and Moody, and usually three or four other players, were from the 18th Ward; the rest, even if not local residents, were at least representing them by virtue of donning the Beltzhoover team's flannels. When folks walked down the hill to McKinley Park on a Tuesday evening or a Sunday afternoon, they would be treated to a high-quality ball game at little cost; and with Mellix on the mound, the game was likely to be cause for a few laughs, too. Most of the fans at McKinley Park were from Beltzhoover, and they reflected the racial proportions of the community fairly closely, with as many whites as blacks in attendance. At the games, they stood or sat next to each other and cheered for the same team. On July 4th, they attended the doubleheader at McKinley Park and also competed in 50- and 100-yard dashes, egg races, ball-throwing contests, and needle-threading and fat-people races for prizes provided by the Montooth Hotel, the McKinley Drugstore, and Goldsmith's Store. The other 18th Ward spectators were usually from the surrounding hilltop neighborhoods of Arlington Heights, Knoxville, and Mount Washington. White Beltzhoover residents supported their team as much as their black neighbors, even if the game was being played against a white squad. In fact, their financial succor was critical, as they could often afford to toss a larger donation into the passing hat than most black fans. When the 18th Ward ventured to play Mount Lebanon, Bellevue, or Latrobe, a dozen or so carloads of backers, black and white, usually made the trek.

There were other compelling reasons for Beltzhoover to back its team, even though the very presence of a consistently good ball club year after year would have been enough cause for most. The fact is that Moody and Mellix were community activists who greatly enriched their neighbors' social life. At a team practice or before a game, dozens of youngsters from the neighborhood would shag flies and pick up pointers from the players.

The 18th Ward Juniors, a youth team made up solely of neighborhood kids, including Mellix's and Moody's sons, played a regular schedule against teams from nearby communities, and some of the players would jump to the senior team after a few seasons. In the winter, a few of these lads would join with the older men on the 18th Ward basketball squad, playing the likes of the Rankin Spartans, the Sharon Elks, and the Keystone Mystics, while their female counterparts took to the hardcourts in a women's league.

There was a political dimension to the 18th Ward's success, too, more so than the mayor throwing out the first ball at a game with the Nashville Elite Giants or other politicians making speeches at club smokers. Ralph Mellix had worked at Westinghouse during World War I, but the daily trip between East Pittsburgh and Beltzhoover took up too much of his time. When two of his buddies got jobs at the Union National Bank in downtown Pittsburgh, Ralph soon followed, working there as a window cleaner. He convinced his supervisor to let him off every day between eleven and two so that he could wait on tables at McCreary's Restaurant, where he attended to Mayor Magee and other politicians. By the end of the year, he had asked the mayor for a job and wound up working at the City-County Building. From 1921 until he collected his pension in 1964, Mellix worked in a succession of city and county departments, usually as a supervisor of janitors and maintenance workers. Then, as now, holding that sort of job in the city of Pittsburgh meant "you were in politics."[64] You were expected to deliver the votes and work for the party of the man who gave you your job.

Mellix certainly understood the workings of the political patronage system and manipulated it for the good of his community. He recalled, "I wouldn't accept no money for what I did. I wanted jobs for my Negro friends and I got many jobs for my Negro friends in Beltzhoover." He also worked toward the desegregation of Warrington Park and neighborhood schools. One project he and Moody undertook was a recreation center at a Beltzhoover school, which some 500 children attended.

Party allegiance was less important than reading the shifting political winds. Mellix began as a Republican and was a sponsor of the Colored Civic Republican Club in the early 1930s, but he followed *Courier* editor Robert Vann's advice to turn Lincoln's face to the wall and in later years worked for the Democrats. He led the 18th Ward club of the Democrats for United Action and once rallied over 2,000 constituents to McKinley Park in a battle he ultimately won against the ward chairman. Delivering the rally's keynote speech was Pittsburgh Mayor David Lawrence. When Lawrence was inaugurated as governor a few years later, Mellix led a local contingent to the ceremonies in Harrisburg. "What I liked about Beltzhoover," Mellix reflected, was that "the colored people stuck with us. They believed in us." Whether that meant jobs or better city services or free soft drinks for the children at ball games, Mellix, and thus his ball club, were involved.

While the 18th Ward team could count on the Beltzhoover community for support, it could not rely solely on the local pool of baseball talent if it wanted to remain competitive. Mellix and Moody were a formidable contribution, and they were joined on the squad by several fine local ballplayers, but a majority of the players every season were from elsewhere in the city or from outlying areas. The 18th Ward team at first was called the Beltzhoover Colored Independents and claimed to be "composed of men from the Beltzhoover district exclusively."[65] But their inability to field a team that would be competitive with the Pittsburgh Monarchs, the Braddock Black Sox, and the New Kensington Colored Elks was acknowledged by a willingness to recruit ballplayers no matter where they were from. The team name changed as the 18th Ward gained a reputation on the diamond.

The team itself was selected each year during spring tryouts, at which twenty to thirty ballplayers practiced before the discerning eyes of Mellix and Moody. About fifteen of them—as many as would fit into the truck that transported them to away games— were given uniforms and constituted the core of the team. They came from New Kensington, Homestead, Duquesne, and the Hill, in addition to Beltzhoover, and many went directly from work to McKinley Park to make the 6:30 P.M. starting time. The commitment to be there was an important ingredient for these teams. "If you played for us, you played for us," Ralph Mellix put it. "There weren't too many of us who played for other teams."

The 18th Ward attracted more than just commitment. Mellix and Moody recruited Wyatt Turner, the fine defensive catcher of the Pittsburgh Crawfords who had been benched when young Josh Gibson checked into the lineup, for their team, and he anchored their nine for the next twenty years. Another former Crawford, Charlie Hughes, was a frequent performer at shortstop.

Two of the most outstanding all-around athletes black Pittsburgh has ever produced played for the club. Joe Ware, born in 1913, acquired the nickname "Showboat" for his flashy play on the gridiron, but he was equally adept at baseball and basketball. Mellix began to follow Ware's career while Joe was starring for Westinghouse High School, and he recruited him for the 18th Ward when Joe was still in school. "When I was sixteen years old," Ware explained, "Mellix came to my dad and asked could I play. My dad told him in so many words that I don't like my boy playing ball on Sunday, but I'll leave him in your hands." The two men were still close friends fifty years later, although Ware chauffeured Mellix then.[66] Gabe Patterson hit the sporting scene a few years later, and like Ware, he divided his energies between the gridiron, the diamond, and the hardcourt. They each played for the 18th Ward for three or four years.

The 18th Ward reunion banquets in the 1950s were cross-sections of sandlot baseball with former Negro Leaguers Ted Page and Euthumm Napier sitting next to the Lucases and the Rideouts, baseball-playing brothers who had grown up in Beltzhoover, or Sellers Hall's sons, Sell, Jr., and Robert, who pitched for them in the 1950s. Sandlot ball was like that, bringing together men and boys from disparate playing backgrounds.

At times the 18th Ward squad jelled and played together as a unit for several consecutive seasons, as was the case when they terrorized the South Hills League in the early 1950s. Other years found wholesale changes as players moved to other sandlot teams or to a Negro League or minor league team. Playing four or five times a week for thirty or more summers meant that just about everyone had a chance to get in some innings. Nor was the

18th Ward a bad team to play for. McKinley Park "wasn't nothing when we first was down there," Willis Moody exclaimed, but "we got that rock pile fixed up." With a locker room and a hot shower, a good league to play in, and every now and then a modest pay envelope, there were a lot worse places to play. More importantly, however, they knew they were going to be on a competitive team, and for many that was what counted most.

After a game, some of the players would go to the Armstrong brothers' beer garden, have a few beers, and "loaf." Mellis and Moody sometimes bought a round, and five or six of the older players' wives would join the party. Beyond that, there was not all that much socializing involved, except for the inevitable interchanges of playing ball together every other night of the summer. Some of the players' families became quite close, while others hardly met.[67]

For away games, the players received transportation money if they were forced to make their own way there. At home games, they were likely to make a few bucks. Not everybody got the same amount, as Mellix and Moody distributed the money based on their own informal incentive system for output. "We'd squeeze ours out, too," Moody remembered. The senior partners of the team took home perhaps twice as much as the players, about twenty-five or thirty dollars on the average— "What you'd call a profit? No indeed," Moody attested—an amount that probably just covered their expenses.

Racial dynamics involving the team were, by and large, good. "Looked like they were glad to see us come around. We didn't have no trouble and we had a few more people turn out than the rest of these teams did," according to Willis Moody. Neither he nor Mellix were positive if a white boy had ever donned the team's flannels, but Moody speculated, "If we would've, I'd have went and got one of the Rooneys."[68]

The 18th Ward team folded in the late 1950s after capturing several championships in the South Hills League. Moody left first, allowing a younger man to replace him in center field as he took a seat on the bench and continued to coach and manage. Mellix made several attempts to retire as an active player, but Moody reflected, "I guess Ralph was so sad he kept going back every year." After the 18th Ward played their last game, the 18th Ward Juniors continued to take the field. Willis Moody's son was coaching them in the early 1980s, more than half a century since the 18th Ward squad first played. By the late 1950s, the senior squad's chief backers, the Armstrongs, had both died and money for sandlot teams everywhere was tight as competition from television and professional baseball kept down the crowds at the twilight games. With the demise of the 18th Ward team, black sandlot baseball's longest-playing squad closed another chapter in baseball's history. "It was a rocky road," Willis Moody recalled with an infinitesimal smile, "but we had a lot of fun."

3 More Sandlot Ball

The younger members of the Crawfords grew up in an inter-racial setting, residing near and playing with whites. Those blacks who came to Pittsburgh later, after the 1920s, entered a different, more racially restricted environment. While black and white migrants to the city shared the Hill and other areas early in the century, by 1930 a definite trend toward segregated neigh-borhoods was underway.

In the 1930s and 1940s residential segregation increased throughout most parts of the city, and clearly identifiable black ghettos emerged. Racial discrimination in housing and a second, postdepression migratory wave combined with white flight to make the Hill the most segregated community in Pittsburgh. Between 1930 and 1970, two-thirds of all blacks in the city lived there, or in Homewood-Brushton, or in East Liberty.

The black population climbed from about 55,000 to 87,000 between 1930 and 1950, while Pittsburgh's total population increased only slightly, from 670,000 to 677,000. The number of foreign-born white residents decreased considerably during these years, from 109,000 to 65,000, as European migration slowed to a trickle due to the immigration quotas of 1924, economic depression, and then a world war.[1]

Large numbers of blacks, however, continued to come to the city. These migrants of the 1930s and 1940s found a black community still seeking internal unity. Black Pittsburgh re-mained without a vibrant business district of its own, and its churches, while numerous, were divided along both spiritual and social lines.[2] Although some political gains were made as blacks followed *Courier* editor Robert L. Vann's advice to vote for the New Deal, these advances were minimal.[3] Most important, steady, skilled, and well-paid work was scarce.

The Great Depression hit area industry particularly hard, and

The portion of this chapter on the Garfield Eagles orginally appeared as "Soaring Above the Sandlots: The Garfield Eagles," *Pennsylvania Heritage* 8 (no. 3, Summer 1982): 13–18.

the subsequent layoffs and underemployment affected blacks more than whites. Although World War II increased the demand for black labor, followed by a generally upward occupational movement during the 1940s and 1950s, black workers as a whole remained confined to unskilled and semiskilled occupations. In the steel mills, for example, despite seniority and the promises of the CIO, most blacks were trapped in labor gangs and in the lower job classifications well into the 1970s. Nor would the area's long-term employment trends offer much chance for improvement.[4]

The construction of housing projects after World War II furthered the shift toward mostly black neighborhoods. The projects were erected, for the most part, in already predominantly black areas or in isolated parts of the city. Blacks comprised 62 percent of Pittsburgh's public housing population in the 1940s; and that figure rose still higher, to an incredible 85 percent, by the 1980s,[5] when more than one-third of the entire black population in Pittsburgh, over 100,000 people, were living in the projects. As the twelfth most segregated city in the northeast in 1940 and 1950, Pittsburgh moved up to sixth by 1960.[6]

A deteriorating racial climate paralleled increasing segregation. A recent study found a greater incidence of civil rights violations and racial violence after the 1930s. Blacks and Italians, for example, had coexisted with a high degree of peaceful interaction since the arrival of the Italians in Pittsburgh in the 1890s. But by the 1930s, blacks and Italians began to avoid each other and previously integrated streets became all-black or all-Italian in a few years. As streets went, so too did communities. The upper Hill, which for decades had been a Jewish and black neighborhood, turned heavily black after the construction of the Bedford Dwellings housing project in 1938. By 1960 the upper Hill was about 98 percent black, and Homewood-Brushton was over 70 percent black.[7]

Those who came to sandlot ball from the mid-1930s on, then, were far less likely to have ever played alongside whites on the streets of their neighborhoods. For them, sports competition against whites ran counter to life as they knew it in increasingly segregated communities. The sandlots continued to offer black Pittsburghers a sense of accomplishment they seldom got at work, in politics, or in the neighborhood. And while the sand-lots similarly provided satisfaction to many working-class and immigrant whites as their communities developed, for the latter, Pittsburgh offered other alternatives for the development of their talents that were not available to blacks.

Beat Yesterday: The Team from Terrace Village

With the dawn of their fourth season, in the spring of 1952, the men behind the Terrace Village (TV) ball club issued an unusual sort of defy. Defies normally challenged all comers to pick up the gauntlet; they were standard on the pages of the *Pittsburgh Courier* and other black papers, giving the various clubs a change to make contact with each other. TV's proclamation was a vow to "Beat Yesterday," a rare public declaration for a sandlot team to make, but then the TV club was an uncommon one. Its housing-project community and interracial character clearly set it apart from the rest.

"In this day of strife, turmoil and unrest all over the face of the earth," the men who built the TV ball club maintained, they were "more determined than ever to promote and provide for the people of our community and surrounding communities an athletic program of good clean sports that through its practice of integration and with the help of Almighty God we might lead the way to a better way of life for all the people. At the same time, providing a solid foundation for these young baseball players who are determined to reach the heights of the diamond."[8] Their slogan, to "Beat Yesterday," meant not only to better their won-lost record but to confront the particular challenges posed by their neighborhood.

The Terrace Village community began amid a sense of hope and renewal. At its October 11, 1940, dedication ceremonies, President Franklin Delano Roosevelt sat smiling in the back of a convertible, playfully teasing a young thumb-sucking boy. The boy's family was about to receive the keys to the first apartment in the new residential complex. Around them stood an estimated 30,000 people as the president cut the ribbon opening the 1,800-unit housing project, then the second largest ever under-taken by the federal government. Terrace Village, which later separated into Bedford Dwellings, Addison Terrace, and Allequippa Terrace, mirrored the racial composition of the surrounding Hill community.

At the time of their construction, the projects addressed the dismal housing situation existing on the Hill and in other Pittsburgh neighborhoods. To many residents, Terrace Village showed that the government could do something about their problems. There was a certain sense of promise about public housing then, for the early projects were conceived in part as a way station to the middle class and thus sought stable, working families as tenants. The men behind the TV ball club embodied the best of that hope.

The club began in 1949, nine years after the projects opened. Like most sandlot clubs, its creation was the work of a small core of activists. The individuals behind the team were, for the most part, black men in their thirties and forties who lived in the projects. Perhaps a dozen men worked to build and maintain the club during its decade of existence, but at the beginning there were three key organizers: Bill Berry, foreman of the janitorial department at Joseph Horne's Department Store; Ocey Swain, a display man at Spear Furniture Company; and Jack Hopkins, a custodian at Fifth Avenue High School in Soho. They were no strangers to the diamond nor had they all hung up their spikes for the final time—Berry continued to play for a few years, hurling for the TV nine. Yet their motives were not simply to build a team that they could play on; rather, they shared a common commitment to youth, to their community, and to sport, a bond that led them to emulate what they saw happening in other parts of the city and to start a ball club for the Terrace Village projects.[9]

At their first meeting in one of the project's community rooms, the three men were pleased to find a receptive audience and a few new recruits, in addition to a well-known gentleman sitting at the back of the hall. Harold Tinker had retired from baseball almost two decades earlier after his sandlot Crawfords beat the Homestead Grays. He returned to sandlot ball for a while, but after a religious reawakening he had decided to "put my time in for the Lord instead of on the ball field." Tinker now lived on a small winding street next to the projects, and when "I saw in the paper that they were organizing, . . . I told my wife, 'I'm just going over there to see what they're doing.' I knew what I was going over for but I didn't want her to think that I was gonna go back." Tinker listened as Berry, Hopkins, and Swain sketched their plans. He recalled: "All I did was sit there and Bill Berry, I'll never forget it, said 'I see we have one of our popular ballplayers and managers in our meeting tonight. I'd like to suggest to our committee that we try to get him to accept the job of managing the Terrace Village team.' I was astonished because I didn't ask anybody or say anything but it was really what I wanted. I told them, 'Well, you probably know that I have retired. I'll think it over and I'll let you know.' "[10]

The addition of Tinker gave the club both a veteran field manager and another articulate spokesman. He reiterated the club's aims a couple of years later in an interview with Earl Johnson for "The Sport Whirl," in the *Courier:* "I have dedicated my life to . . . sports for the youth of this neighborhood regardless of color or creed. Terrace Village wishes to instill in the young men who are members of our organization the will to live a good moral life, and learn to compete with or against anyone regardless of color or creed."[11] Johnson evaluated the club's record from its first few seasons in this light and concluded: "Their record is one of playing ability, excellent sportsmanship and real democracy. . . . Our records of Terrace Village prove that Tinker has followed his creed."

For these four men and a few others the team became a year-round avocation. They worked long hours during the season, and winters found them meeting two or three nights a week to plot fundraising efforts or solicit ads for their programs from local merchants. Their initial fundraising scheme was a raffle, and they followed that up with a program—a folded piece of paper with the player roster, space to keep score, and the names of local merchants on the back—which they gave away at home games. Receipts for their first year's work totaled about $600. "But the great thing about this Terrace Village ball team," Tinker insisted, "was that we had an idea to progress. We had an aim in the beginning that we were going to the top of the heap. We weren't gonna be satisfied with just being a sandlot team. The next year we had a book program just like the Pirates have."[12]

Revenues more than doubled as the men, bolstered by such new additions as George Crooks, Alvin Clark, James Thorpe, and Truehart Peatross, figured out how much money they needed and allotted a certain amount for each to bring in. Sponsors included the usual sandlot backers, mostly merchants with an eye to their trade. Later programs listed over 200 boosters who donated between $2.00 and $12.50 each. These were mostly people from the projects, co-workers, and politicians who wanted to keep their names before their constituents.

Hill's Pharmacy, a Centre Avenue drugstore run by two Jewish merchants, put up the annual $150 league forfeiture deposit, and various other stores donated uniforms with their names on the back and "Terrace Village" on the front. The first uniforms cost $18.75 each (the larger sizes were more expensive). The organizers wanted the team to look "first class when they went out there." "After we got going," Jack Hopkins explained, "we'd go down to the Diamond Market and some of those big places where black people were spending a lot of money and we never had none of them turn us down." Charlie Glick, owner of the Diamond Market, donated four uniforms the second season, but Tinker persisted in his solicitation: "I talked to Charlie Glick three of four times up in his office and he said, 'Tinker, you mean to tell me you guys are gonna be that good?' and I said, 'We're gonna be tops before this thing is over! Glick thought it over and decided, 'If you're gonna be that popular, I'm going to buy the whole set of uniforms!"[13]

The team arranged for nearby Kennard Field as their home grounds and fixed up the ball field. William Wooden, a neighborhood retiree, volunteered to be the groundskeeper. "He went around just like the guys over at Forbes Field. We bought him a jacket like the team and hell, he worked all day out there," Hopkins noted. "He kept that field just as smooth as could be— no pebbles or nothing." "As smooth as a pool table seconded Ocey Swain. Above the field was a building with showers and a pool table, which the team used as a clubhouse. It was a place for the players to relax as well as a dressing room.

Game days meant long hours, especially for Hopkins, who worked on Mt. Washington above the south side of the Monongahela. "I'd leave work and go down the incline to that peanut place near 16th and Penn Avenue," Hopkins recalled, "and get a fifteen-pound bag of peanuts and about eight boxes of nickel candy bars and a gross of Cracker Jacks. I'd carry all that stuff back here, and we'd go and get bags and we'd sit down and bag those peanuts." Bill Berry, in the meantime, would get ten or twelve cases of pop and ice and fill up some coolers. With the help of the players, the men carried their merchandise over to Kennard Field and set up shop behind the backstop. "During the game," Hopkins explained, "me and Swain would be going around selling the peanuts and pop and stuff and in the third inning or so, I'd go around and take up a collection and would give it to my wife to hold up there on the hill till the game was over." After the game, they'd go back to the clubhouse, and "then we'd have to sit there and count the money out and figure out how much we'd spent and what we lost or made and if you were two cents short, Swain would be on you, I'm telling you. We would really be tired and it would be 11:00 or 12:00 and I wouldn't have had no dinner or nothing, every night we had a game." Hopkins got off work at 4:00 P.M. and literally worked a second shift for the team before his day was done. "It wasn't only me," he stressed. "Most of the kids had jobs and they had to come straight from work. The upshot of it was that I worked harder during them years than I ever did in my life."[14]

They all had to work hard. The cost of running a team rose constantly in the early 1950s. For example, in 1952 the team spent over $2,000 on league fees, uniforms, equipment, and umpires. Whenever they lost a baseball, Tinker recounted, "I felt real sad. There goes another $2.75." The men made up losses from their own pockets. "On the Fourth of July, one year," Hopkins related, "—and I'll never forget this as long as I live— we had spent about $300 [Ocey Swain took $275 out of his vacation money and he borrowed another $25 from his wife] buying the stuff, peanuts and all that. Stayed up all night before sacking all these peanuts and getting everything ready. The next morning it's raining like the devil and we got all our money invested." According to Hopkins:

Old Tinker comes up and gets to praying and all and you know, it quit raining around 11:00—no lie. We got all the kids together and they swept the field off and put sawdust down and the groundskeeper came and marked the field and all. We put a tarpaulin up behind the backstop and put our counter there and we ran an extension cord down from one of those corner apartments and put lights on and all that stuff and the sun came out and shined bright that day. We were the only game that was played in western Pennsylvania and we sold all our stuff out. It was one of the biggest days we ever had.[15]

Some fans questioned their motives, claiming, "You walk up and down that hill carrying them heavy buckets and then you mean to tell me you're not taking none of that money!" But most fans came to appreciate their commitment to the team.

The Tuesday and Friday night games were the highlights of the week, not just for the players and the men behind the club, but for the Terrace Village projects. "I think it was the biggest thing they ever had and ever will have," Hopkins asserted. "Everybody looked forward to the ball games. They would start getting out there at 5:30 and that place would be something, I'm telling you." At times the contests drew 4,000–5,000 spectators, and key league games and the July 4th tilts with the 18th Ward were standing-room-only affairs. "It was a good thing," Tinker commented. "They all got to know each other—joshing and carrying on. It was a good healthy community thing." The take, however, did not always reflect the size of the crowd. "When we'd play in Dormont or one of those kinds of places, some of their fans would put a dollar in but most of our fans were poor. They didn't have nothing. Most of them would put a nickel or dime in."[16] Perhaps more important than their fans' financial support was their actual presence, both at Kennard Field and on the road. It gave the team a good feeling, Tinker recalled, to have their people with them.

The unique aspect of the Terrace Village ball club was its interracial character: at times white youths made up a third or more of its roster. No other sandlot team in the area came close to that sort of racial makeup. Some white clubs had an occasional black player, and vice versa, but none sought to consciously cross racial barriers. One of the first decisions made by the men who started the TV team was that "it was going to be for all of the boys in the community, regardless of race, creed or color. . . . We didn't know anything about any particular white boys in the community who wanted to play sandlot ball," Tinker remembered, but the club was certainly not going to rule them out. There were none present during the first practice sessions, but before long one white youth, Lou Diperna, was fielding grounders and taking his cuts in the batting cage. Within a few years there were usually four or five white faces on the bench or in the line-up. Some of them had grown up on the Hill and Terrace Village was the closest thing to a neighborhood team they had. Doc Shanafelt pitched for TV when he wasn't playing for the University of Pittsburgh; Bill Barry lived on Fifth Avenue; and Barry's cousin Billy Caye lived in the lower Hill district. Their experiences confirm that when Tinker said, "I wasn't any more interested in those colored boys than I was in the white boys," he spoke from his heart.

Billy Caye joined forces with TV in 1950, and Joe Studnicki signed on two years later. Both were born in 1932 and grew up playing ball on the streets with teams the youngsters had organized themselves. Studnicki's father was employed at the Jones and Laughlin steel plant, a work force Joe, too, would eventually enter. He played for the Bates Street Hawks, a team made up of the kids on his block, when he was twelve and thirteen years old. The players held raffles to buy their jerseys and caps, and their opponents came from the other streets in the Oakland community. Eventually, Joe joined the Oakland Barons, who also practiced and played on Kennard Field. Someone from TV watched him on the mound one day and asked him to join the team. There were four or five whites already on the roster, among them Billy Caye. Like Studnicki, Caye was from a predominantly immigrant neighborhood. He played for the Fifth Avenue Braves as a teenager and then tried a little fast-pitch softball in a city league. In 1950, Caye and his cousin Bill Barry decided to "get hooked up in a higher class of ball and figured we could make Terrace Village as it wasn't as strong as the other Greater Pittsburgh League teams." TV had some good ballplayers, young men like Norm Gant, Billy Peatross, Henry Ford, and Doc Shanafelt, but there were still openings on the roster. Tinker, in Joe Studnicki's estimation, was "a heck of a guy who knew baseball inside and out." Both Caye and Studnicki claimed that they were treated like anybody else. "The best man played," Studnicki explained, and the men who ran the club knew their baseball and worked hard for the team. Studnicki said that while he never went to parties or the homes of his black teammates, he played cards and loafed at the clubhouse with them. "I went to school and worked at J&L with blacks. It didn't seem strange to be playing ball with them." Caye recalled going to bars on the Hill after games and drinking beer with black teammates, and he said he "never got any trouble from anybody."[17]

No one connected with the Terrace Village club could remember any racial problems outside of a few fans shouting slurs at them. There were occasional team meetings at which the club elders tried "to impress upon [the players] the principles [they] had in mind," but no one actually made too much of the team's interracial composition. Outside of their program notes, TV made its point by playing good, hard ball. Tinker explained, "After our boys come to play with these boys and found out that all they wanted to do was win and they played just as hard to win as they did and that they would sacrifice themselves and that they were always there, this changed the minds of some of them and they became one."[18] At the end of one season the team participated in a Negro Independent Championship series sponsored by the *Courier*. TV won it with a white lad pitching the final game.

For the first two seasons, 1949 and 1950, the TV nine played in the Honus Wagner League. The following winter they applied for a berth in the Greater Pittsburgh League (GPL), which had not had a black team apply since the Edgar Thomson application was rejected in 1939 on the grounds that the ET squad was too good for the league. The GPL, with Dormont, North Pittsburgh, the Kollar Club, Bellevue, and St. Johns, would have had trouble making a similar charge about any area team in 1950. It was considered by area sandlotters as a "fast circuit," and its ranks were filled with former major and minor leaguers. In fact, it was virtually a minor league, with many of its players destined to enter the ranks of organized ball. There really was no higher level of semipro baseball in Pittsburgh outside of the fully professional teams—the Grays, the Pirates, and the Crawfords. Many of the GPL players made as much as they would have with a minor league team, and several teams had payrolls that topped $3,000 a month.

The Terrace Village leaders met three times with officials from the GPL but had a hard time convincing them that the team could play their calibre of ball. At one meeting Tinker directed his appeal to Dormont team owner Billy Fuchs, who he considered the main power of the GPL: "You know what type of team we had with the Crawfords and I'm telling you that we have the potential of coming to the same level that the Crawfords were if we're given a chance." Fuchs responded, "You mean that?" Tinker stood his ground. "I mean that. I wouldn't say it if I didn't mean it. Right now, I think that we could give most of the teams in your league a contest—not all of them—but most of them." Fuchs had battled the Crawfords many times some twenty years before and was on the losing end more often than not. A team as good as the Crawfords would be an impressive draw. "If Tinker feels that way about it," Fuchs reasoned, "maybe we ought to give them a chance."[19] The following week a league representative called to say that TV was in.

Initially the team was badly outclassed, losing twelve of their first fifteen games. They and the other new team in the GPL, the East End Merchants, finished in last and next-to-last place that season. The league was definitely tough. East End wound up in the cellar with a pitching staff from which three men eventually made it to the majors. The following year, TV made it into the first division, and in 1954 they played in the league championship series, which would be Tinker's last hurrah as a manager. He recalled: "We should have won it. Even the people in Dormont told me when we were going out of the park, 'Tinker, if ever a team should have won a championship, your team should have won it.' The last two games we lost to Dormont, we lost in the ninth inning. And in both of the games, the weakest hitter on the Dormont squad was used as a pinch hitter. Don't ask me how Billy Fuchs set them up but this boy came through both times with men on base."[20] When a team doesn't win, the manager usually loses his job. Tinker was voted out at a meeting of the organization and in later years stuck to coaching and his work as publicity director. A succession of managers, including former Crawford and 18th Warder Wyatt Turner, tried their hands at the reins, but none was able to bring home the GPL pennant.

Like most sandlot clubs, TV had substantial political connections, mainly through Fifth Ward kingpin and Allegheny County prothonotary David B. Roberts. When Davey Roberts, or DBR as the press referred to him, died at the age of seventy-five in 1973, he was eulogized as the county's "prothonotary extraordinaire for just under a quarter of a century."[21] Few of the voters whose support put Roberts at the head of the Democratic ticket for those years ever figured out just what a prothonotary was. Born in Soho and reared on the Hill, Roberts built a powerful ward-level machine that was his base for county and state politics. After the briefest of formal educations, he worked behind the counter of a Fourth Avenue fish market, and as a copy boy and then a sportswriter for the *Pittsburgh Dispatch*. In 1926 he was elected a Republican committeeman for the Fifth Ward. Along with Judge Ralph Smith and other progressive Republicans, Roberts switched his party allegiance in 1934 and became a Democrat. Fired from his job with the State Revenue Department by angry Republicans, he was rescued by newly elected Democratic Governor George Earle, who appointed him a workman's compensation referee. DBR endeared himself to working people during his four years as a referee, handing out decisions that consistently favored the injured worker. Now Democratic committeeman for the Fifth Ward, Roberts was its de facto leader. In 1943 he was elected the first Democratic prothonotary, or chief clerk of courts, and was subsequently reelected five times. Generally credited with running the office efficiently although somewhat autocratically, in 1944 he was charged with forcing employees to join the newly organized Prothonotary Employees Association of Allegheny County and to pay dues of anywhere from $12.50 to $50.00 a month. His colorful political career came to an end when internal disputes within the state Democratic organization led them to dump him in 1967.[22]

Sport fell within DBR's venue both as a ward politician and as a matter of personal interest. At one time Roberts managed the J. F. Malones, a sandlot baseball team for which Dr. William McClelland, his political ally and later commissioner of Allegheny County, pitched. The Malones were backed by the father of one-time Pittsburgh district attorney James F. Malone, Jr.

Roberts also coached the Bloomfield Deans and the Hills' Or-
deale Club, and he was a regular at Forbes Field.

Although Roberts had moved from the Fifth Ward to a more
prosperous Brookline neighborhood, he maintained an address
in the ward and was regularly elected one of its committeemen.
With its 40,000 registered Democrats and high turnouts on
primary and election days, the Fifth Ward was a strong power
base. Roberts, the very essence of a ward leader, was held in high
esteem by his black constituents, giving them both circus and
bread. In 1958, for example, his prothonotary offices hired more
blacks than all the other county offices combined.[23] Countless
residents obtained jobs, legal relief, and rent and grocery money
from DBR's offices. Jack Hopkins observed that if a black youth
wanted to go to college, Roberts was the one to go to for a
summer job. In fact, Hopkins's own son and one of Ocey Swain's
daughters worked for Roberts while attending school. At Easter
and Christmas he regularly distributed candy and toys to children on the Hill. In short, Roberts was the man to see, and in a
majority of cases he delivered.

The Terrace Village ball club, according to Tinker, saw
Roberts as "our main connection." His picture and a message of
support were on the back of the program, for which he usually
donated $100 instead of the customary $50. DBR was the featured speaker at TV awards banquets, to which "he came early,
stayed late and had a whale of a time," according to the *Courier's*
Earl Johnson. On Labor Day in the 1950s, he sponsored the
annual David B. Roberts Memorial Trophy baseball game for
black teams, and his Independence Day celebrations were the
community's social event of the year.[24]

Since his election as a committeeman in 1926, DBR had seen
to it that the city hosted a gala Fourth of July celebration on the
Hill. With martial music, oratory, fireworks, and a street dance,
the celebration drew virtually the entire population of the Hill
into the streets. The highlight of the day was a baseball game in
which Terrace Village and the 18th Ward usually competed for
another trophy Roberts provided. Crowds of 5,000–10,000
watched these two predominantly black teams tangle year after
year in closely matched games. The winner received the trophy, a

small check, a dozen baseballs, and local bragging rights. Whether or not Roberts actually funded the day's festivities was less important than the fact that people credited him with its occurence, making DBR a popular figure with considerable political clout. Harold Tinker summed up Roberts's interest in the ball club: "It gave him a lot of support from the people. He wanted their votes, you know. All them fireworks and bands and dancing out in the street, he had it for a purpose. He kept the people. He had them in his hand." Roberts made things easier for the TV club with his donations, trophies, and field permits, while his identification with the team kept him in good stead.[25]

The Terrace Village club never reached the heights it aspired to in its 1952 program, for the Greater Pittsburgh League was too tough, and the best the team could manage was the runner-up spot. The squad was fairly evenly divided between men in their late twenties and thirties and youngsters on their way to the top. Several of the older players stayed with the team throughout its decade-long history, while many of the youngsters used it as a stepping-stone to other GPL or minor league clubs. Both Joe Studnicki and Billy Caye were offered better financial deals with other GPL clubs, and Caye played briefly in the New York Giants farm system. Jimmy Watts, Billy and Maurice Peatross, Josh Gibson, Jr., and Norm Gant were but some of the black Terrace Villagers who played their way into organized baseball in the 1950s as the major leagues belatedly opened their farm clubs to black players. TV simply could not afford to provide its players with a steady income, although when a lucrative exhibition game came their way, the players did receive a pay envelope. For the most part, however, GPL finances worked against them: the home team garnered the entire gate, which helped teams outside the city that could charge admission. But TV lacked the well-to-do financial sponsors of other league teams and was forced to rely on passing the hat in an economically depressed community.

Terrace Village's accomplishments came as much off the field as on it. Before the team folded in the 1960s they were regarded as the most adeptly run sandlot squad in black Pittsburgh, and the team and the men behind it were respected by black and white opponents alike. Their legacy was to cast aside the shib-boleth that prevented blacks and whites from playing on the same side. TV represented their community in a way no other team in the 1950s even attempted to match. At least in some ways, they did manage to "beat yesterday."

On the Gridiron: The Garfield Eagles

Baseball came first, but it is only a summer game. Its place in the seasons has much to do with its charm. In March and April, after sport's *tiempo muerto,* many fans and players are willing to endure occasional cold snaps and icy spring rains. But in the fall, each sunset foreshadows the season's end as baseball runs its course. Some pursue the sport year-round, in Cuba and Mexico, Puerto Rico and Venezuela, barnstorming through the American South and California, like migratory workers chasing the sun. But few can do that, so most put away their gloves and spikes as the leaves turn brown. For many, sport is over until next year; for others, the gridiron replaces the diamond.

Football was a relative latecomer to the American sporting scene, evolving from rugby and incubating within a handful of colleges and universities in the late nineteenth century. When football established its own place in the seasons, it did so primarily as a collegiate sport; its professional adjunct was a financially insecure, mostly ignored sideshow. In black Pittsburgh, as in much of black America, football had little presence until the early twentieth century, well after baseball had established itself as *the* sport of the black community. Throughout the first half of the century baseball was more extensively played, and with a higher level of sophistication, than football.

Baseball's roots were set deep into the American soil before football emerged on the sport scene, and there was no reason for black America to view things differently. Baseball is a far cheaper sport to play on an organized basis than football. (Certainly, children are able to play each with a minimum of cost and a premium on resourcefulness, but as the level of play advances, more expenses are involved.) Equipment and medical insurance alone demanded greater funding to maintain a football squad than a baseball team in the 1920s or 1930s. There also was the general lack of any football tradition in the black South. Migrants to Pittsburgh brought with them not only their fondness for baseball but the skills to play the game, honed by years of action in the cities and towns of the South. By contrast, few of them had ever played football before moving northward. Moreover, once they got there, blacks were less than welcomed in the prime football training camps—the schools. If not on the streets and in the sandlots, a boy who wanted to play football in black Pittsburgh or western Pennsylvania would do so through his school. Blacks were not uniformly barred from these teams, but they were informally discouraged from participating. There were usually at most two or three blacks on a Pittsburgh high school squad throughout the 1920s.

Despite this inauspicious beginning, football became as popular as baseball in black Pittsburgh as the twentieth century progressed. At first, many black boys were introduced to the game by their white friends or, in some cases, by the schools. Those who acquired an understanding of the game's dimensions were able to teach their contemporaries and the next generation the rudiments of football.

Gabe Patterson learned the game on empty lots on the Hill, playing with a racially mixed athletic club he and some other boys aged eleven to fifteen organized themselves. The Wesley Giants, named for the street their young captain lived on, challenged similarly organized teams. Patterson graduated from the Giants to the Schenley High team, where he quickly became known as a swivel-hipped halfback who could do it all. Like Patterson, Larnell Goodman's football education came by playing with his older white and black friends. But when Goodman left the predominantly white Polish Hill to attend Schenley, the coach told him he was too small to make the team. Benny Jackson, Ray Irvin, and several of their black friends from Garfield heard the same thing at Peabody. Along with a couple of white friends, this Garfield group had constituted a pick-up team that played squads from adjoining neighborhoods while still in grade school. They all went out for the Peabody High team but the coach kept only a few of them on the roster. The rest, averaging less than 140 pounds each, could make little protest against the coach's argument, even though some thought the decision might be racially motivated. Most blacks playing high school ball in the 1920s, like Patterson or Fred Clark at

Oliver or Joe Ware at Westinghouse, saw few other black faces in the huddle. They were a select group, and as such some of them parleyed their gridiron skills into football scholarships at Howard and other black colleges. A very few even played professional football, although the black presence there was never more than tenuous until after World War II.[26]

As youngsters like Patterson, Goodman, Jackson, Clark, and Irvin matured, there were fewer and fewer ways for them to continue playing football. While their white friends could become part of a growing sandlot, collegiate, or professional football network, there were few outlets for blacks. Indeed, what there was they created largely on their own. Their fields of play, as with baseball, were the sandlots. There, black Pittsburghers built an autonomous network of football teams and informal championships. Black youths learned the sport and their older teammates closed the gap between the races' ability to play the game. Some blacks played for white sandlot clubs, usually as paid performers for a crucial game or when the betting was particularly heavy. Gabe Patterson and Joe Ware were called on many times to spark a flagging offense for such teams as the Carrick Eagles or the Tarentum Firemen. But few teams made even the slightest pretense of presenting themselves as integrated squads. The exceptions were usually high school teams that played together for another season or two after graduation.

There were never more than half a dozen black football teams on the Pittsburgh sandlots in any one season during the 1920s and 1930s. Even with their longer rosters, the sum total of black players was less than during the baseball season. Teams were neighborhood-based in the 1920s, but as the years passed, squads began to recruit players from all over western Pennsylvania. In comparison with the far more plentiful white sandlot teams, the black squads were underfinanced, poorly trained, and usually outcoached. But not for long.

The Delany Rifles Athletic Club fielded one of the earliest black squads. Organized in 1908 by Captain Frank Steward, the Rifles professed to maintain themselves as an independent quasi-military organization. They named their team for Martin Delany, black Pittsburgh's most prominent citizen in the nineteenth century and a political thinker who is regarded by some as the father of American black nationalism. The Rifles complemented their social activities with a full panoply of athletics. Stocked with prominent black Pittsburghers, including attorney and organizational president Steward, baseball promoter Sellers Hall, and recreation worker James Dorsey, the Delany Rifles football team took on Wilberforce College and other local gridiron teams. The Rifles reflected their elitest "Old Pittsburgh" social base and contrasted markedly with most sandlot clubs. Teams like the East Liberty Scholastics, the Phoenix Club, the Saratoga Athletic Club, and the East End Athletics might have been able to compete with the Rifles on the playing fields, but their members were largely drawn from a different social class.[27]

It was not until the 1930s that black football teams proved that they were the equals of their white sandlot opponents. The club that showed the way was neither the well-financed Rifles nor even a team from the populous Hill district. Rather, the squad that made it to the top came from a relatively small black enclave in the mostly white neighborhood of Garfield.

The Garfield Eagles were often called the Homestead Grays of football, although a more apt comparison would have been with the Crawfords. The Eagles took to the gridiron with much the same verve as the Crawfords took to the diamond. For almost two decades, from 1928 until the mid-1940s, this sandlot eleven played the best football of any black team in western Pennsylvania. During those years, the Eagles were more than just a football team, however. The core of the Garfield community's social life, and for many their primary reference group outside the family, the Eagles left their mark as much off the field as on it.[28]

Garfield is a hilly, working-class community in the eastern part of Pittsburgh, about the size of Beltzhoover. Its black population exceeded 1,500 by 1930, out of a total population of 8,400, but it never grew much bigger until the construction of a housing project in Garfield in the early 1960s. By then the white population had begun to drop off and blacks constituted a larger portion of the community. At the time the Eagles were started, blacks comprised a little less than one-fifth of the neighborhood, a figure that would remain fairly stable during the team's two-decade history. Blacks often lived side by side with white families, but as one climbed the streets toward the top of Garfield Hill, the frequency of black faces increased. Although there were certain difficulties, such as shopping along Penn Avenue, Garfield's main thoroughfare, black residents expressed general satisfaction with the neighborhood and with race relations there. Black and white children played together, and many of their fathers worked alongside each other in the mills and factories in the nearby Lawrenceville district. That "there was none of this racial hatred we have today" is a common theme in recollections of the neighborhood by its black residents.[29]

The dozen or so black youths who formed the Garfield Eagles in the late summer of 1928 had grown up with each other. There were three pairs of brothers among its organizers, and most of the others were next-door neighbors; all of them had played in pick-up games with groups from nearby neighborhoods when they were twelve and thirteen, and when they entered Peabody High, most of them tried out for the team. Only Lee and Rink Davis and Merle Thacker made the team, however. The rest were left with only one real alternative if they wanted to continue playing football—to start their own team. Thacker is generally remembered as the first to suggest the idea. Even though he and the Davis brothers had earned high school jerseys, they continued to play with their friends on the newly formed sandlot club. Thacker proposed the name Garfield Eagles, and a local dynasty was born.

Of the original members, some were in high school and some just out. At 20, Ray Irvin was the senior member. Irvin worked as a janitor at a downtown office building, although employment in the early years of the team's history, which coincided with much of the Great Depression, was not usually the norm. The depression came early to black Pittsburgh and it came heavy, too. Most team members who were not in school were out of work or underemployed. They had time, though, and were willing to spend it to become part of a football team.

Their first task was to find a coach. Ed Lewis's running exploits on the cinder track of Peabody High had made him into a local hero of sorts.[30] He lived in the same row of houses as Ray Irvin and knew most of the players, and he agreed to take on the job only after cautioning the team that he knew little about the game of football. Lewis recognized immediately that the group as a whole was not in the best of shape. While he could do little about their tactical or strategic development, he could run them into condition. Thus, he had them on the field practicing twice a week and running wind sprints nightly.

A group of white Garfield boys known as the Garfield Merchants contacted Ray Irvin and challenged the Eagles to a game. Irvin was already acting as business manager, a post he would never relinquish. He booked the game for the neighborhood's Fort Pitt playground. The Eagle players knew enough about each other to assign themselves positions. A few, like Rink Davis and Thacker, had impressive natural ability; and the rest had, at least, the benefit of Lewis's conditioning program. While it wasn't a lot, it was enough to turn back the Merchants on the third Sunday of September 1928. The Eagles pushed the ball across the Merchants' goal line once, and though the conversion attempt failed, they held on for a 6–0 win. "We were sticking out our chests, then," center Ray Irvin attested.[31]

During the rest of that year the Eagles won some, lost some, and learned the game by playing it. Their sense of themselves was molded in part by the common sacrifice of their training regimen and in part by playing the last seven games on the road against white teams. They played .500 ball and showed that they could succeed off the field, too. Finding sponsors and raising funds to keep the team going were important victories for a group of young men who were not exactly setting the world ablaze elsewhere. In addition to learning how to play football, they learned something about themselves and their potential to make things happen.

Their second season was much the same as the first, with only a slightly altered cast of opponents and players. But during their third year the Eagles underwent a radical transformation. The main difference when the Eagles returned to their Fort Pitt playground practice site in the summer and fall of 1930 was Joe Barranti. Barranti was neither black nor from Garfield. His in-laws wondered why, if he had to coach, he could not coach a white team. Joe had grown up in Overbrook, a white neighborhood south of the Monongahela River, and had played for

Carrick High School, which in the 1920s meant strenuous training, daily practice, and an emphasis on execution.

The brother of one of Barranti's friends ran Kramer's Drugstore in Garfield, which had a mostly black clientele. It was there
that Barranti encountered Ray Irvin, and when his football background came up, Irvin asked if he might be able to lend a hand.
Barranti replied, "Let's go up on the field and we'll see what you
got." Outside of a "nucleus," he found that "they didn't have
nothing, not even enough guys to scrimmage."

In the summer of 1930, with the economy still plummeting,
the Eagle players and their new coach had plenty of time to
practice. Barranti instituted evening workouts from six until
eleven or later, four times a week. When the squad ran plays they
parked two cars on the field with their headlights on so they
could see what they were doing. Outside of a few players like
Rink Davis and Ralph Roy, who had picked up certain basic
skills, Barranti was confronted with a team that was sorely
lacking in the fundamentals. He demonstrated how to block and
tackle and ran them through drills until they had it right. The
players built their own tackling dummies, ran through tires, and
flung themselves on the ball in fumble drills. Barranti added a
couple of innovations to their single-wing offense, mainly some
fakes, reverses, and the popular flying wedge. The squad only
averaged 145–150 pounds per man, so Barranti taught them
how to finesse their way past frequently heavier and stronger
opponents. When it rained or he thought they needed it, Barranti held practice in the basement of one of the team's supporters. There his board drills illustrated different plays and how to
defense them, elevating the team's understanding of game strat-
egy to a level not usually found on the sandlots. Former Eagles
are near-unanimous in crediting Barranti with the team's breakthrough into the top ranks of sandlot ball.

There was yet another dimension in Barranti's relationship to
the team. "The man would do anything in the world for us,"
Benny Jackson remembered. "He even had a brand-new car he'd
lend to us." His wife, Gertrude, often drove players home from
practice and once was stopped by a policeman who could not
understand what she was doing alone with a black man after

midnight. Joe taped each player's ankles before games, and after a victory his culinary feats were celebrated as much as his coaching. His homemade wine and spaghetti dinners in Buck Phillips's Garfield home became part of the team tradition.

During their first year under Barranti's tutelage, the Eagles won five games, lost three, and tied two. As word of his coaching skills spread, blacks from other neighborhoods came to try out for the team. For the next two seasons the club went undefeated, compiling a cumulative record of twenty wins, no losses, and five draws. The Eagles built a reputation as the champions of black Pittsburgh, and many of their crucial plays became part of sandlot lore. One can still hear a spirited description of Ralph Roy returning a punt eighty-five yards through the mud against the McKeesport Crimsons to win a game in the Eagles' first undefeated season, or a play-by-play account of Rink Davis scoring all thirty-four points in the Eagles' shutout of Marshall Tech in the final game of the season.

The Eagles went from a team composed of only Garfield residents to a squad that drew on all of black Pittsburgh. Their reputation and active recruitment attracted the best black players in the area. In their seventeen seasons, over 300 men donned the orange and black jersey with an eagle on the front. Some played for a season or two, others for a decade or more. At first they came without much in the way of a football background, but increasingly the team tapped the best high school graduates around. Fred Clark, Fuzzy Tolbert, and Johnny Moore joined the Eagles after their high school careers had ended. Moore, a tall, muscular youth who played at the quarterback position without the benefit of headgear, also was the first baseman for the Pittsburgh Crawfords. Pete Rembert, an all-city center at Schenley High, and Muscles Harris, an all-district tackle at McKees Rocks, were mainstays on the Eagles' line in the 1930s. Rembert went from there to Bluefield College on a football scholarship and returned to coach the team. Harris, who could allegedly throw the ball from end zone to end zone and who also wrote cheers for the team's cheerleading squad, matriculated at Alabama State after several years with the Eagles.

Frequently, men who had played football at one of the black colleges would join the team afterward. And as the Eagles reached the calibre of many black college teams, some of their players, like Rembert and Harris, earned college scholarships based on their play. Steubenville High School star Puck Bergwin played at Western Reserve College and then "spread destruction throughout the American Football Association" for the Newark Tornados, a short-lived pro team that was willing to use an occasional black player, before he joined forces with the Eagles for a season.[32] Gabe Patterson, who played Negro League baseball and Canadian League football with the Montreal Alouettes, sparked the Eagles' potent offense after graduating from Schenley High and finding his coach's promise of a college scholarship to have been a false one. In the backfield he was often paired with Jack Johnson, a fortyish fullback who kept a cigar in his helmet to chomp on in the huddle.

The Eagles' roster expanded to forty or more players, so the team could field four platoons, if necessary. Many of the players basically participated in practice only, as the starting eleven often played both offense and defense and substitutions were rare. But even if they didn't see much action in games, mostly everyone showed up whenever the team came together, obviously enjoying the practice sessions and the camaraderie. Their average team member's weight increased until the Eagles were regarded as heavyweights. They took on the best teams in western Pennsylvania and even numbered a few black colleges among their opponents. At times they were members of the West Penn Conference or the Honus Wagner Heavyweight Conference. Over seventeen seasons and 164 games, the Eagles won 98, lost 47, and tied 19. In 1943 and 1944, as in 1931 and 1932, they went undefeated.

Along with the changes on the field came changes on the bench. Joe Barranti left the squad after three years to work full-time for Gus Greenlee, owner of the Crawford ball club. Barranti had already been working part-time in Greenlee's numbers business, and in the summer of 1933, Greenlee proposed that Barranti form a professional black football team under his ownership. Greenlee thought that a football squad would fill the seats in his newly constructed stadium on the Hill, Greenlee Field. Barranti assembled fifteen to twenty men and began team workouts in August. After a dozen practices, Greenlee lost interest and dissolved the team before it ever scrimmaged. Barranti came back to the Eagles temporarily but found the players' commitment to practice not up to his standards and left shortly thereafter. He was succeeded by a number of men from the neighborhood who lent a hand, as did former college players and prospective college coaches. The two who coached the longest had both played for the Eagles: Peter Rembert served in the late 1930s, and Henry Yandel took over when Rembert left to accept a coaching job at a black school in the South.

"When we got Yandel," Gabe Patterson argued, "he upgraded the football team 100 percent." Yandel attended Coach Shaughnessey's clinics at the University of Pittsburgh, where all the big-time college coaches met to discuss plays and game situations. Patterson continued, "Yandel got to know him and he got to know Yandel and he began to input into these sessions as much as he was getting out of it." While Rembert had been a straight running-play coach, Yandel introduced the T-offense. In Patterson's estimation, Yandel "changed the whole outlook of sandlot football in the city." He had the Eagles calling audibles at the line of scrimmage and using flare passes and triple pivots with the quarterback handing off the ball on an end-around play. His offense was essentially the same one the colleges and the pros were employing, and it impressed the other sandlot teams. "With him," Patterson attested, "it became a twenty-four hour game 'cause it was nothing for him to call you in the middle of the night and say, 'I just thought of a play and I know it's for you.' The man ate and slept the game. One night he kept the whole backfield out until five o'clock in the morning teaching us the audible signal play. He'd pound and pound until you got it." Yandel quit his job to devote more time to coaching and eventually lost his family in the process. In Gabe Patterson's estimation, "He was really only alive when he was on the football field." Under him, the Eagles recaptured the élan of the Barranti years, going undefeated in back-to-back seasons and capturing the West Penn Conference title in both years.[33]

If Joe Barranti and Henry Yandel introduced the Eagles to a sense of discipline and commitment on the field, the players also evinced a new sense of themselves off it. They were the ones who started the team, and although they received important help from older members of the community, they always basically ran the club themselves, with finances and bookings largely under their control. Of the dozen young men present at the team's creation, most stayed with the club until World War II called them away. Some found the calibre of play to be over their heads after the first few seasons but nevertheless remained active in some way. Ray Irvin, for instance, realized that a 110-pound center who went against 200-pound defensive tackles was "just foolish [for] being in there." So Irvin worked behind the scenes, booking games and handling the logistics of a fairly complex club. He, Benny Jackson, Lee Davis, and a handful of others constituted the backbone of the squad. The team would have been measurably weaker, if it could have survived at all, without their participation.

The expenses for a football squad were considerable in the 1930s, often running to several thousand dollars a year. For the first few seasons the Eagles took the field in an assortment of cast-off shoulder pads, pants, and helmets, and no one player was ever fully equipped. A decent set of equipment, team jerseys, and medical insurance required that the players raise money in greater amounts than they were accustomed to dealing with. During the season, tape, footballs, gas money and carfare, oranges, and cleaning bills were regular expenses.

The players met this challenge themselves. They printed placards announcing their schedule and found local merchants and individuals to subsidize them. They solicited booster donations and often dug into their own pockets to make ends meet. As they gained confidence in their ability to raise money, they also diversified their ventures. Through a connection at the police station on the Hill, the young Eagles were able to buy confiscated moonshine for less than the prevailing price and sell it at a profit to folks having Saturday night socials in Garfield. Calling themselves the Garfield Eagles Social Club, they held a constant stream of parties throughout the year, some at the Elks or Loendi clubs but most of them at somebody's Garfield residence. Ray Irvin dutifully recorded the finances of these affairs in a set of nickel composition books, the now tattered pages of which indicate not only the expenses for a band and refreshments but also the take at the door. Some parties brought in only a few dollars; their annual street fair, however, often garnered several hundred.

Each summer the club roped off a section of Broad Street for a week-long street fair. With sawdust on the street and Japanese lanterns strung between the light poles, Broad Street was temporarily transformed into an outdoor ballroom. An eight-piece jazz band played nightly and hundreds of couples, black and white, danced under the stars. Those not interested in dancing could play the carnival wheels or buy ice cream. Emmanuel Phillip's home was along the roped-off stretch, and in his cavernous basement, which the team used as a clubhouse, "team members were selling moonshine faster than the beer gardens were selling whiskey."[34]

All of these fundraising efforts were supplemented by the Eagles' gates receipts, mostly when on the road. The site of their home grounds, the Fort Pitt School playground, made it difficult to collect much at the gate because of the city ordinance against charging a set admission fee. The team thus made more when they traveled, though Irvin's records show them receiving guarantees of only twelve to thirty dollars the first few seasons, amounts quickly devoured by their expenses.

The force behind these money-making ventures was the Garfield Eagles Social Club, the organizational embodiment of the team off the field. The club's seven officer positions rotated informally among the core of those team members who were most committed to the squad. Many of the wives were active, and monthly meetings often attracted twenty-five or thirty people who helped to make plans and figure out how to implement them. The club was a learning experience for most of the participants, teaching them how to handle large sums of money and organize impressive social events. It continued well into the 1960s, even though the football team had disbanded by the mid-1940s. When the social club was dissolved as well, several of its members carried their organizational experience to the Elks and various black community organizations.

Football tends to inspire intense loyalties among those who play it together, and the Garfield Eagles were no exception. "It was an atmosphere where we were all for one and one for all," Gabe Patterson remembered. "If we were in the streets and saw one of our guys doing something wrong, we'd go up to him and take him out of the situation and tell him he's wrong and that was it. If he was having difficulty at home or with his woman or what not, we'd settle it." If there was an economic hardship, players dug deep into their own pockets and helped out. When a man was short on rent money, his teammates threw a Saturday night social for him. By taking a cut from the poker game and selling fried chicken, chitterlings, and greens, these house-rent socials combined festivity with self-help. "We had like a woman-man relationship between men. No half-way—no b.s.," Patterson testified. "It was for real. You could talk about things among the fellows more freely than you could with someone else." Sitting around the clubhouse playing cards and telling tales, "we would discuss from rags to riches—something like this thing they got now that's group therapy."[35] Several players described the Eagles as a family and the players as brothers.

As a family, the Garfield Eagles fit snugly into the community. They directly touched the lives of most blacks in Garfield, and many of the whites, too. Benny Jackson recalled that several local shopkeepers, especially the few black ones, helped out "when they saw we was trying to do something to stay out of trouble." The Evans family owned a few houses and a grocery store where blacks in the neighborhood shopped. When the club needed money to meet a guarantee to a visiting ball club, Mrs. Evans took it out of the cash register. If the gate was sufficient, they repaid her; if not, she let it go. Other men helped coach or drove one of Buck Phillips's four rubbish trucks to various parts of the city and outlying areas to transport players to and from practice four nights a week. Two local men, one white and one black, served as the linesman and referee at home games. A neighborhood doctor often accompanied them to away games and half a dozen girls led cheers. Finally, a fairly large percentage of residents, both black and white, came to their socials and street fairs and rooted for them at home and away games.

The main backer of the team, both financially and in terms of fatherly counsel, was Emmanuel ("Buck") Phillips, the man many referred to as the "Mayor" of Garfield. The offspring of a French railroad engineer and a part-black, part-Indian woman in the late 1880s, Phillips moved to Garfield around 1911. He worked for local merchants prior to a venture into the hauling business, first with horses and buggies, later with trucks. He became one of the two or three most substantial black businessmen in Garfield and was active in his church as well. The "Mayor" gradually assumed the role of de facto leader of black Garfield, and even though he never ran for office, he did canvas for votes and act as a broker between residents and the Tenth Ward chairman, Charles Martin. According to his son Vernon, he saw politics as a way to take care of things in the community. Phillips was responsible for finding jobs for between forty and fifty people who were released from prison under probationary programs, and neighbors, both black and white, turned to him when they were in need of financial or legal assistance.

Buck Phillips's oldest son, Johnny, was one of the original members of the Garfield Eagles and his father offered to help the team in any way he could. The family's three-room basement with a shower served as the team clubhouse and dressing room. "We loafed there," Benny Jackson recalled. "We'd all bring whatever we had, a few potatoes, a piece of meat, and we'd make a big stew and eat there. Not even go home for dinner." When the team needed funds, Phillips reached in his pocket and asked how much. His political ties helped the team obtain a permit to play at Fort Pitt and later a changing room and grandstands for that field, and on more than one occasion he got players out of trouble with the police. When the team was attacked in Brentwood, it was Phillips who told them, and about twenty whites who joined them on the field, to form a circle so that nobody could get at their backs; then he led them all to safety.[36] In the aftermath, when the town mayor threatened to ban Sunday sandlot ball, it was Phillips who persuaded ward leaders to intercede. In return for these city services, Phillips and the players knocked on doors and worked the polls.

When it came to decisions regarding the team, Phillips turned matters over to the players. "He wanted to help," Vernon Phillips explained, but "he didn't want to run it." When asked to describe Buck Phillips, more than one former player said he was like a father. "He was it!" Benny Jackson attested. "He had a lot of nerve and heart and backed us all the way. We'd listen to him, too. Probably go to him first with a problem." "I adored him as much as I did my own father," was how Ray Irvin put it. "He was the one who would sit down and explain to you. If you was right, he'd let you know. If you was wrong, he'd chew you out."

World War II disrupted sandlot ball in black Pittsburgh, the Eagles being virtually the only black gridiron eleven left in the city after the 1941 season.[37] The draft and enlistments cleaned Garfield out overnight, tearing holes in the roster; and by then, Buck Phillips and many of the original members were less active in the team's affairs. A group of younger players, including Larnell Goodman and Gabe Patterson, began to assert themselves, and in 1942 the team moved its home games to Ammon Field on the Hill. By 1945 the team's name was no longer the Garfield Eagles but the Pittsburgh Eagles, and during the war they severed all ties with the Garfield Eagles Social Club, most of the club members being in the service.

In part, the split was due to the growing presence on the team of players from outside Garfield and the separation of many of the older members due to the war. Yet there was also a division over the financial arrangements. At first, no player received anything for playing and no one thought anything of it. After all, they were playing for fun. But as the level of competition and the amount of money involved both increased, the team leaders began to offer some players a small sum to play. Western Reserve sensation Puck Bergwin, for example, was paid to play on a game-by-game basis. There is a great deal of disagreement among the surviving members of the squad as to how these financial arrangements were worked out, and there was likely just as much confusion then. Despite the relative openness of the organization, not everyone was fully aware of the goings on at the business end of the operation. Ray Irvin explained, "During my administration as business manager, we gave what we thought the individual was entitled to—production was the main thing and we didn't show no partiality against anybody." But the pay scale was not generally accessible to team members, and that in itself added to the growing tension.

Larnell Goodman, for example, believed that Buck Phillips was making money on the club and objected to what he perceived as an inequitable distribution of funds to a handful of players. He described the move to the Hill as a players' revolt in which the younger members gained control over the money and split it up on a cooperative basis. Others disputed his argument that Phillips made money, contending that, to the contrary, Buck Phillips donated considerable sums to the club and got little in return. Vernon Phillips asserted that 5,000 or more fans at a game did not necessarily translate into much money at the gate. He and Benny Jackson viewed the team's downfall as the desire of some of the players to get paid. "We never got a dime. All we got was fun and we ate a lot," Jackson maintained, but "some of the guys who came later wanted to know on Sunday what the guarantee was first thing to figure their cut out." Despite these long-standing differences of opinion, however, there is surprisingly little bitterness left when former Eagles discuss the move to the Hill. Buck Phillips wrote to Benny Jackson, then away in the service, about the changes and told him that Larnell Goodman and the others wanted to buy the equipment. "I didn't feel bad," Jackson explained. "No hard feelings. I was glad to get rid of the equipment and see it used. I went to see them play over there in the Hill and kidded around with them." For Jackson and most of the rest, the Eagles had run their course as a Garfield team. There was little desire to hang on to it any longer.

The Hill-based Pittsburgh Eagles maintained their on-the-field traditions throughout the 1945 season. But, cut off as they were from their Garfield roots, the team disbanded within a few years. They no longer had the extensive behind-the-scenes support of the Garfield Eagles Social Club, which, unlike the football team, stayed in Garfield and lasted into the 1960s. Furthermore, in the postwar boom of American sports, black athletes were finding increased acceptance in college and professional ranks. That meant that a team like the Eagles encountered increasing competition for players. While sandlot ball experienced a resurgence in the late 1940s and early 1950s, long-term trends were about to bury it. The Eagles were not there for sandlot's last hurrah, but by going out in peak form, they left as they played, with a touch of grace.

Belonging to the Garfield Eagles changed each player's life. The team became the main reference group for many members, who went through a series of bonding experiences, from hard practice sessions to coping with defeat and then unexpected

success. The Eagles also carried the players through economically depressed times and left them with not only the old aches
and pains of a football career but a better sense of organization,
themselves, and the role of sport in black Pittsburgh. The Eagles
were, perhaps, the most important black institution in Garfield
during the 1930s. The team also touched the lives of a fairly
large portion of the neighborhood's black population and was
the only agency that could bring most of the community together in one place for any event. It was the first black enterprise
to gain widespread acceptance among Garfield whites, representing a breakthrough of major proportions for black Garfield.
Evaluating its impact on racial consciousness is difficult, but
clearly the Eagles forced many to consider, at least temporarily, a
new side of black Pittsburgh. Its athletic and social legacies are a
part of the oral history of the city, a subtle counterpoint to
today's sportsworld.

Black and White on the Sandlots

They call it stormy Monday, but Tuesday's not as bad when
there's a ball game after work to chase away the blues. In its most
elemental form, sandlot ball was a game to anticipate and play,
with its attendant frustrations, disappointments, transcendence,
and exhilaration. It was a matter of emotions and exertions, and
it was simply to experience them that most players took part—
for play, not for pay. Although a fair number of black and white
sandlotters benefited monetarily, including tips from bettors and
other perquisites, few actually prospered from the game.

The range of professional sport for black Pittsburghers, while
expanding in the 1920s and 1930s, nonetheless remained fairly
limited. Black professional baseball's financial rewards paled by
comparison to those of white organized ball. The Negro
Leagues were more capitalized and stable than the black sandlots, but players, fans, and backers continually moved between
the two. A black ballplayer could aspire to reach the black
majors, and once there, he could find an income unattainable by
most black workers. But no black ballplayer, even the most
highly paid, ever got rich from baseball. For many it was a year-
long occupation, with winter ball being played in the Caribbean.

Those who did not play winter ball usually sought work instead, mostly in service and labor positions like the majority of urban black Americans. In Pittsburgh, a ballplayer like Ralph Mellix, the 18th Ward mainstay who hurled throughout western Pennsylvania as a free lance, could pocket a sizable sum. But Mellix was an exception. Few survived for very long on their sandlot pay alone, although sandlot gave them something they'd never find in a paycheck.

White sandlot ball was not a going economic concern either. The difference in capitalization, however, provides one of the sharpest contrasts between black and white ball. Baseball's development in black America was retarded by slavery, which left it far behind white baseball both in terms of experience and finances. Blacks had few opportunities to play ball and organize teams until after the Civil War. This lack of a playing tradition meant that blacks' knowledge of the game was behind that of white players for several decades.[38] Black baseball caught up in terms of quality of play but never came close to white ball's economics. The closer sandlot ball was to pick-up games among neighborhood youth, the less money mattered. But as groups like the young Pittsburgh Crawfords or the Fifth Avenue Braves matured, they needed to raise increasing amounts of money. That was easier to do in the relatively more affluent white community than in black Pittsburgh. White spectators generally contributed more to the passing hat than blacks, even at contests involving a black team. Moreover, relatively more white teams were located in suburban or rural areas where it was possible to charge an admission fee. At forty cents a head, Bellevue could count on $500–1,000 from each home contest.

Community support was critical to sandlot ball, and white communities were generally able to contribute more. The men who ran the 18th Ward and Terrace Village clubs were porters, janitors, clerical workers, and laborers. White clubs like Bellevue, Dormont, and North Pittsburgh had local merchants behind the bench. Dormont, a perennial contender in Pittsburgh's fastest sandlot circuits, could count on Billy Fuchs, a well-to-do printing company owner; North Pittsburgh counted on Bus Garlick, an upholsterer. While these men were hardly titans of industry, their incomes, and hence their financial ability to help their clubs, were considerably more than those of men like Harold Tinker, Jack Hopkins, or Ocey Swain. Bellevue, for example, had a booster club that required members to donate at least $300 annually. It is small wonder that Bellevue could afford a payroll of more than $3,000 a month during the 1950s.

Better financial backing allowed white sandlot ball to form more stable leagues and go to greater lengths to recruit talent. When Mount Washington went into the final game of a seven-game play-off series with Dormont in 1957 and needed a pitcher for the deciding contest, they simply flew in a former pitcher of theirs who was stationed with the army in Iowa. That would have been impossible for a black team.[39] The difference meant better equipment, and when and where there was a pay envelope, a bigger amount in it. "They'd have a sack of bats and we'd have two or three," was how 18th Ward manager Willis Moody put it. While black clubs like the 18th Ward and Terrace Village were sometimes able to give their players $4–5 a game, their white opponents, like Dormont and North Pittsburgh, were paying theirs $25–30.[40] Billy Caye, who played for both white and black clubs, made $225 a month playing with Muscogee during a brief stay in the minors in the early 1950s. He returned to area sandlots after realizing he was not going to make it in organized ball and received $200 a month playing for Bellevue in the Greater Pittsburgh League. No black Pittsburgh club ever dreamed of paying a player anything close to that.

At its higher levels, white sandlot ball overlapped with organized baseball. The latter had organized itself into a tightly structured, narrowing hierarchy extending from the lowly Class D minor leagues to the lords of baseball, the American and National leagues, in the early years of the century. While a majority of minor league clubs in Class D, C, and B, and often A, operated at a loss, Class AA and AAA clubs were profitable ventures. Consequently, the ledgers of most minor league clubs were not that much different than sandlot clubs in the Greater Pittsburgh League. Nor did the men behind these minor league teams make a direct profit from them, any more than a man like Billy Fuchs did, though minor league clubs certainly had a beneficial economic impact on a small town or city and sandlot backers accrued some indirect commercial benefit from their sponsorship. Sid Herlong, a Florida congressman and past-president of the Class D Florida State League, estimated that a year of Class D ball ran about $40,000 per club, with revenues recouping only three-fourths of the costs. He noted that in his league and probably elsewhere, "Boys in class D don't play baseball for a livelihood. They play because they like baseball. Boys who are not in organized baseball [i.e., those on the sandlots] make just as much money as they would in organized baseball and work part time on the side."[41] While the young men Herlong mentioned also played because they wanted to make it to the major leagues, he was basically correct in his assessment. Many played Class D ball long after any hope of reaching the big time had been exhausted. The lower levels of organized ball at least gave them an opportunity to continue playing.

In Pittsburgh and in the Northeast, which had a far smaller number of minor league franchises than the South and Southwest by the late 1940s, the sandlots were a more realistic way to continue playing. A player could live at home, hold down a job, and play before family, neighbors, and friends. The money sandlot provided sometimes even equaled a minor league paycheck, but even if it didn't, it mattered little, given the reasons that most had for playing. Black sandlot baseball overlapped with its professional game, too, but the economics were on a reduced scale all the way down the line.

One of the biggest differences between the lower levels of the minors and the sandlots was the age of the players. Organized baseball signed young prospects and the player then progressed through the minor league system at a rate determined by his ability and the particular needs of the club that owned him. The minors were largely stacked with young men in their teens and twenties. The sandlots, however, recognized nothing beyond ability and were filled with men of all ages. While youth was hardly absent from the sandlots, men in their thirties, forties, and frequently fifties were regulars. Many were former minor leaguers who had gone as far as they could in organized ball and had returned to the sandlots to keep on playing.

Sandlot's roots in white Pittsburgh were deeper than those of black sandlot ball, stretching back to the middle of the nineteenth century. Baseball boomed in the city after the Civil War as demobilized military units, neighborhood, and workplace teams met in local and regional rivalries. Only rowing, with its twenty mill- and community-based clubs, rivaled baseball's appeal, though both sports were firmly embedded within a working-class milieu in which Pittsburgh's skilled craftsmen set the tone. In the decades following the war, the crafts exerted their greatest influence ever in Pittsburgh politics, cultural life, and work-places. Loosely linked to taverns, fire companies, politicians, and merchants, sport intertwined male sociability with drinking and gambling. This sporting network was decidedly noncommercial and nonprofessional, however, and it was partially due to its strength that support for a professional baseball club in Pittsburgh was slow to materialize. The first attempt to establish a pro franchise folded in 1878, the team being unable to compete on the field or at the gate with the stronger independent clubs.

Sport in Pittsburgh reflected a political cast, but it was class, not ethnicity, that counted most. Teams brought together men of similar occupation, worksite, or neighborhood, the latter often wedding the different ethnic subgroupings of a community to a common sporting bond. Ethnic sport was more the domain of the turners and later the sokols and falcons (Poles).

The political and workplace influence of craftsmen began to wane in Pittsburgh during the 1880s and 1890s, and that ultimately had its effect on sport. The reorganization of work in the steel industry undercut the strength of the crafts, and the mills increasingly turned toward the new immigrants from southern and eastern Europe. The last working-class regatta on a Pittsburgh river was held in 1887, and when the sport reappeared it was the domain of the college-educated. Pro baseball, meanwhile, returned to the city in 1882, and this time it was there to stay.[42]

Sport in twentieth-century Pittsburgh became more commercialized and professionalized, but blacks and many immigrant and industrial workers remained largely outside the new mass culture. The sandlots remained their focus, and for some immigrants, the gymnasium of their fraternal association was also central.

Although white sandlot ball awaits its historian, certain comparisons between black and white sandlot ball seem valid. Like many black clubs, white teams were often sponsored by ward politicians and, especially during the 1920s, area industry, churches, and settlement agencies. Some of these teams reflected a particular ethnic cast and probably lent an element of ethnic cohesion and identity to their communities. But by the 1930s few white clubs were ethnically homogeneous. White sandlot clubs frequently recruited on a citywide basis with talent, not nationality, the critical factor. While these clubs served similar social and community functions to those of black teams, white communities were not as dependent as black communities in finding on the sandlots some compensation for the economic, cultural, and political discrimination they faced elsewhere.

Sandlot ball was at its strongest in Pittsburgh between the two world wars. The century's second global conflict, however, disrupted sport in America and activity on the sandlots was greatly reduced for the duration. Sandlot, suppressed during the war, came back stronger than ever afterward and experienced a decade-long resurgence before the final curtain came down. While World War I was followed by an unprecedented expansion of sandlot ball, along with the boom in collegiate football and professional sport, World War II led to an era in which professional sport took full control, forcing the sandlots to the wall. At first, as teams like the Pittsburgh Corsairs and the Wilmerding Alumni took to the gridirons, it appeared as if sandlot ball was returning to form. But neither of these teams, nor the 18th Ward, the Garfield Eagles, or Terrace Village, survived the 1950s.

No one force killed sandlot ball. It simply died out due to a combination of factors that ranged from changing economic and social conditions to new cultural patterns and the transformation of professional sport. The emergence of television, the more complete integration of high school and college ball, and the long-awaited racial breakthroughs in pro sports contributed to the sandlots' demise.

Sandlot ball is now little more than a collection of fading memories. Yet for almost a third of this century, the sandlots offered black Pittsburgh a chance to control its own sporting life, an opportunity it did not waste. During these years, teams like the Pittsburgh Crawfords and the Garfield Eagles represented black Pittsburghers both to whites throughout western Pennsylvania and to themselves. On this terrain, at least, blacks proved themselves the equals of whites. They gave blacks in Garfield, Terrace Village, Beltzhoover, and the Hill good entertainment and a source of enduring pride. Led by a core of sport activists like Bill Harris, Harold Tinker, Ray Irvin, and Willis Moody, black Pittsburgh built a sporting network that was renowned throughout the region. That network may have crumbled during the 1950s, but its legacy is in part the continuing fascination of black Pittsburgh with sport.

4 Professional Black Sport and Cum Posey

Black sport in America has never fully escaped its heritage of slavery. Even while gaining some measure of autonomy during the early decades of the twentieth century, black professional sport remained undercapitalized, subject to the manipulations of white owners, agents, and promoters, and relatively powerless to control its own destiny. This was less evident in Pittsburgh, however, where black professional sport edged closer toward its outer limits of growth, both on the field and at the gate, during the 1930s and 1940s. For more than a decade Pittsburgh was the center of black professional baseball in the Americas. Its two finest teams, the Homestead Grays and the Pittsburgh Crawfords, helped to push black baseball to its highest competitive level, while their black owners, Cumberland Posey and Gus Greenlee, maneuvered behind the scenes to establish the game on a sounder footing.

A confluence of factors made black pro ball in Pittsburgh relatively more autonomous than elsewhere. Both the Grays and the Crawfords were rooted in the city's black sandlots, and despite becoming professional outfits they remained tied to that sandlot scene in myriad ways. Black Pittsburgh's allegiance thus was never in doubt. Moreover, both the financial backing and the leadership for these teams derived from the black community: the money came largely from the numbers game, the biggest black-controlled business in the city; and the leadership was provided by Cum Posey, the city's most astute black sport entrepreneur, and Gus Greenlee, its main numbers banker.

Black control of pro sport carried with it political implications for black Pittsburgh. Posey and Greenlee were active politically in their respective communities, in part cashing in on their roles as sporting figures. A less tangible benefit of black control was the tremendous pride and self-respect that the Grays and the Crawfords brought to the wider black community. They were to all of black Pittsburgh what the Eagles were to Garfield and the

18th Ward to Beltzhoover. Blacks from any of Pittsburgh's neighborhoods could claim the Grays and the Crawfords as their own and compare them favorably to the best teams that white America could offer.

Black Players, White Control

In the pre–Civil War South, black men fought in the prize ring, raced horses, and trained fighting cocks for their white owners. A few who excelled in athletics, like the legendary bare-knuckled heavyweight Tom Molyneux, were able to parley their expertise into personal freedom.[1] But Molyneux and Chicken George, the cockfighter of *Roots* renown, were exceptions. Most black men competing in athletics did so under the control and discretion of white slaveholders. If blacks played their own sports in "the world the slaves made,"[2] there is little record of it.

After the Civil War, blacks continued to compete in commercialized sport, but the jocks did not own their mounts and the boxers and cockfighters usually fought in white-controlled arenas and pits. In the South blacks were all but eliminated from professional sport by the end of the nineteenth century. Jim Crow social legislation banned mixed bouts in the prize ring and virtually ended interracial competition on the ball field. Black jockeys, who had dominated Southern racing in the late 1890s, were scarce a decade later. In the North, exclusion was not so much the result of legislation as a set of de facto practices subscribed to by organized baseball and other sports. Where once a score of black athletes had played on white professional ball clubs, not one could be found on the roster of a white team by the dawn of the twentieth century. Professional black athletes were relegated to the "underground" of sport—the sandlots and the prize ring. But a crucial difference existed between sport in the North and the South: if excluded from the more organized levels of professional sport in the North, blacks there at least could compete on all-black squads against white athletes on the sandlots and in semipro ball; by contrast, interracial competition remained a dead issue in the South until the 1950s.

Black Americans were quick to organize their own amateur teams and competitions after the Civil War, and this spirit of self-organization ultimately spilled over into the professional sphere, where the legacy of slavery was the most bitter. Since the owners, not the players, of most turn-of-the-century ball teams arranged the games and handled the finances, and since making a profit was decidedly important to both owners and promoters, early black professional teams were faced with severe underfinancing, if they depended on the economically depressed black community, or control by white capital. Furthermore, few blacks had the necessary background in promotion or the political, social, and financial connections that would make professional sport a profitable venture.

Robert Peterson argues in *Only the Ball Was White,* a pioneering study of black professional baseball, that a few black teams began paying their players as early as the late 1870s or 1880s. The first fully salaried black team was probably the Cuban Giants, formed by the headwaiter of the Argyle Hotel in Babylon, New York, in 1885 to entertain the summer guests who stayed at that Long Island resort. While the team's founder and the players were black, when the Cuban Giants took their act on the road they did so under white financial management— a typical arrangement in black professional baseball.[3] By World War I there were black teams operating more or less on a professional footing in most large cities outside the South, but few were able to attain either a large degree of financial success or a modicum of stability. Such teams came and went, and efforts to form leagues in 1887, 1906, and 1919 were soon aborted.

Denied access to organized white baseball leagues after the 1890s, black teams nonetheless were forced to continue to rely on white ownership to remain viable. Late in the 1933 season, W. Rollo Wilson, *Courier* sportswriter and later commissioner of the Negro National League, answered a reader's letter voicing apprehension about the role of white owners:

As for fear about white interests controlling Negro baseball—why, they have always done that.

Mighty few teams have been entirely financed by Negro capital, if you want to know the truth. There have been many instances of so-called Negro "owners" being nothing but a "front" for the white interest behind them. And then many teams have always been owned by white promoters or investors.

Name some of the greatest teams of the years agone—the Lincoln Giants, the Lincoln Stars, the Brooklyn Giants, the Bacharachs, Baltimore Black Sox, the Cuban X Giants, the Philadelphia Giants, the Leland Giants, the American Giants, the Kansas City Monarchs. The money of white men made these clubs.[4]

Wilson's roll call of black teams backed by white money was by no means complete, but it underscores the significance of white capital.[5]

Capital shortage was not the only serious problem confronting black baseball. Barred from the white organized leagues and unable to make a go of it solely in their own regional or national leagues, black teams were forced to play a never-ending series of games, many of them on the road against other sandlot and semipro teams. When the Pittsburgh Crawfords or Homestead Grays were scheduled to face the New York Black Yankees in a two-game series in New York, they would barnstorm their way there and back, squeezing in as many semipro tilts as possible. Gus Greenlee and Cumberland Posey were adept enough businessmen to arrange their teams' games in the area, but booking contests in cities like New York and Philadelphia was not that simple. Semipro ball in these large metropolitan areas was usually the fiefdom of a local promoter who monopolized the action in his territory through control over key teams and parks. If black clubs could have afforded to construct their own stadiums or been able to independently arrange rentals with the owners of organized baseball's parks, some of these agents' influence would have been curtailed. But few black clubs ever had that luxury,[6] so the agents persisted in redirecting a large share of black baseball's profits into their own pockets.

Baseball promoters were especially strong in the East. A swing through New York City could last two or three weeks, with the visiting black club never playing the same opponent twice. Playing enough matches often made the difference in meeting the payroll and paying the hotel bill. Nat Strong in New York and Ed Gottlieb in Philadelphia had controlling interests in their cities' black franchises as well as ownership and sway over the top-drawing semipro clubs and the best places to play. While they were frequently regarded as avaricious businessmen who preyed on black baseball, black teams could not ignore them.

Nat Strong was part-owner and booking agent for Dexter Park, one of the premier independent ball parks in the country, located in Queens. The Bushwicks, perhaps the most successful white independent ball club in the nation, played their home games there, and Strong had a piece of their action, too. The Bushwicks often drew more fans than their major league rivals and paid salaries higher than any minor league and some major league teams. A game with them at Dexter Park was a financial plum. Strong also owned part of the Brooklyn Royal Giants and the New York Black Yankees, and he booked the Harlem Stars, the Bacharach Giants, and Alex Pompez's Cuban Stars. A black club wanting to do business with Strong did so on his terms: for example, he refused to book black teams into Dexter Park except on a guaranteed fee basis, not giving them the option of a percentage of the gate. Strong could virtually make or break a club in the lucrative New York market.[7]

Eddie Gottlieb's realm was Philadelphia, where he built a reputation as a promoter and coach. His South Philadelphia Hebrew Stars, a basketball team he founded and coached, won professional championships in several leagues from the late 1920s through the 1940s, and when Gottlieb took on the Philadelphia Warriors, he coached them to the championship of the National Basketball Association in the league's first year of play.[8] Although Gottlieb refused to allow blacks to play on any of his basketball teams, he was quite willing to take an active part in black baseball. In 1933 he became a joint owner of the Philadelphia Stars with Ed Bolden, a black man. The Stars, formerly the Hilldale Club, had been run by black businessman John Drew, who was unable to keep the team solvent after refusing to pay a 10 percent agent's fee to play in New York City. Gottlieb simply took his 10 percent off the top. With booking rights to New York's Yankee Stadium, in addition to his Philadelphia interests, which included control over Shibe Park, Gottlieb was a formidable force indeed.

Wendell Smith accused Gottlieb of having a stranglehold over the Negro National League and took him to task in a *Courier* article entitled "The Strange Case of 'Brother' Gottlieb . . .":

Not too many years ago, a character by the name of Eddie Gottlieb was sauntering around the streets of Philadelphia, posing as a promoter. He had his office in his hip pocket and nothing in his head but some ideas about exploiting Negroes in sports. In those days he was a very humble character and the sports mob classed him as . . . a man free of prejudice. That's the way it usually is with guys who see a chance to "move in" and "take over" in such cases. They establish themselves as liberals first. . . . That's the way it was with "Brother Eddie." He was the Negro's friend. . . . He knew how tough it was to get along because other people had been booting his people around for thousands of years, too. . . .

So "Brother Eddie" got in good. He became a fixture in Negro baseball. He made piles and piles of dough as an owner of the Philadelphia Stars. . . . Then somebody organized the Basketball Association of America, a league of the pro court world. "Brother Eddie"—our friend—was named the coach and manager of the Philadelphia Warriors, an entry in this new league. That's where he showed his true colors, however. "Brother Eddie" is running that team now, but has forgotten his old friends. He refuses to give them a chance to play on his team. He contends he can't find a Negro good enough. He hasn't tried to find one, of course, and we all know that.

"Brother Eddie" has . . . disrobed as a liberal. Today he's a prejudiced, biased man. He's a traitor of sorts in the world of sports. He will have nothing to do with Negro basketball players in the winter months. When baseball season starts, however, "Brother Eddie" will be back with us. He'll be operating his Philadelphia Stars and raking in the dough of Negro baseball fans.[9]

Cumberland Posey of the Homestead Grays castigated both Gottlieb and Strong in the summer of 1933 when he attacked Eastern booking agents. Posey had recently witnessed the demise of a league he had helped to found, and he argued that "it was not the fault of the club owners of the East-West League which caused the downfall of the league in 1932. It was the economic conditions aided by Nat Strong and Ed Gottlieb and their tools in colored baseball." Posey objected to the 5 percent that Gottlieb demanded for all games in the East and the 10 percent he took when a black team played a white club in the East: "It is said that Strong and Gottlieb control the booking of all the white clubs of the East, and any clubs not wanting to deal through them are blacklisted East of Harrisburg. The downfall of Harrisburg Giants, Hilldale, Original Baltimore Black Sox, and Newark Browns can be traced to these men. Keenan of Lincoln Giants dropped out before he would deal with them and give them their ten percent." Posey called for black club owners to band together to approach park owners directly and to "shake off the sinister influence of the great booking agents of the East."[10]

If Nat Strong and Eddie Gottlieb stood accused of the economic exploitation of black baseball, Syd Pollock and Abe Saperstein drew the additional charge of making it out to be little more than a minstrel show. Saperstein made as much, if not more, money out of black sport during the first half of the twentieth century as anybody in America. World-renowned for his Harlem Globetrotters basketball team, his introduction to black sport was through baseball. He was a force to be ignored only at great peril. Operating out of Chicago, Saperstein was booking agent for the major black teams in the Midwest. The Negro American League was his fief for a time, and traveling clubs were virtually compelled to deal with him to secure the better ball parks and choice dates. For his troubles Saperstein took a percentge of the gate, as he did for black baseball's showpiece, the East-West Classic, during the 1930s and 1940s. His 5 percent cut of this black all-star game was payment for his promotional activities in Chicago, where the game was held, but the fee had all the earmarks of a pay-off to play in Abe's territory.[11]

During Gus Greenlee's brief ascendancy within the Negro National League, Saperstein was uncharacteristically subdued; but with Greenlee's departure, he returned to form. Allied with a shifting group of black and white team and park owners, Saperstein prospered even when black baseball as a whole did not. When his former associates in the Negro American League forced him out of their ranks in 1942, he attempted to organize his own league for the 1942 season. Cum Posey dubbed it "Abe Saperstein's Protective Association": "He is out to keep control of the independent baseball parks of the middle west. To do this he must show the owners of these parks that he can furnish them league attractions. Thus Abe Saperstein's Protective Association. Perhaps you or I would do the same thing if we were in Saperstein's position and saw ourselves losing over $3,000 in Cincinnati and $1,500 as our share of the East-West game, besides other lucrative promotions."[12] Although Saperstein sometimes held direct interests in black teams, like the Birmingham Black Barons and the Ethiopian (or Cincinnati) Clowns,[13] he profited more through his control of bookings and parks.

There had been a comical element to black baseball ever since its early professional days, when teams and promoters both recognized that white fans were attracted by the novelty of watching blacks play ball. Some touring black teams emphasized the entertainment aspect and developed routines, or reams as they were sometimes called. While there was likely a degree to which these reams played to the racial stereotypes held by many white spectators, for the most part the humor exalted rather than demeaned the ability of the black players. Reams might emphasize the smooth, often slick style many black players brought to the game. However, the Ethiopian (or Cincinnati) Clowns, the Zulus, and to a lesser extent Abe Saperstein's Harlem Globetrotters, all employed Stepin Fetchit–like routines.

Syd Pollock's Clowns operated under several different names, and Saperstein used them as a ploy to eliminate the Negro American League franchise in Cincinnati when he formed his own league in 1942.[14] Pollock claimed that he was only the general manager of the Clowns and that a black man, Hunter Campbell, was the true owner. *Courier* sportswriter Wendell Smith argued that if, indeed, Hunter Campbell was the owner, he was not only guilty of all the charges directed at Pollock but of additional scorn.

As a Negro, Campbell should realize the danger in insisting that his black players paint their faces and go through minstrel show reviews before every game.

I am sure Mr. Campbell realizes that every Negro performing in public life stands for something more than the role he is portraying; that every Negro in the theatrical and sports world is somewhat of an ambassador for the Negro race, and that whether he likes it or not, is reponsible to 13,000,000 people for his actions. . . .

If Hunter Campbell fosters this type of aggregation, then he should be exposed and the world should know about him. I don't know Mr. Campbell, but I find it difficult to believe that he, a Negro, advocates and perpetuates an organization which is detrimental in any way to the cause for which we are all fighting—racial advancement.

If such is the case, then we should label Mr. Hunter Campbell— "The Fifth Clown-ist of the Negro Sports World!"[15]

Despite continual criticism by the black press, Saperstein and Pollock, like Strong and Gottlieb, carried on with business as usual. That they did so at both the expense and public image of black baseball underscored the powerlessness of the organized black leagues. A stable, prospering black league could have loosened the stranglehold of the white agents by intervening directly in the booking process. Yet in the absence of such an institution, even Cum Posey had to admit that the agents were almost a necessary evil. Arguing that, "No booking agent, white or colored, should have the powers these men have," Posey nonetheless acknowledged that, outside of his Homestead Grays and a few other teams, "the rest of the clubs would be in an awful fix without these same booking agents."[16]

Men like Strong, Gottlieb, and Saperstein were as much a reflection of black baseball's problems as the cause of its woes. Chronic undercapitalization and the unsteadiness of both the teams and leagues made black baseball ripe for exploitation. But it was not simply a case of sophisticated white businessmen profiting from an incipient black venture—there were black baseball men who were every bit as calculating as Nat Strong and Abe Saperstein. Perhaps the fairest assessment of Strong's, Gottlieb's, and Saperstein's historical contribution to black sport is that they aided in the capital formation of black baseball yet retarded the development of a viable, autonomous black sporting life.

The Negro National League

Rube Foster, Cumberland Posey, and Gus Greenlee each challenged the stranglehold of white owners and agents over black baseball but were unable to completely break their grip. Foster, the first to mount a campaign, was described in 1970 by Robert

Peterson: "If the talents of Christy Mathewson, John McGraw, Ban Johnson and Judge Kenesaw Mountain Landis were combined in a single body and that body were enveloped in a black skin, the result would have to be named Andrew (Rube) Foster."[17] Foster had migrated from Texas soon after the turn of the century, pitching his way north. In a match-up with Rube Waddell, the white Hall of Famer with the Philadelphia A's in 1902, Foster picked up the nickname Rube in addition to the victory. His contribution to black baseball, however, extended far beyond his outstanding pitching record. Quick to pick up the administrative dimension of the game, Foster entered the owners' ranks in 1910 when he formed a partnership with a white Chicago saloon keeper named John Schorling, who was Chicago White Sox owner Charley Comiskey's son-in-law. The two men took over Frank Leland's Giants and renamed them the Chicago American Giants. Leasing the old White Sox's home grounds at Thirty-ninth and Shields, the Chicago American Giants became the toast of black Chicago. The best known independent black team in the Midwest, they often outdrew both the Cubs and the White Sox on dates when the Second City's three best teams played at home.[18]

In the second decade of the twentieth century Chicago was a strong baseball town. Black teams played in a popular city league where crowds of 15,000–20,000 were common. White pros like Johnny Evers, Joe Tinker, and Johnny Cling often played in these games under assumed names, picking up some money on the side and fooling very few of the fans with their aliases. By the First World War, Rube Foster governed black baseball in Chicago, controlling not only his own team but, indirectly, many semipro outfits for which he handled all bookings; even a few of the better white semipro clubs, like the Duffy Florals and the Logan Squares, booked through Foster. His relation to black baseball in the Midwest became much like that maintained by Nat Strong in the East.[19]

With the temporary eclipse of white semipro ball at the end of World War I cutting into his business, Foster determined that the solution to his own problems and those of black baseball in general was to launch an independent black league. In the winter of 1919, with the ashes of the summer's devastating Chicago race riot barely cold, Foster proposed an eight-club Negro National League (NNL). The owners of the Kansas City Monarchs, the Chicago Giants, the Cuban Stars, the Detroit Stars, the Dayton Marcos, the St. Louis Stars, and the Indianapolis ABCs joined him in the first successful effort at organized black baseball. As president and secretary of the NNL, Foster welded the clubs into a viable league, almost single-handedly holding them together during the early years. The financial records that survived indicate that, at least for some years, the NNL was a mildly profitable venture; for example, league games drew over 400,000 fans and took in almost $200,000 at the gate in 1923.

Foster managed NNL affairs and collected 5 percent of the game receipts to cover his expenses and recompense his efforts. But the league was largely a Midwestern affair and failed to make inroads in the East, where agents like Nat Strong, who controlled black baseball there through his Eastern Colored League, reigned supreme. Largely the creation of one man, the NNL could not survive Rube Foster's personal troubles. Stricken by mental illness in 1926, he was committed to an institution, where he died in 1930. His team, the Chicago American Giants, was sold by the remaining owner, John Schorling, to a white florist in the spring of 1928. Foster's larger project, the NNL, collapsed soon afterward, and by the end of the summer of 1932 there was no major black league functioning in America.

The struggle to form black leagues and develop autonomous black professional sport did not die with Foster. The focus of these efforts moved eastward to Pittsburgh, where two of black baseball's most remarkable leaders, Cum Posey and Gus Greenlee, in turn fielded two of its stellar clubs, the Homestead Grays and the Pittsburgh Crawfords.

Cum Posey, Black Sport Entrepreneur

Cum Posey did more than make people think about the little Monongahela River town of Homestead for something other than its steel mills and the epic labor confrontation of 1892. He was, as much as any one man could be, the architect of sport in black Pittsburgh. Posey was born in 1891 in "respectable"

Homestead, amid trees and residential streets, blocks above the crowded, migrant ghetto ward where most Homestead blacks lived. When his father, Captain Cumberland Willis Posey, Sr., was buried with full Masonic honors in 1925, he was eulogized as one of Pittsburgh's most prominent and wealthy black men.

The son of a Maryland minister, "Cap" Posey had spent most of his life on the river. He found employment as a deck sweeper aboard a ferry on the Ohio and Little Kanawha rivers, and by studying the ship's engines he eventually earned his license as an engineer, no small feat for a black man in the 1880s. Leaving the river for Homestead's hills and a new career in a nearby shipyard, the elder Posey supervised the construction of vessels that would ply Pittsburgh's rivers. By the turn of the century he had diversified his business dealings, investing in various coal companies for which he worked as an executive. His Diamond Coke and Coal Company became the largest black-owned business in Pittsburgh. Thus, he was able to bequeath to his children access to the "Old Pittsburgh" black community and exposure to the wheeling and dealing of venture capital. The latter was a rare experience for a young black during the boom and bust cycles of turn-of-the-century American capitalism.

The senior Posey's business ventures alone would have marked him as one of black Pittsburgh's foremost citizens, but he chose to further solidify his status by serving as president of the prestigious Loendi Club, the Warren Methodist Episcopal Church, and the *Pittsburgh Courier*. He also belonged to the "appropriate" secret societies. The *Courier* noted his death at the age of sixty-seven as the passing of a "pioneer in industry."[20] His eldest son and namesake was to become a pioneer of another sort.

The young Cum Posey gravitated to the Hill's black sporting scene, often playing for the "roughneck" element against teams more representative of black Pittsburgh's upper crust. Taking to the gridiron for the Collins Tigers and breaking into the line-up of a handful of sandlot nines, Cum Posey became known for something other than his class and family background. He not only participated in Homestead's sporting program but coached its basketball squad.[21] Later, Posey enrolled at Holy Ghost (renamed Duquesne University) and Penn State. As one of the few black students at either school, his acceptance was made easier

by his light complexion and athletic prowess. His sporting exploits began to attract attention, but according to Wendell
Smith, ".... an adventurous and turbulent spirit brooked no
faculty interference with his desires and he never stayed anywhere
long enough to get the recognition which might have been
his."[22] The sportswriter called Posey the "outstanding athlete of
the Negro race" during the late 1920s, "perhaps the most colorful figure who has ever raced down the sundown sports trail."[23]

But it was neither on the sandlots nor in the collegiate arena
that Cum Posey first gained a national reputation. Instead, the
crowded, steamy gymnasiums and second-floor dance halls of
club basketball brought him recognition. Basketball in the early
twentieth century was still in its infancy. Games brought together
teams from disparate settings, as semipro, collegiate, and social
club quintets clashed on a match-by-match basis, mixing most of
the nation's basketball in an interracial concoction in which the
best teams played their way to the top.

In Pittsburgh, black basketball teams were handicapped by
limited floor space. Twice weekly, for two hours a night, the
Washington Field House was open to blacks, with "every colored
boy in Allegheny County who owned a pair of rubber soled
shoes on the floor at the same time."[24] Pittsburgh was definitely
in the backwaters of the basketball world in those years, but the
city nonetheless made its presence felt in a game Posey remembered as the "first colored game ever played in Pittsburgh."[25] The
contest pitted Howard University's 1911 black collegiate champions against the Monticellos, a local team that had come
together that season under Posey's tutelage. Joining Cum in the
Monticello line-up were his brother See, recreation worker James
Dorsey, baseball promoter Sell Hall, and Walter Clark. In a game
played under intercollegiate rules for the first half and YMCA
rules for the second half, the Monticellos upset heavily favored
Howard and vaulted into the national limelight.[26] After traveling
to New York City, the nation's basketball capital, and beating all
challengers, the Monticellos soon gained informal recognition
as the nation's top team.

Over the next few seasons the Monticellos and several other
black and white teams established basketball on a semipro basis
in Pittsburgh. The players received anywhere from a few dollars

to seventy-five dollars for a game, depending on the size of the crowd. Posey's quintet, eventually known as the Loendi Club because of its association with the local black social club, began to rent the Labor Temple on the Hill for combined basketball game and dance fetes. With Pittsburgh now a stopping place for the nation's best teams, the Loendi Club's reputation grew. The cast of players changed, as did the name of the squad, but the five-foot-nine, 140-pound Posey remained in the line-up, equally adept at guard and forward. Its floor general during the game, Posey managed the finances and promoted the team off the court.

Romeo Dougherty, the dean of black American sportswriters, never tired of writing of "those exciting days when Posey, America's greatest Negro basketball player . . . raced upon the hardwood, applauded by both friend and foe." A team seeking supremacy had to go up against Posey's team.

The Alpha Physical Culture Club, the "Red and Black Machine" of the St. Christopher's club of St. Phillips Parish, St. Cyprian, Laetitia, Brooklyn's "Grave Diggers" of the Smart Set under the pugnacious little "Rush" Lord, the Owls, the Imperials, Independents and Vandals of New Jersey, all knew of the glory awaiting them by decisively defeating that team moulded from the original Monticellos and with the toughest of steel cast in the caldrons of their own Pennsylvania.

There they stood, strong as the Rock of Gibralter, thumbing their noses at New York and defiantly sending word from the "City of Smoke" that they could always make the Gay Gothamites do the Pennsylvania Polka to the tune of Betts, Gilmore, Rickmond, Hall, "See" Posey, "Pimp" Young et al![27]

Combining black collegiate stars like George Gilmore of Howard and William ("Pimp") Young of Lincoln with local talent like Greasy Betts from the Homestead steel mills, Posey's Loendi Club played and beat the top teams in the country and put together four consecutive seasons without a loss to another black club. Loendi claimed honors as the "colored world's champions" for five years during the 1920s,[28] and its local rivalries with Jewish teams like the Coffey Club and the Second Story Morries were the highlights of the winter sports season in Pittsburgh.

Cum Posey had not only assembled a championship team and

played the game with such verve that no black sportswriter considered naming an all-star quintet without including him, he also established basketball on a more professional footing. What he did not learn on the captain's knee, he picked up firsthand promoting basketball in Pittsburgh and New York City. His experiences helped to make him one of the most successful black sport entrepreneurs in history. But basketball was entering a temporary downswing in the late 1920s, and when the game later returned to form, it was Bob Douglas's New York Renaissance team rather than Posey's Loendi Club that soared above the rest. By then Cum Posey had turned to another game—baseball.

The Homestead Grays

The Homestead Grays did not spring fully grown from Cum Posey's head, even though many people thought he exerted an almost Zeus-like control over black Pittsburgh sport in later years. Instead, they emerged from turn-of-the-century sandlot ball. In 1900, a group of black Homestead youths, some of whom worked in the mills, formed a squad to take on white neighborhood and workplace teams. Calling themselves the Blue Ribbons, they played a few seasons with moderate success and continued for the next decade to field a squad each season. Their Blue Ribbon label was discarded in favor of a new name, the Murdock Grays, but the team itself remained a Homestead-based outfit.

In 1910 the players met in John Freyl Alexander's home and reorganized the team, electing Alexander their nonplaying president and Jerry Veney their manager. The team also voted themselves a new name, the Homestead Grays. Veney, like his younger brother John and several of the original team members, had migrated to Homestead before 1900 and found jobs at the Homestead Steel Works. (Veney eventually became one of the first black narrow-gauge engineers in the works and retired from the mills in 1935 after forty years of service. His brother John worked as a diesel engineer, putting in forty-seven years at the Homestead plant.) With Benjamin ("Brother") Pace, Henry ("Rube") Saunders, Bud Brown, Robert ("Doug") Hobson, and a few of their friends and workmates filling the line-up, the squad led by Veney and Alexander became a popular local attraction. It also managed to achieve its main objective: allowing the players a chance to play and enjoy themselves. The team played for fun, but also to win, which it did. In 1913 the Homestead nine won forty-two games in a row against area opponents.

The Grays operated on a cooperative basis, sharing both costs and the proceeds from the gate. As they improved on the field, they were able to induce ballplayers from other teams to join them: Cum Posey, Buddy Clay, and Chief Walton left the Ripley Giants, the Pittsburgh Giants, and the Clay Giants respectively to sign up with the Grays. The team itself was vulnerable to overtures by other teams because the manager, Jerry Veney, preferred to pass Sunday in prayer and meditation and thus did not schedule any games on that day. Other team members marched to a different drummer and hired themselves out to rival teams for Sunday games. Sell Hall's Pittsburgh Colored Giants especially coveted the Gray's players, and his solicitations began to disturb some of the team members who did not share Veney's views of the Sabbath. By 1916 the controversy over Sunday play was resolved when Alexander and Veney stepped aside. Charles Walker, who had begun his career as the Grays' batboy, was elected president; he was to stay with the club for the next few decades. Young Cum Posey became the captain and soon the team's manager. He and Sellers Hall, who decided to join the club after failing to raid it, booked its games until 1918, when Hall went his separate way.

During the early years the Grays made room for a trio of performers who stayed on the roster as the team rose not just to the top of the Pittsburgh sandlots but to the heights of the baseball world. Mo Harris, Charles ("Lefty") Williams, and Oscar Owens were the kinds of players on whom dynasties are built. Williams, for example, pitched for the club during the next eighteen years, hurling an incredible seventeen no-hitters and posting twenty-nine victories and no defeats in 1930. By the early 1920s the Grays began putting their players on salary to keep rival squads like the Pittsburgh Keystones from enticing some of their men away.[29]

The Grays became legendary in the years when there were few

good black teams in baseball, and they did it with an occasional white boy on the team. Ziggy Walsh, a local lad, caught for them before accepting an offer to play in the Appalachian League,[30] and Johnny Pearson, who Posey considered perhaps the greatest all-around athlete to come out of Homestead, played with the Grays before moving up to organized ball.[31]

Cum Posey was an astute observer of the changing sports scene. Returning to Homestead at the end of his academic career, Posey worked for the Railway Mail Service, a job he kept until 1920. Dividing his time between work and a deepening involvement in sport, he promoted and managed the Monticellos and then the Loendi Club, gaining an appreciation of the finances of sport. He also developed contacts with promoters, sportswriters, and owners that held him in good stead for the rest of his life. His close study of sandlot baseball in Pittsburgh convinced him to quit his job with the Railway Mail Service and plunge full-time into a sporting career.[32] The Coolidge years proved to be a time of rapid growth for American sport amid general economic prosperity. Black Pittsburghers, like most recent immigrants to Pittsburgh, shared only marginally in the overall economic prosperity, but they were not left behind as America's sporting enthusiasm mounted.

Posey, who had joined the Homestead Grays as an outfielder in 1911, was managing and promoting the squad by the time the United States entered World War I, and he owned the team by the early 1920s. His contribution to the Grays was twofold: he put the best possible team on the field, and he made the team into a profitable business venture. To construct his Homestead dynasty he gathered together a core of Pittsburgh's best sandlot players. Most of the original Homesteaders were soon forced to the bench, some choosing to leave the club. Posey then added a number of pitchers with national reputations and some of the best ballplayers ever. By the mid-1920s, local men like Vic Harris, Jap Washington, Willis Moody, Oscar Owens, and Mo Harris were leading the Grays to victories over teams from Bellevue, Homestead Steel, the Martin Club, and Honus Wagner's Carnegie Elks.[33] Within the next few seasons the infield was strengthened by the addition of Bobby Williams, formerly a shortstop for Rube Foster's Chicago American Giants, and the pitching staff was bolstered by Posey's recruitment of Sam ("Lefty") Streeter, a veteran of several NNL campaigns.

If any new player signaled Cum Posey's commitment to making the Grays the best team possible, it was Smokey Joe Williams. Williams's career spanned two centuries, and many have cited the six-foot-five-inch Texan as the best black pitcher ever. He signed with the Grays for the 1925 season, a forty-nine-year-old veteran of more than twenty-five seasons in professional black baseball, and pitched for the team until 1932. Still the master of the mound in his early fifties, Williams won regularly for the Grays, no-hitting a strong Akron semipro club in 1928 at the age of fifty-two. When the *Pittsburgh Courier* polled thirty-one students of black baseball in 1952 for their all-time team, Williams led the voting for its pitcher, named on almost two-thirds of the ballots.[34]

During Williams's first season the Grays played 158 games before a collective crowd of several hundred thousand fans, winning an amazing 130 times, losing only 23, and having 5 games end in a tie. The following year, 1926, their record after 114 games was 102 wins, 6 losses, and 6 draws, including a stretch of 43 consecutive victories. The Grays celebrated their unprecedented streak with a banquet at their Wylie Avenue clubhouse. With a jazz piano backing up the baritone of Bob Cole and the harmonizing of Jimmie Hays, former manager of the Baron Wilkens Club in New York, the players and their wives or sweethearts danced, dined, and listened to the remarks of attorney Wilbur Douglas, the evening's toastmaster, and *Courier* editor Robert Vann, the main speaker. Charles Walker, the Gray's co-owner, had promised the affair if the team won 28 games in a row. Posey went one step further, awarding gold baseballs, emblematic of a championship club, which he had promised if the team won 35 games without a loss. The most remarkable aspect of the evening was that it marked not the capstone of the Grays' baseball brilliance but simply another step on their way to greatness.[35]

The following April, while preparing to meet a team of American League all-stars promoted by Earle Mack, son of Philadelphia A's manager Connie Mack, the Homestead team added two more nonpareils to their line-up.[36] To field a team that would compete against the likes of Washington Senator star Goose Goslin, the Philly's Lefty Grove and Walter ("Big Train") Johnson, the Grays signed Oscar Charleston and John Beckwith. A right-handed slugger, Beckwith could play any infield position. Charleston, one of the highest paid black players in the early 1920s, played or managed in the black leagues for three and a half decades. He was a superb fielder and an exciting hitter, one of the first Negro League veterans selected to the Hall of Fame.

Cum Posey's recruiting efforts did not stop there. As an independent team not subject to the rules and regulations of organized black baseball until 1929, the Grays were not bound to respect another team's contracts, nor did they face a league commissioner's ire. When a player he wanted was available, Posey went after him. Martin Dihigo, whose bust at Estadio Latinoamericana in Havana is inscribed simply "El Inmortal," played for the Grays, as did Cool Papa Bell, Judy Johnson, and Willie Foster. These men, and others like them, were among the best ballplayers in the world, and Posey was largely successful in attracting and keeping them. In July 1925, after representatives of the Baltimore Black Sox and the Atlanta Black Crackers had tried to recruit some Grays and left with little to show for their efforts, *Courier* writer William G. Nunn, Sr., cautioned: "For the information of all players and fans in general, the Homestead Grays have played to more paid admissions than ever before in their history. Posey has the happy facility of satisfying his men. They are perfectly contented to play with him. Watch yourselves, you Easterners. 'Tis a long alley that doesn't have an ashcan in it somewhere, and if Posey comes East, he'll not return empty-handed. All rules work two ways."[37]

Secure in their position as the dominant black team in the tri-state region, the Grays dismissed efforts to get them to join leagues or agree to a nonraiding pact. Organized black baseball, sensitive to the threat an independent team like Posey's presented, tried to bring the Grays into their fraternity, but Posey resisted all entreaties. "Any player on the Homestead Grays who desires to change to another club is free at all times to change," Posey wrote in the *Pittsburgh Courier* in 1926, "and any good player who is in any club in either league will be offered a contract when the Grays' management feels they need this player."[38] He brooked no opposition in his drive to make the Grays the best team possible.

Posey put up with little interference off the field either: by the 1930s he held sway over black baseball in the area. As the Grays evolved from a Homestead club of industrial workers playing in their free time to the toast of the Pittsburgh sandlots, they became an excellent draw, the best and most popular local black team. The Grays were in great demand by white tri-state semipro and sandlot clubs, which realized that when the Grays played the fans came in droves. Posey understood this better than anyone and parleyed the team's drawing power into financial success. He often received the much-sought-for-but-rarely-granted rain guarantee from area teams, meaning that the Grays received a minimum payment even if the game was rained out. And in those days, when the grass was real, rainouts were more frequent. The Grays could also persuade opposing teams to give them a higher than usual percentage of the gate since they drew such big crowds.

Other concessions were extracted, too, and Posey was even accused of convincing certain white teams to refuse to book other black teams on penalty of losing their games with the Grays. Joe Ward, a columnist with the *Chronicle Times,* wrote to the *Courier* in 1925, calling for an investigation of Posey's methods: "The entire trouble between the colored teams in this section is that the Homestead Grays, or rather their manager, has built up a good drawing card, and is fearful that another good club might interfere with the club's progress. I have proof that the manager of the Grays has stipulated in his bookings of certain games that his club will not play there if another colored club is booked."[39]

When Tom Brown's All-Stars signed a contract with Syd Pollock's Cuban Stars for a Sunday game at Forbes Field, while the Pirates were on the road, the agreement stipulated that the game would be the first the Cubans played in Pennsylvania, and their posters advertising the game said as much. "Well, Cum Posey got ahold of that," veteran sandlotter Ralph Mellix remembered, and he "booked the Cubans for Saturday," the day before they were to play Brown's All-Stars. Brown went to court to attach the proceeds from the Saturday game but was unable to win legal relief. He complained that Posey monopolized the region's sandlot ball for black teams, and Mellix, who had played for Brown, agreed: "The Grays had a monopoly in the tri-state. They didn't want no other colored team to get going around here."[40] Sellers Hall took Posey to court, too, alleging that he and co-owner Charles Walker had breached a partnership contract with him. Hall helped promote the Grays during World War I and even invested a small sum in the club, but he left the squad in the summer of 1923 at a time when the Grays were losing money. Posey and Walker argued that they had never entered into a partnership agreement with Hall, who himself could offer no hard evidence to the contrary. His appeal to put the Grays into receivership was subsequently denied and Posey was left unchallenged for another decade.[41]

As the Grays steadily improved and began to play Negro National League and Eastern Colored League (ECL) teams on their way across the Alleghenies, local black sandlot clubs found that it was becoming easier for them to book games with teams the Grays had previously monopolized. Certain black clubs began to work with Posey, lending him extra players for days when he had booked two games at the same time and needed black bodies to fill in his line-up or bullpen. The Grays blazed a trail through white communities, which previously had been wilderness to black teams, securing dates and taking their pick of local white opponents. Other black teams soon realized that the brilliance of the Grays bathed them in a more flattering light, too: by stimulating white interest in black baseball, the Grays helped all black clubs. White fans wanted to see their club tangle with black teams, and attendance at these matches was usually high. When six of the best black sandlot teams in the area decided to form the Greater Pittsburgh Colored Baseball League in the spring of 1930, they acknowledged Posey's influence by choosing him to head the league.[42]

Gradually, Posey began to exert the sort of influence over Pittsburgh's black sandlot and semipro ball that Rube Foster had in Chicago. And when the mantle of leadership of the Negro National League slipped off Foster's shoulders after his hospitalization in 1926, Cum Posey tried to pick it up. In January

1927, when the NNL and the ECL both approached Posey with an offer of affiliation, Posey answered them in his weekly column, "The Sportive Realm," which was carried in the *Courier* and other black papers. Calling for the owners to "desert the smallness which has stood out so prominently in past years," he suggested that instead of joining a league, the Grays would agree to play two league teams twice a month at Forbes Field as the league clubs made their jumps between the eastern and western circuits. He also offered to respect league contracts if league teams would agree to honor his. Posey refused, however, to return Oscar Charleston to the Harrisburg Giants, offering them compensation instead.[43]

When the leagues objected to his terms, Posey wished them good riddance in his next column.[44] But, eager to test his Grays against the other national black baseball powers, he finally joined the American Negro League in 1929. The ANL was made up basically of the same teams as the ECL, which had dissolved the previous season. Playing sixty-five games against the Baltimore Black Sox, the Lincoln Giants, Hilldale, the Cuban Stars, and the Bacharach Giants, the Grays posted a less than distinguished winning record that left them in the middle of the pack. When the ANL did not return for its sophomore season, the Grays went back to independent, barnstorming baseball. If the ANL had been a bust, it was still a learning experience for Posey, who addressed organized black baseball's problems in his columns. On the field the Grays got better and better, their 1930 and 1931 teams ranking with black baseball's best ever.

On the eve of the 1931 season, Cum Posey diagnosed baseball's health against the backdrop of the depression. "The 1931 baseball season among the colored clubs of the nation has never had a more dreary outlook," he warned, yet he argued that businesses conducted in a "safe and sane manner" would weather the storm. "Baseball at this time needs men with much knowledge of all things connected with the operation of big-time baseball." After describing the qualifications such men needed— remarkably similar to his own—Posey wrote a prescription for baseball's ailments that covered schedules, salaries, agents, and the general deportment of the game's protagonists. While the Grays and the Kansas City Monarchs already had a full schedule of games for the 1931 season, Posey cautioned that the other clubs should not wait too long before taking steps toward a new association of clubs and putting their affairs in order.[45]

Posey sought to fill his own prescription the following season by spearheading the formation of the East-West League. Besides the Grays, the conference included the Detroit Wolves, which Posey also controlled, the Cleveland Stars, the Baltimore Black Sox, Hilldale, the Newark Browns, and Alex Pompez's Cuban Stars. Posey's administrative scenarios were as advanced as could be found in the world of black sport, but the league was severely undercapitalized and a more inauspicious year for beginning such a venture would have been hard to find. Pittsburgh, Detroit, Cleveland, Newark, Philadelphia, and Baltimore were all hit hard by the depression, their citizens unable or unwilling to turn out in the numbers that might have made the league viable. The Detroit franchise folded in early June, and despite efforts to cut back on costs by slashing player salaries, firing its full-time umpires, and curtailing the schedule, the league itself failed to make it through the summer.[46]

Defeated in his efforts to make the East-West League a viable one, Posey crawled back to Pittsburgh and prepared to resume his feast, both financially and sportively, on a local fare of sandlot clubs. But he had not reckoned on a new diner at the table, someone who was trying to help himself to the main course. The man with the appetite was Gus Greenlee, whom Posey had denied a franchise in the East-West League. Greenlee and his Crawford ball team were about to mount a challenge for black sandlot supremacy in Pittsburgh.

The Edgar Thomson Works team, called ET, was coached by Olympic medalist Earl Johnson. Several of the ET players jumped to the Crawfords in the late 1920s. Back row (left to right): Ted Sledge, ?; Neal Harris, Claude Johnson, Rudy Hughes, ?; Charlie Becotas, —— Watson, Earl Johnson. Front row (left to right): ?, ?; Gus Neville, Ernest Terry, Harold Tinker, ?; William Kimbo, ?. *Photograph courtesy of Harold Tinker.*

Gus Greenlee, Hill numbers baron and owner of the Pittsburgh Crawfords, behind the bar of his Crawford Grill. *Photograph reprinted from* Bulletin Index *(August 18, 1938).*

Josh Gibson began his baseball career on the sandlots of Pittsburgh and ended up in the Hall of Fame. *Photograph courtesy of Josh Gibson, Jr.*

The Pittsburgh Crawfords, champions of the city's recreational league in 1926, pose on the steps of the Carnegie Library on Wylie Avenue. (Left to right): William Smith, Teenie Harris, Johnny Moore. Back row (left to right): Nate ——, Bill Harris, Harry Beale, Buster Christian, Jaspar Stevens. *Photograph courtesy of Harold Tinker.*

Champions Negro National League
1935

The Pittsburgh Crawfords, champions of the Negro National League in 1935, pose in front of Greenlee Field on the Hill. With future Hall of Famers Oscar Charleston, Judy Johnson, Cool Papa Bell, Josh Gibson, and Satchel Paige, this Crawford team may have been the best ball club ever. Left to right: Oscar Charleston, Jimmie Crutchfield, Dick Seay, Sam Bankhead, Bill Harvey, Sam Streeter, Bill Perkins, Chester Williams, Theolic ("Fireball") Smith, Harry Kincannon, Judy Johnson, Cool Papa Bell, Leroy Matlock, Ernest ("Spoon") Carter, Josh Gibson, John Washington, Satchel Paige, unidentified rookie pitcher. *Photograph courtesy of the National Baseball Library, Cooperstown, N.Y., and Jimmie Crutchfield.*

Harold Tinker and four of his Terrace Village players. Left to right: Wilbur Brown, Norman

The Terrace Village braintrust ran one of the region's earliest integrated sandlot teams in the early 1950s. Left to right: Wilbur Brown, Bill Berry, William Crooks, Harold Tinker, ?, Jack Hopkins, Ocey Swain. *Photograph courtesy of Harold Tinker.*

Willis Moody (left) and Ralph ("Lefty") Mellix made the 18th Ward, black
Beltzhoover's team, one of Pittsburgh's longest running sandlot acts. Both men
played Negro League ball and sandlot ball in addition to organizing this community
club. *Photograph courtesy of Mrs. Ralph Mellix.*

Vernon, Annie, Elizabeth, and Buck Phillips (left to right) on Broad Street near Buck's home, the basement of which served as the clubhouse and dressing room for the Garfield Eagles. Known as the "Mayor" of Garfield, Buck Phillips was one of the area's most influential black businessmen. *Photograph courtesy of Vern and Catherine Phillips.*

The Garfield Eagles graced western Pennsylvania's sandlots as the premier black eleven for almost two decades. *Photograph courtesy of Ray Irvin.*

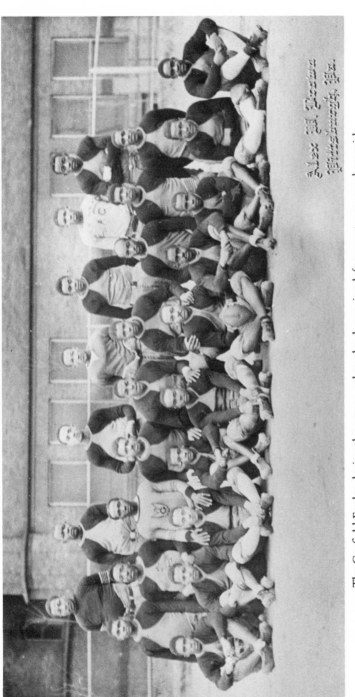

The Garfield Eagles during the 1930s, when the depression left many team members with little more to do than practice and play football. *Photograph courtesy of Benny Jackson.*

The Monticello basketball squad included Cum Posey (front row, second from left), a stellar player in early twentieth-century basketball and later black Pittsburgh's most successful sports entrepreneur. *Photograph courtesy of Zerbie Dorsey.*

The Homestead Grays, shown here in 1913, began as a team of black steelworkers. Cum Posey (middle row, third from left) eventually became the team's manager and then its owner. *Photograph courtesy of Mrs. Cumberland Posey and Carnegie Library of Pittsburgh.*

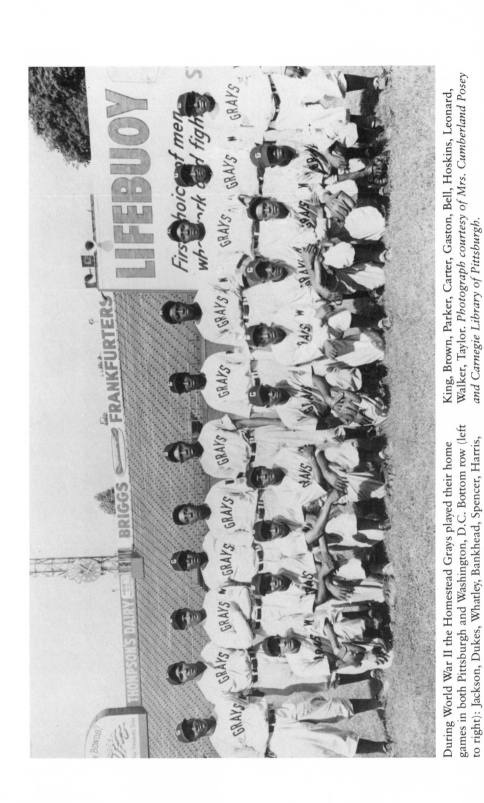

During World War II the Homestead Grays played their home games in both Pittsburgh and Washington, D.C. Bottom row (left to right): Jackson, Dukes, Whatley, Bankhead, Spencer, Harris,

King, Brown, Parker, Carter, Gaston, Bell, Hoskins, Leonard, Walker, Taylor. *Photograph courtesy of Mrs. Cumberland Posey and Carnegie Library of Pittsburgh.*

5 Gus Greenlee, Black Pittsburgh's "Mr. Big"

Almost everyone in black Pittsburgh knew Gus Greenlee in one way or another. Some patronized his nightclubs, others drank his bootleg liquor, and many more played their pennies or dollars on his numbers. Hill voters felt the shock waves from Greenlee's Third Ward Voters' League, while black Pittsburghers all over the city voted for the candidates he backed. Many went to him when they needed coal, groceries, or money for rent, and more than a few benefited from never-to-be-repaid loans to set up a business or attend college. They cheered his stable of boxers, especially John Henry Lewis, the first black American light-heavyweight champion of the world, and often paid their way into Greenlee Field to see the array of sporting events he promoted. And during the 1930s, black Pittsburgh knew Gus Greenlee as the owner of one of baseball's finest teams, the Pittsburgh Crawfords.

Two of Greenlee's brothers became doctors and a third practiced law, but Gus dropped out of college after a year and wound up becoming black Pittsburgh's "Mr. Big." With over 200 pounds padding his six-foot-three-inch frame, Big Red, as he was also known, commanded attention. Physically, he resembled the slightly lighter-skinned Dan Seymour, who made a career out of movie roles like Angel Garcia in *Key Largo* and Abdul in *Casablanca*. But Greenlee never settled for bit parts. As one of Pittsburgh's most influential black men, the caliph of "Little Harlem" stayed strictly on center-stage.[1]

Marion, North Carolina, where Gus was born in 1897, was a small Southern town split fairly evenly along racial lines and dependent on textiles and furniture for its economic sustenance. Gus's mother, the bastard child of a prominent white man, instilled in her children a sense of racial pride. Gus's father, a masonry contractor who had built the courthouse, the town hotel, and a good deal more, was, in the words of his youngest son, Dr. Charles Greenlee, "the black of the county."[2] He urged his sons to play baseball and go to college. While Gus enjoyed the game as much as his brothers, he ran afoul of his father's wishes that he attend school. "Gus wasn't easily disciplined and dropped out his second year in college," his brother recalled. "After that, he was on the dogs with father." In 1916, Gus Greenlee joined the migration northward, hopping a freight train to Pittsburgh where an uncle lived.

Gus didn't bring much with him in the way of material goods. In Pittsburgh he shined shoes, pushed a wheelbarrow at a construction site, and labored as a fireman at Jones and Laughlin's Southside Works; he also worked as a hack driver for an undertaker and soon bought a taxi of his own. When the United States entered the fray in Europe, Gus shipped overseas with the 367th Regiment. Armed with a machine gun, he saw action at Verdun and took a piece of shrapnel in his left leg at St. Mihiel before returning to Pittsburgh.[3] After the war he found Pittsburgh to be fertile ground for racketeering, as Prohibition and the Coolidge prosperity created opportunities for men and women who were willing to take a few risks. Gus returned to his taxi driving but diversified his cargo. Known around town as "Gasoline Gus," he bootlegged liquor in Pittsburgh and its satellite mill towns. Homestead, a hotbed of gambling and assorted other vices, was a regular stop. Soon Gus made the transition from supplying the liquor retail to serving it at his own speakeasy. He would run at least one club for the rest of his life.

The Paramount Club, Greenlee's first tavern, was situated on Wylie Avenue in the Lower Hill, just above downtown Pittsburgh where the Civic Arena now stands. The area was occasionally referred to as Pittsburgh's tenderloin, or vice section, because it tolerated interracial social activity at a number of Prohibition-era night spots. The Paramount, itself labeled a notorious "black and tan cabaret," was closed down by the police in 1922.[4] Reopened by Greenlee and a man named Kid Welch in 1924, the Paramount advertised refined entertainment and the music of the Paramount Inn Orchestra, reputed by the *Courier* to be the city's best band. The club continued to cater to blacks and whites alike, and its proprietors ran afoul of the law when a local paper alleged that young white girls were "running wild" in this "plague spot of a city infested with vice."[5] But Greenlee was not deterred for long by revocation of the Paramount's dance license; his customers were back on the floor before the end of the year. Meanwhile, Gus branched into the promotional end of the entertainment industry. With Bill Cleveland he formed the Musical Booking Agency, headquartered on the Paramount's third floor. Cleveland's connections with local clubs and Greenlee's assets made for a most auspicious undertaking, according to the *Courier*.[6] Greenlee was also proprietor of the Workingmen's Pool Hall on Fullerton Street, in which he invested over $5,000 in tables and accoutrements. Clearly, he was one of black Pittsburgh's more substantial businessmen.[7]

In addition to the Paramount, Gus ran the Sunset Cafe, a popular Bohemian resort where he feted Duke Ellington and his band with a banquet following a local performance in 1933.[8] But his favorite establishment was the world-renowned Crawford Grill, the Hill's classiest night spot and a mecca for jazz aficionados.[9] The Grill was the setting for countless late-night jam sessions, with musicians who had finished their gigs elsewhere dropping by to play until dawn. Open all hours of the night despite strict Pennsylvania blue laws, the Grill was a popular saloon offering daiquiris that were reputed to be to Pittsburgh what La Floridita's were to Havana. The Crawford Grill built much of its reputation on the sport and entertainment notables it attracted, though its patrons in general were drawn from a much wider audience. An evening's crowd included both blacks and whites, and black customers were usually fairly representative of a cross-section of the city's black population. Visiting Negro League ballplayers, members of black Pittsburgh's elite, and workingmen unwinding after a shift could be found at adjoining tables, if not actually drinking together.

When the owner was feeling particularly expansive, the Grill was closed so Gus could cater one of his private affairs. After two friends returned to Pittsburgh from a month-long hunting trek in Canada, Gus hosted a "Feast of the Nimrods." His master chef, Harold Winslow, prepared an eight-course meal, beginning with blue points on the half-shell and featuring bear as the main course. The guest list included Pittsburgh's black leadership: attorney and later judge Homer Brown served as the master of ceremonies, Alderman Harry Fitzgerald, Constable Pappy Williams, and the editors of the *Pittsburgh Courier* all attended, along with *Post-Gazette* theater critic Harold Cohen, his party of white friends, and some groups from as far away as Akron and Cleveland.[10]

White sportsmen were frequent visitors to the Grill, and for many it was *the* place to go after a night at the fights or the ball park. Art Rooney, owner of the Pittsburgh Steelers and a close friend of Greenlee, and his entourage often stopped by, as did those whites who were comfortable in interracial settings. On weekends the Grill was packed, and all three stories were opened to accommodate the crowds.

The Crawford Grill was more than a classy nightclub for blacks or a place where whites could find good jazz.[11] It was also the hub of Greenlee's far-reaching and varied operations. Seated at the bar, Gus received visitors and offered counsel in the style of Rick Blaine in *Casablanca*. And like Rick's Café Americain, the Crawford Grill was the scene for many a whispered conversation tinged with illegality.

The Numbers Racket

Gus Greenlee's main enterprise, and black Pittsburgh's economic staple from the late 1920s through the 1940s, was the numbers game, a lottery in which bettors wager that the three-digit number they select will be the number that "hits" that day. The odds of picking the winning number are 1 in 1,000, since that's how many different combinations are possible, but the bettors usually collect at a substantially higher rate, between 500-to-1 and 600-to-1. The winning number is arbitrarily drawn or determined, usually based on figures from the stock exchange, commodity sales, or selected races at a particular track. Ideally, that number is beyond manipulation. A bettor can wager any amount desired, and in the early decades of the century it was not uncommon to gamble a penny or even a half-cent on a number. Hence, the numbers have long been regarded as the poor man's lottery.

The origin of the numbers game has been clouded by the

passage of time. Some observers have suggested that its precursor was European peasant village drawings. Games like the Italian lottery, which involved the selection of a three-digit number, were played on the Lower East Side and other New York City neighborhoods in the early twentieth century.[12] But there was another game in evidence in the United States as early as the Civil War, called policy, and it was also a forerunner of the numbers game. Policy gambling spread rapidly during the post–Civil War decades and became the predominant form of lottery gambling in this country until the 1920s.[13] Played in the black sections of New Orleans in the early nineteenth century, policy traveled northward with the migrations during the World War I years. Some believe that policy got its name from bettors wagering money they had initially intended to use to pay the premiums on their insurance policies.[14] In policy, the bettor wagers that anywhere from one to four numbers will be selected out of a can, known as the policy wheel, containing balls or pellets numbered from one to seventy-eight. The odds and payoffs are determined by how many numbers the bettor tries to hit. In some cities, particularly Chicago and St. Louis, policy remains the predominant form of illegal lottery wagering, but in most northern cities the numbers eclipsed policy during the 1920s.

A third possible point of origin for the numbers game is the Caribbean basin, where *la bolita*, a two- or three-digit numbers game, has been played at least since the 1920s. Some students of the game argue that West Indian blacks invented *la bolita* and subsequently popularized it as the numbers game in the United States; others argue that both the numbers and *la bolita* originated in the United States and were transplanted to the islands in the 1920s. At any rate, West Indians were prominent in the expansion of the numbers game in the United States during the 1920s.[15] One West Indian migrant, "Madame" Stephanie St. Clair, was known as the "Policy Queen of Harlem," and her fortune allegedly topped the million-dollar mark. Fellow West Indian Caspar Holstein, perhaps Harlem's wealthiest numbers banker, built a reputation as the benefactor of black charities and the patron of black artists and writers. In the *Colonia España* in Brooklyn, José Enriquez Míro, William Brunder, "Big

Joe" Ison, and Alex Pompez all established prosperous numbers operations during the 1920s. Míro had left his native Puerto Rico at the age of fifteen, arriving in the United States in 1917 and working as a laborer until his entry into the numbers business in 1926. He was soon reputed to be backing games in Boston and Philadelphia in addition to those in Harlem and gained fame as the Puerto Rican "King of the Numbers." Pompez, a Cuban from Tampa, became better known as the proprietor of a traveling Cuban baseball team and later as a scout for the New York Giants. For these West Indians and their brethren, *la bolita* or the numbers provided a path to wealth.[16]

Whether it was policy, *la bolita,* or the numbers, and whether it was located in Chicago, New York City, or the islands, this enterprise was primarily black-controlled, although many poor and working-class whites put their pennies and nickels down on a number they thought might hit. A look at the history of the numbers game in Pittsburgh depends on the credibility of peoples' memories, and, as with most illegal matters, those who know don't say, while those who say don't know. However, popular mythology and a few published sources hold that Gus Greenlee and his sidekick, Woogie Harris, brought the game to Pittsburgh in the mid-1920s.[17]

Charles Greenlee, Gus's youngest brother, argued that Gus "invented the numbers while he and Alex Pompez [owner of the Cuban Stars] were down in Cuba training a ball club and saw them playing *la bolita,* a Cuban game. . . . They came back and got the act together. Gus started booking the butter and eggs here and Pompez started booking the butter and eggs in New York."[18] Ralph Koger, who worked inside Greenlee's operations, offered a slightly different version. He believes that Effa Manley, owner of the Newark Eagles and the wife of Abe Manley, a successful Camden, New Jersey, numbers banker, picked up the idea while touring the islands. She transformed *la bolita* into the numbers game and then alerted other black baseball owners to its financial possibilities. Koger said that Dick Gauffney, a gas station owner who was peripherally connected to the sporting scene in Pittsburgh, began booking numbers and would turn to Gus and Woogie for help when he "got hit heavy and didn't have the money to back it."[19]

William A. ("Woogie") Harris was born in the Lower Hill in the 1890s. Like most young men he played sandlot ball, but it was as a card player and a gambler that Woogie left his mark. His expertise was especially evident at "skin," a rapidly played card game popular among Jews, Italians, and blacks in the 1920s and 1930s. While Gus and Woogie were certainly responsible for popularizing the numbers game in Pittsburgh and making it a going concern, it is unlikely that they introduced it to the city. Greenlee could not have encountered the game through a tie-in with black baseball during the early or mid-1920s since he was not involved with a team until 1930. It is possible, however, that either he or Woogie knew the Manleys, Alex Pompez, or other racket-related entrepreneurs through their own business activities.

Clarence ("Knowledge") Clark, sometime political analyst for the *Courier* and a confidant of Greenlee, thought that Swifty Howard, a dining car waiter on the milk run between Pittsburgh and New York, was the first to book numbers in town.[20] Howard wrote a few hundred dollars worth of numbers each trip and turned them into a numbers bank in Harlem,[21] but he did not establish a Pittsburgh-based numbers operation. The first to attempt that, according to Clark, was a Dr. Cottman, who began booking numbers out of a Centre Avenue office. Cottman's lottery lasted a year, until a number with "a big hit came out on him and he folded."[22] Several months later, Carlton Hays came to town and discussed the basics of the numbers game with several Wylie Avenue regulars. Hays had been connected with the game in Philadelphia; his brother Jimmy was a local cabaret entertainer. Among those who listened to Carlton Hays were Dick Gauffney, Bill Snyder, Woogie Harris, and Gus Greenlee.

Each of these men began booking numbers, but the extent of any collaboration among them is difficult to ascertain. The numbers game caught on quickly among the mostly poor and working-class black and immigrant residents of the Hill. The attractive payoff, the possibility of betting a penny or less, and the excitement the game added to daily life all contributed to its popularity. Soon people known as runners were working for Greenlee, Harris, and the others, each day collecting wagers from people they knew and turning over the bets, marked on numbers slips, to a collector, who in turn handed them to the head of the operation, the numbers banker. The runner and the collector retained a percentage of the action, called the "play." Sometimes a runner or collector added to their take by holding back some slips and the money bet, gambling that those numbers would not hit. Many a numbers man, rather than pay off a winning number, skipped town or simply refused to pay, and the bettor had little recourse. In Philadelphia, for example, where a "Numbers Epidemic" had seized the black population, one banker alone netted profits of more than $200,000 in a single year. It came out in court that whenever a well-played number hit, the banker arranged with the local precinct to raid his bank so that he could avoid paying off the bettors. The banker, however, regularly paid off the police and ward politicians.[23]

By the late 1920s numbers betting was widespread and was no longer solely a black phenomenon. People of all races, ethnic backgrounds, and classes were playing their hunches or betting their systems. A *Pittsburgh Press* story estimated that during 1928 "nearly two millions of dollars flowed into the coffers of the city's 'number kings.' "[24] This lucrative business occasionally caught the eye of the legal system. For example, both Harris and Greenlee were fined $100 for illegally operating a lottery in 1926. Nor were they the only ones, but the fines were merely financial slaps on the wrist, given the profits of the game.[25]

The reliability of the numbers industry in Pittsburgh was never more severely tested than on August 5, 1930. "Walk up to an old time numbers writer," journalist Ray Sprigle observed in 1936, "and say real quick, 'eight-oh-five.' Watch him turn pale, his knees go wobbly. See him gasp for breath."[26] Bettors play particular numbers for an almost unlimited number of reasons. Some bet numbers corresponding to a dream which they determine by using a 'dream book' written especially for numbers betting. In the 1950s and 1960s, Willie Mays's batting average was a common bet. Many frequently play the day's date; consequently, the number for August 5 would be 805 (eighth month, fifth day). In 1930 that number drew an exceptionally heavy play. Sprigle wrote that "every book in town was loaded up to the gills with money on 805," and the number hit.[27] He continued: "The numbers racket in Allegheny County stopped dead in its tracks.

Books folded up like nobody's business. Jittery numbers barons rented hotel rooms in Cleveland, Philadelphia, Atlantic City and as far away as Chicago, where they could jitter in seclusion, safely sequestered from hordes of eager Pittsburgh numbers players who had 'hit' on 805 and wanted to be paid off."

Some numbers men never returned, and one ditty of the day ridiculed a prominent absentee: "805 was a burner. Where the hell is Jakie Lerner"[28] On the Northside the book paid off at half the normal odds, but elsewhere there was no payoff unless the number had been played with Gus Greenlee or Woogie Harris, the only books to pay off completely on 805. They pawned virtually everything they had and mortgaged their homes to raise the cash. It is impossible to determine either how many bettors wagered on 805 or how much their winnings should have been, since the numbers was too decentralized and fragmented a trade and bookkeeping was prudently kept to a minimum. Clarence Clark recalled William Snyder later confiding that his payoff from 805 would have been "a couple of hundred thousand." Snyder never recovered, but Greenlee and Harris snapped back within months. While most numbers bankers and writers were subsequently discussed with anger and contempt, Gus and Woogie were treated with a newfound respect.

With the numbers game in a shambles, Harris and Greenlee not only maintained their own trade but picked up much of the play of their defamed or departed rivals. For Gus and Woogie, 805 was an immediate financial disaster but a long-term god-send; it was the springboard by which they jumped to a position of dominance in the numbers business, not only on the Hill, but in many sections of Pittsburgh and throughout the tri-state region. For several months Harris booked numbers as far away as Washington, D.C., sending his younger brother Teenie to collect. Headquarters were either at Harris's Crystal Barbershop on Wylie Avenue, the nearby Crawford Grill, or the numbers bank, complete with cashiers' windows and a lounge for the runners, that Greenlee ran in downtown Pittsburgh across from the courthouse. None of the men I interviewed knew the exact size of Greenlee's and Harris's take, but most believed that it quickly grew to at least $20,000–25,000 a day, and some thought it was probably much higher. Everybody agreed that Harris and Green-

lee, in the words of Sam Solomon, a long-time numbers entrepreneur, "had it all."

Woogie Harris and Gus Greenlee operated their legitimate
businesses in addition to their numbers trade from closely situated establishments on Wylie Avenue. They lived side-by-side in
impressive residences on Frankstown Avenue on the outskirts of
the city and were often seen out on the town together. In the
minds of many, especially when talk turned to the numbers
game, they were partners. Not so. Charlie Hughes, one of black
Pittsburgh's premier ballplayers and a shortstop for Greenlee's
Pittsburgh Crawfords, captured the essence of their relationship
when he called them "cut-buddies"—not partners in the formal
sense, but friends who shared both good and bad. If one did
exceptionally well in some venture, he might cut the other in for
a share; similarly, one turned to the other when in trouble. The
two men cooperated not only in the numbers game and during
the after-hours but in the larger role they and their numbers
capital played in black Pittsburgh during the 1930s and 1940s.

As Gus and Woogie gained prominence following 805 and
their numbers trade grew to impressive dimensions, three interrelated developments occurred. The first was that a score of
imitators appeared in neighborhoods throughout the city during
the early and mid-1930s. The numbers was not a difficult game
to set up on one's own, and both Gus and Woogie were willing
to lend a helping hand. Some of these new operators were
independents, making their own book, while others worked
more on a franchise basis, paying a piece of the action to Gus or
Woogie, turning in their play, or laying off excessive wagers on
heavily played numbers with them. Even those who turned in
their play were tempted to keep at least some of the wagers
themselves; the odds were simply too much in their favor to
make it a high risk. While some of these men expanded either
Greenlee's or Harris's influence, others began to cut into their
trade.[29]

The second development, the entry of a gangster element into
the business, was part of a national phenomenon as former
bootleggers moved in on the policy and numbers games with the
end of Prohibition. In many cities blacks were either pushed out

of the numbers or forced to accept a secondary role in their own operations.[30] Before 1926 the speakeasies and trade in illegal alcohol in Pittsburgh had been operated on an independent basis with appropriate payoffs to the police and ward leaders. But in 1926 this relatively peaceful racket found itself confronted by what the *Pittsburgh Press* called the "descent on the city of Capone-like gangsters."[31] The arrival from Chicago of "big shot" racketeers ignited a battle for control of the city's more than 1,100 speakeasies. Gangland slayings, almost unknown before 1926, became monthly occurrences; in 1932, 100 killings related to the struggle for control remained unsolved. The gangs failed to consolidate their hold, however. Thwarted in their efforts to gain sway over Pittsburgh bootlegging, these racketeers were also unable to penetrate the numbers as their brethren in other cities had done.

The third key development was the incorporation of the numbers into the city's long-standing alliance between its racketeers and its politicians.[32] Ward chairmen frequently took a direct role in the regulation of vice and racket activities in their district; in turn, the racketeers not only cut the politicians in financially but provided services around election time.[33] In Pittsburgh, the long alliance between the rackets and the politicians, which had germinated in the late nineteenth century under the political hegemony of Christopher Lyman Magee and William Flinn, was further consolidated with the election of Charles Kline as mayor in 1925. Investigative reporter Ray Sprigle, commenting on the role of the rackets in the election, noted: "Vice is organized along ward lines as in politics and vice and politics are organized as a single entity. In every ward and every precinct the man who handles the vote is the man who handles the bawdy house concessions and the gambling privileges. . . . The leaders of the political machine which rules Pittsburgh have made the ward chairmen of each ward the supreme vice dictator of his district."[34]

During the summer of 1932, Mayor Kline attempted to centralize the numbers business by creating a single large bank with a head administrator. He also tried to reduce the payoff on a winning number from 600-to-1 to 500-to-1.[35] While he was able

to consolidate his control over vice and incorporate most racketeers into his political machine, thus preventing the emergence
of a single rackets boss, Kline was unable to remain in office.
With his departure and the transition to Democratic party rule
in Pittsburgh during the 1930s, the politicians' lock on the
numbers weakened and the business reverted to its decentralized, neighborhood-based ways. The numbers man continued to pay various forms of obeisance to the ward boss, but
no single numbers operation took over. Independent or "outlaw
books" were common, and most operated as long as they paid
the "nut," as protection money was called. In this laissez-faire
atmosphere, punctuated by occasional raids, the numbers men
prospered.

The failure of the gangsters to establish themselves meant that
the numbers was generally devoid of violence. Secure ties with
ward politicians and police meant the numbers game was virtually ignored. "Nobody seems to care much whether the numbers racket flourishes or not," Ray Sprigle concluded.[36] Although temporarily checked by the depression, the volume of
business swelled with the introduction of direct cash relief. Numbers writers knew almost to the hour when the relief or WPA
checks were due and made their appearances accordingly. As the
amount bet each day grew, the numbers came to employ some
5,000 people either on a full- or part-time basis in the city.[37]

The money paid for protection and the difficulty in fighting
"outlaw bookies" and independents cut into the profit margin of
Greenlee and the other bankers. And while they might have been
writing more business, they were paying off more, too. Further,
the emergence of white numbers writers meant that limits were
being imposed on the growth of Greenlee's territory. Gus and
Woogie were confronted with increasing competition, sometimes
from men they had introduced to the business themselves. They
were also forced to seek political alliances and to accept the
reality that if they got too big the politicians could cut them back
to size easily enough. For Greenlee this recognition led to a foray
into ward politics on the Hill and a long-term friendship with
State Senator James Coyne, the Republican kingpin in Allegheny
County.

Coyne's power base was in the Oakland section of town, where his Monaca Club, a gambling parlor and speakeasy, operated free of restraint across the street from a police station. Greenlee and Pittsburgh Steeler owner Art Rooney were two of Coyne's most ardent supporters. When Coyne ran for county commissioner in 1931, their baseball teams, the Pittsburgh Crawfords and the Northside Civics, played in uniforms with "Coyne for Commissioner" stenciled on the back.[38]

Rooney and Greenlee shared an allegiance to Coyne as well as a close friendship and a common stake in the rackets/sport/politics nexus. Both took sandlot teams and made them over into their sport's dominant franchises, the Crawfords in the 1930s and the Steelers in the 1970s. Rooney, a ward chairman, "ran the numbers on the Northside," according to a former Pittsburgh homocide detective. "He was the head man. I worked over there and he had bookmaking establishments, too."[39]

Rooney tells of a late-night rendezvous with Coyne and Greenlee at the Crawford Grill. The three were sitting in a backroom discussing an impending election when a young woman stopped by and whispered into Gus's ear that she wanted some money. When Greenlee refused her, the woman retorted, "That's not the way you talked last night, honey." Greenlee replied, "Last night was last night. When I'm hard, I'm soft. When I'm soft, I'm hard. Beat it." Believing that the matter had ended, the three men returned to their agenda when an ashtray came flying by, narrowly missing the senator's head. Greenlee chuckled but Coyne, rattled by the affair, demanded that they hold their meetings in Oakland from then on.[40]

If Greenlee in particular had merely enriched himself from the numbers and engaged in the conspicuous consumption characteristic of the successful racketeers of his day, there would be little to the relationship between his economic livelihood and his role in black sport. But his broad and lucrative economic base allowed him to play a vital part in the development of black Pittsburgh and its sporting life—one that led a black Pittsburgh athlete to refer to him as the "Jesus of Negro sport" and another to assert that Gus and Woogie together would "go down as the people who kept Pittsburgh on the block as far as blacks were concerned" during the depression.[41] Black Pittsburgh saw Gus not as a racketeer, an exploiter of the black community, but as a "sportsman"[42] and someone to turn to when you were in need. In interviews with almost a hundred long-time members of the black Pittsburgh community, only one indicated any hostility toward Greenlee; the others spoke of him in glowing terms. Walt Hughes, a former sandlot athlete, remarked, "Gus Greenlee was a beautiful man . . . a wonderful person who'd help anybody." Joe Ware said simply, "Gus? One of the best." Gabe Patterson commented that Greenlee was the "best man I ever knew. He never looked down on nobody. I never heard nobody speak bad about him. No way. If somebody needed help after they got into whatever they went into, Gus would be right there to help out."

When a black family on the Hill needed money for rent, groceries, a truckload of coal, or to pay the doctor's bill, they often went to Greenlee. "He was never slow when a fella needed a favor," Ted Page remembered. "His hands were just as fast as you could hope they would be when he'd come across people who needed help." At Thanksgiving and Christmas, Greenlee dispatched employees with turkeys for hundreds of Hill families, and during the depression he ran a soup kitchen across the street from the Crawford Grill. Walter Rainey, a self-professed "bitter enemy" of Greenlee's because of a political conflict in the early 1930s, remembered him "standing there in the restaurant cooking food and just giving it away to the people all up and down the street."[43] Rainey added that Greenlee paid for a number of black youths to go to college, too. Many of these acts were not dissimilar to the services an effective ward chairman provided.

Gus's numbers revenue became a primary source of black-controlled investment capital for black Pittsburgh. After the sudden collapse of the Steel City Bank in 1925, black Pittsburgh was without a bank of its own—except, that is, for the numbers bank. Greenlee and, to a lesser extent, Woogie Harris thus were black Pittsburgh's bankers. When loaning money Gus did not ask for collateral, and most of his intimates agreed that very few loans were ever repaid. The money wagered on the numbers continued to find its way back to the black community in the form of college tuition loans and start-up money for hotels, bars, restaurants, and legal and medical practices. Gus acted as an informal patron to black musicians and even set up "Old Hot Sauce" Williams in the barbecue business.[44]

Greenlee and Harris also contributed money to black causes and candidates. Gus supported Mary Bethune in her struggles at Bethune-Cookman College and Pittsburgh's Homer Brown when he first ran for the state legislature. "Hadn't been for them," Joe Ware argued, "the campaigns for the first blacks in Pittsburgh wouldn't have happened."[45] Greenlee also allegedly bailed the *Pittsburgh Courier* out of financial trouble on one occasion.[46] "He was a sucker for do-gooder causes," Clarence Clark added, and he gave to sandlot clubs, black nurses, and "just anybody who asked him."[47] When it came to sport, Gabe Patterson said, to Greenlee it "didn't matter what kind of athlete you were . . . Gus loved you and you'd get his money."[48]

While treatment of the numbers game as a positive force in the development of the black community conflicts with the more traditional account of the numbers as a predatory racket, there is yet another aspect of the numbers' role to consider, that of its relation to black sport. Simply stated, whether it was Negro League baseball, boxing, or sandlot ball, numbers money was often a vital source of funds and it is doubtful that black sport would have survived without it. Negro League teams like the Grays, the Crawfords, Alex Pompez's Cuban Stars, and the Newark Eagles were only some of the pro clubs relying on numbers money; John Henry Lewis and Joe Louis were but two of the many black boxers whose careers were funded by the same source. The reason the numbers loomed so large in black sport was relatively simple. As Charlie Hughes, a veteran of both sandlot and Negro League ball, explained, "It was where the money was."[49]

These teams and athletes in turn bolstered the political image and capital of men like Greenlee and Posey and the black community in general. Posey and Greenlee were considered sportsmen and, to some extent, race men. They were well connected politically and powerful, in part because of their public image as sportsmen. Posey took part in Homestead borough politics and addressed race issues in his newspaper column. And while few people doubted that Greenlee's political activity was designed to protect his illegal interests, just as few denied that Gus energized and financed black Pittsburgh sport. Like Posey his sporting contributions opened new cultural terrain for black Pittsburgh.

Ultimately, both men and the teams they were associated with paved the way for blacks to compete successfully with and against whites, which itself had enormous political ramifications for black America.

Gus Greenlee became a major force in black Pittsburgh's sporting life during the 1930s. He slipped quietly enough into the sporting scene at first, but before long he virtually subsidized sport in the black community and added more than a little lustre to Pittsburgh's image as a sporting town.

The Pittsburgh Crawfords

During the 1930 season, Steve Cox, who worked at the sporting goods store where the Crawfords bought much of their equipment and who also booked many of their games, offered to buy the team for $1,000. Reasoning that a black man might offer them more, the Crawfords approached Gus Greenlee. According to Bill Harris, who had returned to the Crawfords after a stint with the Homestead Grays, Greenlee at first declined, claiming to know nothing about sports. However, he did offer the team money, transportation, or whatever else they needed. They persisted in attempting to convince him to take over ownership of the team, and a week later Greenlee called them together and told them that not only had he decided to buy the team, but he was putting all the players on salary. Harris recalled: "Man, gee whiz! A salary. We just blew up. A salary! So he says, 'I'm going to give you all the same price—$125 a month. And if you say you're better than this or whatever it might be, I'll raise your salary.' That was a dream to us. We never thought about no salary. We just wanted to play ball."⁵⁰

There are several possible explanations why Gus Greenlee decided to buy the team. Clarence ("Knowledge") Clark, who spent more time in Greenlee's company during the early 1930s than he did attending classes at a nearby college, claimed that the decision was partly political. Greenlee was in the middle of a hotly contested campaign and wanted to outfit the Crawfords in uniforms bearing slogans aimed at getting voters to cast their ballots for James J. Coyne for county commissioner and Andrew Parks for district attorney. Clark also contended that Greenlee's advisors figured the ball club would serve as an effective blind for money earned through the numbers racket, money that might otherwise attract the attention of federal tax investigators.[51] It was likely, too, that the genial Greenlee simply could not turn down the players' request. Once associated with the club, he became increasingly fascinated with their potential.

In a move to make the Crawfords the best team in black baseball, Greenlee sent for veteran Atlantic City Bacharachs' shortstop Bobby Williams to manage the club. Williams then began recruiting established ballplayers from other cities and teams, including Sam ("Lefty") Streeter, a southpaw hurler for the Cleveland Buckeyes who relied on his big bending curveball to no-hit a strong Book-Shoe team in his first outing with the Crawfords.[52] He was soon joined by Jimmie Crutchfield, Chester Williams, Pistol Russell, and Satchel Paige.[53] As the newcomers were added to the roster, they displaced many of the local boys and men who had been playing for the Crawfords, just as some of them had moved out the kids from the McKelvey and Watt playgrounds a few years before. Bill Harris explained: ". . . everybody thought the team would stay as it was, like the young Crawfords. Then this guy [Williams] came in and began to weed us out and get his old friends in. But he got a good ball club out of it—a beautiful ball club—one of the best in the world."[54]

None of these managerial and personnel changes derailed the Crawfords' impending confrontation with the Homestead Grays for baseball bragging rights in black Pittsburgh. Although the Crawfords had lost their first match with the Grays in 1930, Greenlee's presence added a new dimension to black baseball, and the papers reported that betting on the game was heavy.[55] The Crawfords' supporters were disappointed, however, as their team was drubbed 9–0.

Before the teams met for the third time, according to Harold Tinker, Greenlee told the players they would have to quit their jobs and play ball or quit the team and go to their jobs. Like most of the Pittsburghers on the team, Tinker had continued to hold down his regular job at RKO even though Greenlee had put the team on salary. Since the new owner gave them a couple of weeks to think things over, and since Tinker's ambition had always been to play on a team that beat the Homestead Grays, he said nothing.[56]

The third meeting between the Crawfords and the Grays turned out to be Tinker's last day as an active member of the team. Down three runs early in the game, the Crawfords sent their newest member, a lanky right-handed pitcher named Leroy ("Satchel") Paige, to the mound. "And I'll tell you," Tinker reminisced, "the Grays had one of the best shooting teams in sandlot, but they hardly hit a foul ball off of Satchel the rest of the game. He was mowing those guys down like mad. He was throwing nothing but aspirin tablets—fastballs. He hadn't developed all that fancy stuff then. So we beat the Grays. I think we beat them 6–5 or something."[57]

During a twilight game that same day, Tinker approached Greenlee:

I came in between innings and went over and sat down beside Gus. I said, "I got something to tell you." He said, "What is it, Red?" They called me Red. I said, "I had an ambition and I realized that ambition today." Gus said, "What are you talking about?" And I said, "I had an ambition to beat the Grays with a ball team that was developed by us and we did that today. You gave us an ultimatum to either quit our jobs or quit baseball and I have to quit baseball, because you don't pay me enough to support my family. Gus said, "Kid, think it over. You don't want to do that." And I said, "Yes, I do." He thought it over and said, "I'll tell you what I'm gonna do. As long as you feel like playing, you come up and dress every Sunday that we play, and I'll pay you. Just for dressing and sitting." So I did, through the rest of that year I came up with them on Sunday. But that was my last game with the Crawfords.[58]

Within a few years only Charlie Hughes, Harry Williams, and Harry Kincannon were still on the roster. Josh Gibson, who had been lured away by the Grays, returned later in the 1930s via a trade. Tinker, Bill Harris, Wyatt Turner, and the other players drifted away or lost their spots on the roster to better ballplayers. Harry Beale, who had been with the team from its inception and had taken over most of the administrative tasks before Greenlee made the scene, died of tuberculosis a few years later, at the age of twenty-four. The *Courier* reported early in 1932 that the original members of the Crawfords were rumored to be regrouping and seeking entry into the City League,[59] but nothing ever came of it. The Crawfords of the sandlots were now Gus Greenlee's Pittsburgh Crawfords, a professional club boasting some of the finest players in baseball.

After his club beat the Homestead Grays, Greenlee applied for membership in Cumberland Posey's East-West League. But Posey, who enjoyed a monopoly of sorts over black baseball in Pittsburgh, did not welcome a competitor who could mount a serious challenge to his control. He set stiff terms for a new franchise: Greenlee would have to sign a five-year contract with the league, the terms being that Posey would not only decide what dates the Crawfords got for their local games but which players would remain on the squad; furthermore, Posey or his brother Seward ("See") would be installed as the team's manager. The terms were clearly unacceptable to Greenlee. In retrospect, Posey realized his hard-line bargaining was a mistake, for Greenlee upped the ante considerably and Posey soon found himself without a league, only a handful of his best players, and in dire financial straits. Greenlee wanted the Crawfords in a league, and if Posey wanted to deny him entry into the East-West League, he would form a circuit of his own. Nor could Posey stop Greenlee from successfully raiding the Gray's roster and constructing the foremost black-owned baseball stadium in America, on Bedford Avenue on the Hill.[60]

Between 1932 and 1937, black baseball's two titans battled for control over the game both in Pittsburgh and across the nation. Although his 1931 Crawfords were already an impressive aggregation, Greenlee sought to turn them into the best possible team. From Detroit he signed John Henry Russell and Cool Papa Bell; Walter ("Rev") Cannady and Judy Johnson were enticed to leave Hilldale; and from Posey's Homestead Grays came Oscar Charleston, Ted Page, Ted ("Double-Duty") Radcliffe, and Josh Gibson. The lure in each case was a larger paycheck.[61] A picture hanging in the National Baseball Museum at Cooperstown, N.Y., shows the 1936 Crawfords, champions of the Negro National League the year before, kneeling in front of their Mack bus, which is parked beside Greenlee Field. With Oscar Charleston, Judy Johnson, Cool Papa Bell, Satchel Paige, and

Josh Gibson in the line-up, a quintet eventually selected for membership in the Hall of Fame, the Crawfords became possibly the best baseball team ever assembled for regular season play.

Greenlee not only built a stellar nine, he constructed a stadium to showcase their talents. Black baseball teams had long been without playing fields of their own, leaving them at the mercy of white stadium owners who rented to the black clubs when their own teams were on the road. Arguing that black teams needed greater control over their own schedules, in the fall of 1933 Greenlee negotiated for a plot of land owned by the Entress Brick Company on Bedford Avenue,[62] obtained zoning modifications, and relocated a number of bodies that had been buried on the site. With his accountant, Robert Lane, serving as secretary and his numbers protege, Joe Tito, as treasurer, the new Bedford Land and Improvement Company broke ground for Greenlee Field that winter. Six months, $100,000, seventy-five tons of steel, and fourteen railroad cars of cement later, Greenlee Field was ready. Its red brick walls, laid by black bricklayers, encompassed a playing field alleged to be the largest in western Pennsylvania. After a game against Vandergrift, a white semipro club, the official opening of the ball park occurred on April 30, 1932, with Greenlee's Crawfords going up against the New York Black Yankees.[63] The mayor, the city council, and the county commissioners were all in field boxes around the first and third base lines as *Courier* editor Robert Vann, who delivered the dedication and led the crowd in a standing ovation for Gus Greenlee, strode to the mound to throw out the ceremonial first pitch. With bands playing and 5,000 fans cheering, the Crawfords and the Black Yankees tangled in a pitching duel that was won by the visitors when Ted Page scampered home with the game's lone tally in the top of the ninth inning.[64]

The finest independent ball park in the country, and one of the few black-controlled ones, Greenlee Field hosted an array of sporting events and earned the title of Pittsburgh's "Sports Center." Wilberforce College, the national black football champion in 1931, played a Thanksgiving Day game against West Virginia State there in 1932, the first such contest in Pittsburgh's history. With a seaboard special rolling in from the East Coast and chartered buses and motorcades bringing in alumni and fans from all over the East, the game was an important social event for Pittsburgh's black middle classes. That it ended in a scoreless tie did little to detract from the social whirl accompanying it. On other occasions, soccer matches and fight cards helped to fill the stands. Paid admissions at Greenlee Field during its first year totaled 119,000, with baseball accounting for almost 60 percent of the gate.[65]

Gus Greenlee had a team and a place where they could play; now he needed a league within which the Crawfords could test their mettle. His club's record in 1932 had been ninety-nine wins against thirty-six defeats, but he was no longer satisfied with barnstorming against the best available opponents. Consequently, he resurrected the Negro National League in 1933. Despite its wobbly rebirth during the absolute depths of the depression, the league surpassed all previous efforts at organized black baseball and survived until the late 1940s. Made up of teams from both the East and Midwest during its first four seasons, the NNL became a strictly eastern circuit in 1937 with the formation of the Negro American League (NAL) in the Midwest.

The new NNL broke ground for black professional sport, achieving a measure of financial stability and a public presence unprecedented for a black sporting venture, thanks mainly to its architect, prime innovator, and president during the first five seasons—Gus Greenlee. Perhaps his biggest contribution was the creation of an annual all-star game, the East-West Classic, in which black baseball's best players displayed their talents. The first East-West game, played in Chicago in 1933, featured an East line-up dominated by the Crawfords and the Grays, with nine of fourteen East players who made it into the box score that day coming from one of the two Pittsburgh clubs.

In both 1933 and 1936, the two seasons for which attendance figures are known, the Crawfords played before over 200,000 paying fans, a total audience larger than that of most other black clubs.[66] Attendance was boosted by various promotional gimmicks, including the sale of season's passes, a drawing for a Ford sedan, and cosponsorship with various social organizations of benefit games. Greenlee even convinced 1936 Olympic champion Jesse Owens to travel with the club and race against a thoroughbred in pregame festivities. Owens, who returned to the United States from the Berlin games a hero to black America, had difficulty translating his Olympic gold into financial success and thus was receptive to the plan. Charles Greenlee, who handled the logistics of these races, explained that they always chose a gun-shy horse, one likely to rear up at the crack of the pistol, so that by the time the horse settled down, Owens had an insurmountable lead.[67]

Despite these schemes and the presence of crowd-pleasers like Satchel Paige, Cool Papa Bell, and Pittsburgh's own Josh Gibson, and a juggernaut of a club on the field, the Crawfords were less than a financial success. No verifiable records have survived, although Cum Posey claimed in a 1937 newspaper column that his rivals lost $16,000 in 1932 and another $6,000 in 1933.[68] Bookkeeping was lax, as were Greenlee's accounting practices in general (numbers bankers were never known for keeping records that could later enter the public realm). But if the Crawfords were losing money, it was likely because the team's payroll was the highest in black baseball. The two best-paid Crawfords were Satchel Paige and Josh Gibson. Paige was an attraction in himself, and the announcement that he would pitch guaranteed a crowd virtually anywhere the team played. Gibson was not as flashy as his headline-making battery-mate, but his performance on the field was remarkable, and at bat he was seen as the Babe Ruth of black baseball.

Josh Gibson's career began on the sandlots of Pittsburgh's Northside. Few people suspected that the well-proportioned lad playing with the Northside Red Sox was only fifteen, for he looked and played like a man. After a few seasons with the sandlot Crawfords, Gibson was recruited by Cum Posey, who introduced him to the world of black professional baseball as a member of the Homestead Grays. There, Gibson began to build his reputation as black baseball's premier hitter, swatting seventy-five home runs in 1931 against an array of semipro and pro competition. Although his statistical record is incomplete, eloquent testimony to his greatness can be found among a generation of fans and players. Until his tragic death in 1947 at the age of thirty-five, Gibson hit the ball out of parks all over the United

States, Cuba, Puerto Rico, Venezuela, the Dominican Republic, and Mexico.

Gibson's career represents the strongest possible indictment of white organized baseball. After Walter Johnson and a group of his Washington Senator teammates attended a spring training camp game between the Homestead Grays and the Newark Eagles in 1939, Johnson talked with *Washington Post* sportswriter Shirley Povich. "There is a catcher," Johnson commented, "that any big league club would like to buy for $200,000. I've heard of him before. His name is Gibson . . . and he can do anything. He hits the ball a mile and he catches so easy that he might just as well be in a rocking chair. Throws like a rifle. Bill Dickey [the New York Yankee Hall of Famer who, during his 1928–46 career, was regarded as one of white baseball's best catchers] isn't as good a catcher. Too bad this Gibson is a colored fellow."[69] Jim Murray, in a column about "The '42 Phils That Weren't," discussed the potential starting line-up Bill Veeck could have fielded if he had not been foiled in his attempt to buy the Philadelphia franchise and stock it with black ballplayers: "You want a catcher? How about Josh Gibson? This man just might have been the greatest hitter who ever lived. There's little doubt he's the best catcher. He died in an asylum—some say because he went out to the ball park one day and saw Joe Garagiola on a major league team and the whole horrible meaning of prejudice came over him."[70]

In 1932, Gus Greenlee enticed Gibson to return to the Crawfords by offering a substantially higher salary than Cum Posey could afford to pay him. For the next five seasons Gibson teamed up with Greenlee's other new recruits to make the Crawfords one of baseball's most talented clubs. Before the 1937 season, however, Gibson left the team, traded to the Crawfords' cross-town rivals, the Homestead Grays, for catcher Pepper Bassett, apparently as a result of an ongoing salary dispute. He reported to spring training with the Grays, but like a number of his former teammates Gibson opted for a change of scenery and left the Grays before the season got underway.

Even with the departure of Gibson, the Crawfords were on the verge of becoming a baseball dynasty when the chaotic politics of a Caribbean island intruded. Black American ballplayers had long graced the diamonds of Caribbean basin countries, where their skills were appreciated by fans whose sense of color was less distorted than that of white organized ball in the United States. In Cuba, Puerto Rico, Panama, Mexico, or Venezuela, a black American could receive higher pay than he would for playing ball in the States. Furthermore, he usually encountered far less racial antagonism and discrimination. There was often the added bonus of playing with and against white Americans, giving the players a chance to prove themselves in head-to-head competition.

For most black players, heading south was less an alternative to the Negro Leagues than a continuation of the baseball season. When fall brought the NNL campaign to an end, many players headed to the West Coast where baseball was still being played. After baseball died there, the islands were the next stop. Baseball, for many black professionals, was a year-long proposition. They usually either played ball or sought another job until spring training. Many looked forward to winter ball in the Caribbean, for it offered not only higher pay but a more leisurely existence than the frenetic barnstorming of a typical summer in the States.

The respective baseball seasons of the islands and the United States occasionally overlapped, giving rise to competition for black American ballplayers. Black baseball's southern flank was defenseless before the unexpected raids that hit in the spring of 1937. The first attack came in March, when Cuban ballplayers Martin Dihigo and Lazaro Salazar persuaded five players to forego the 1937 NNL campaign in favor of playing ball in the islands. Two of the five, Bill Perkins and Thad Christopher, were members of the Pittsburgh Crawfords. The league denounced this "Cuban raid," and Gus Greenlee sued the jumping players and sought injunctions against Dihigo and Salazar.[71] The second and more costly raid came within weeks from Cuba's neighbor, Hispaniola, an island divided for centuries between French-speaking, soccer-playing Haiti and the Spanish-speaking, baseball-playing Dominican Republic.

"En este letrina, Trujillo es el jefe," is scrawled on the door to the bathroom by the visitors' dugout at Quisqueya Stadium in

Santo Domingo, about the only place Rafael Trujillo still has clout. Trujillo gained his spurs during the United States Marines' occupation early in this century. He finally seized power in 1930 and spent the next thirty years as *el caudillo* of the Dominican Republic. Trujillo's megalomania knew few bounds: he renamed the highest mountain on the island, two provinces, and even the capital city after himself. By the end of his reign the entire country had become his private estate.

From the 1930s and the inception of league play until his death in 1961, Trujillo cast a shadow over his country's favorite pastime. He intimidated the best players into performing for one of his two teams and stopped several from attempting to ply their trade in the States. In 1937, however, he faced considerable political opposition from the port city of San Pedro de Macoris. Not the least of his problems was that his major opponent in an upcoming election was closely identified with the San Pedro ball club, which was challenging the Ciudad Trujillo team.

San Pedro, by importing a number of Latin and American ballplayers, had put together a team that was sweeping through the Dominican league and heightening Trujillo's opponent's visibility to the sports-conscious electorate. Consequently, Trujillo responded in kind, sending his emissaries abroad to recruit the best players available. Before long they had garnered a handful of players from Cuba, Panama, and Puerto Rico, headed by the latter's Peruchin Cepeda, the preeminent Puerto Rican ballplayer of his times. Trujillo, however, was not satisfied, so his men went to New Orleans, where the Pittsburgh Crawfords had arrived for spring training. Their goal was Satchel Paige; their lure, a considerably larger amount of money than Paige could earn by playing ball in the NNL that summer. Paige resisted their entreaties but Trujillo's henchmen were not to be deterred. Eventually their offer of cash broke down his sense of obligation to Gus Greenlee, with whom he had frequently engaged in hold-outs, contract-jumping, and cut-throat negotiations. Greenlee, infuriated by Paige's latest escapade, instituted legal proceedings and vowed to have him barred from the NNL. Paige, meanwhile, appraised Trujillo's competition and realized he could use some help. He called his former Crawford roommate Cool Papa Bell and asked him to join Trujillo's squad. Bell proceeded to persuade over a dozen NNL ballplayers to join him on a flight to Santo Domingo, then called Ciudad Trujillo.

A total of eighteen American-born blacks played for Trujillo's team, nine of them Pittsburgh Crawfords; a tenth, Josh Gibson, was given a salary for two months of ball with Ciudad Trujillo that was second only to Paige's. While Trujillo's all-star outfit won the island championship, helping him to remain in power until 1961, when the CIA helped terminate him, Gus Greenlee fumed. Why had his players, who Cum Posey had called the highest paid in black baseball, "more petted and pampered" than all the others, decided to leave? Cool Papa Bell later argued that Greenlee's numbers operation had been hit repeatedly by the police that year, causing Gus's largesse to dwindle. Furthermore, with baseball subject to the economic downturn of 1937, many of Bell's teammates were looking for a way out, and Trujillo's offer was too good to turn down.[72]

The NNL, under Greenlee's control, at first threatened to bar these players' return to black ball in the United States. But Paige, Bell, Gibson, and the rest were simply too valuable to send into exile, so they were welcomed back and fined one week's salary. Few of them ever made it back to the Crawfords. Paige, Bell, and some of their Crawford teammates became the nucleus of a barnstorming attraction, the Trujillo Stars, winning the *Denver Post*'s annual championship for teams outside of white organized ball. Gibson returned to the Grays, to whom he had been traded the previous season. The Crawfords finished the first half of the 1937 season in next-to-last place and were never the same again.[73]

As if his dismal team standing was not bad enough, Greenlee and the NNL were in the middle of a protracted battle with booking agent Nat Strong and the white semipro clubs he controlled in the East. The NNL retained Eddie Gottlieb, the white owner of the Philadelphia Stars and a booking agent in his own right, to represent them in all dealings with independent clubs east of Altoona. The league's sense of timing was poor, however, for most teams were struggling simply to survive and black pro ball was playing to its smallest crowds in league history. Amid dismal financial conditions, the NNL's united front against Nat

Strong crumbled, and Greenlee found himself increasingly on the outs in league disputes involving the owners of the Newark Eagles, the New York Black Yankees, and the Grays, all of whom were now allied with the resourceful owner of the Philadelphia franchise, Ed Gottlieb.[74]

To make matters even worse, the Crawfords' chief rivals, the Homestead Grays, won the 1937 league championship. Despite the drain on his resources and the challenge to his leadership, Greenlee vowed that he was in organized baseball to stay. "I want it clearly understood that I am not resigning as Chairman of the Negro National League," he stated. "You may rest assured, however, that there will be a re-organization and the NNL will be placed on a solid foundation in 1938."[75] And perhaps he would have remained an active participant in black baseball if other forces had not combined to convince him to leave the game after the 1938 season, foremost among them being the decline of Greenlee Field.

The ball park Greenlee built never achieved the level of patronage necessary to turn a profit. The depression undercut attendance, as did the failure of the builders to install an awning over the grandstand, which could have shielded fans from inclement weather. Greenlee had approached several black businessmen in the community to invest in such a project, but he could not drum up sufficient interest. That he was unwilling to put up the money himself lends credence to Cool Papa Bell's belief that he was in some financial difficulty at the time. John L. Clark, the Crawford's publicist during the 1930s and a *Courier* columnist, said that it was probably due to the fact that the men who ran the ball park, from the money handlers to the rental agent to the groundskeeper to the head of the concessions stands, showed a marked preference for hiring whites, with disastrous results. Blacks who paid their way into Greenlee Field saw that their money was going to support whites, not blacks who would presumably recirculate that money in the black community, and they made a conscious decision to stay away.[76]

That Greenlee, considered a "race man" by many, allowed such hiring practices suggests that by the late 1930s he had lost some control over his own enterprises or at least was not taking an active interest in them. "Gus's weak point was that he didn't like anything old," Charles Greenlee explained. After the Crawfords climbed to the top, Gus retreated from active participation in team affairs. Roy Sparrow, John Clark, and finally his brother Charles took over the business end of the operation. Clark drew dire conclusions from the failure of Greenlee Field.

Regardless of what mistakes were made, or who made them, a purer racial interest should have been manifested to keep Greenlee Field out of the list of failures. And since there was no single individual, or group of individuals, blessed with that foresight, that courage to be a part of the thing and correct the faults, it is safe to say Pittsburgh is no place to attempt big things for Negroes.

Greenlee Field joins the list of banks, industries and other enterprises which should not be again attempted in this city for the next 100 years.[77]

Meanwhile, the Housing Authority selected the site as the future location for, in Clark's words, its next "colored colony." The wrecking ball was soon at work, and Bedford Dwellings, a housing project, stands today where the Pittsburgh Crawfords once played.

With Greenlee Field dismantled and the once-great Crawfords a pale reflection of their former selves, Greenlee began to disengage himself from black baseball. In February, before the start of the 1939 season, he resigned as chairman of the NNL (the league promptly passed a resolution making Greenlee its honorary president).[78] Two months later he called it quits with the Pittsburgh Crawford Baseball Club. His parting remarks were published in the *Courier*.

After a careful study of the baseball outlook, and in a review of my experience and losses of the past seven years, I have concluded that my resignation from office as president will serve the best interests of all concerned.

Greenlee Field has passed into history, and we have no home grounds that we can control. We can no longer plan for the day when improved industrial conditions will appear and make more profitable athletics in this section. . . . The Pittsburgh Crawfords baseball club had developed a warm friendship and enthusiastic following east of Pittsburgh. I had planned to be active this year if a major league park could be secured in New York or Brooklyn. Since this is impossible, I can see no good judgment in moving the club to a city west of Pittsburgh.

Then, too, owners in the NNL have violated their pledges in respect to players. It is safe to say that 95 percent of my roster has been approached with offers from different owners. . . .
Perhaps new blood will bring new ideas and new weapons.[79]

A group of white Toledo businessmen took over the Crawford franchise in the NNL and retained Oscar Charleston as manager. But despite their claim that most of the 1938 team would be signed, Toledo failed to field a team and the Crawfords became part of history. Gus Greenlee was out of baseball—at least for the time being.[80]

The Fight Game

When Greenlee resigned as chairman of the Negro National League in 1939, he did so in part because of boxing interests. In 1935 he had bought the contract of a twenty-one-year-old light-heavyweight who had recently decisioned Maxie Rosenbloom after sending him to the mat repeatedly. A versatile boxer with a hard-hitting right hand, John Henry Lewis came to Pittsburgh and moved into Greenlee's Frankstown Avenue residence. In the coming months Gus built a boxing camp in his backyard, complete with an eighteen-foot ring, cottage for Lewis, and a dormitory for his other fighters. Retaining Dandy Allen and Larry Amadee, one of Joe Louis's former trainers, to supervise his fighters, and Frank Sutton to see to their diets, Gus soon managed a stable of almost a dozen young boxers.

Gus wanted a fighter in each of the eight weight classes and consequently accepted some aspirants with less than impeccable credentials. James Bell hiked a hundred miles from Evansburg, Pennsylvania, when he heard of Greenlee's camp. According to Charles Greenlee, when asked who he had ever beaten, Bell replied, "I didn't beat nobody, but I hit a mule with my fist once and knocked him down."[81] Joining the "Mule Killer" in camp was a young man from Brazil who Charles Greenlee claimed wasn't even good enough to lick him, and "Silent" Stafford, a deaf and dumb featherweight from Savannah, Georgia, with a crushing right and the sort of human interest angle the press craved. Other fighters in Greenlee's "House of Sock" were competent pugilists like Red Bruce and Jim Thompson, but the star of the entourage was clearly John Henry Lewis.[82]

Not long after Greenlee took over Lewis's contract he persuaded Mike Jacobs, whose Twentieth Century Sporting Club controlled boxing's upper weight classes, to promote a title match between his fighter and light-heavyweight champion Bob Olin, to be held in St. Louis on October 31, 1935. Lewis was due for a shot at the throne as he had already beaten heavyweight champ James Braddock, former light-heavyweight champ Maxie Rosenbloom, and Olin in nontitle fights. Black boxers had long been shut out of title fights in the higher weight classes. In fact, the only black man to win the light-heavyweight title until then was Battling Siki, a French Senegalese who won the belt with a victory over George Carpentier in France in 1921.

The first championship affair in St. Louis in almost forty years, the Lewis-Olin fight was also the first mixed bout in that Mississippi River city to be sanctioned under Missouri's recently liberalized boxing codes. The black challenger had Gus Greenlee in his corner as well as the support of more than twelve million black Americans whose "secret ambition [was] to see . . . John Henry Lewis, the light-heavyweight, win the world's championship."[83] It was rough going in the early rounds, however, as Olin took the fight to his Phoenix-born challenger and had Lewis reeling. *Courier* sportswriter William Nunn reported from ringside:

It was a cyclone of action . . . a whirlwind of fists. . . . Olin set the pace from the very start and before two minutes of fighting, had rocked Lewis to his toes with a barrage of rights and lefts.

What a start! Whites were on their [feet], scenting that the Arizona brown boy was in trouble. Colored rooters appeared to be in a trance. We know that more than one silent prayer wafted its way on high during those tense moments.[84]

The end of the first round found Lewis still on his feet and able to wobble back to his corner, where he slumped on his stool. The second round was virtually a repeat of the first, but it was a different story in the third as Lewis started flicking a left jab to Olin's face. He drew blood with each jab, got in a left hook to Olin's jaw, another left, and then hammered him with a right. Olin never fully recovered, and from the third through the fifteenth rounds Lewis scored at will. Soon the referee's shirt was smeared with Olin's blood, but the champion refused to go down, finishing the fight on his feet. Lewis, the winner on all cards, became the first American-born black to win the light-heavyweight title. In Pittsburgh, as elsewhere, the black community celebrated.

John Henry Lewis was the only black champion at any weight class that year, and Gus Greenlee was the first black man to manage a black champion. That distinction did him little good when "some crude-looking gentlemen" from Chicago paid a visit to his hotel room that night and attempted to persuade him to turn over a chunk of the purse, noting that his head looked better on his shoulders than it would in a burlap sack at the bottom of the Mississippi. Gus obligingly sent someone for the money, but when the courier failed to return in the allotted time he exhibited some fancy footwork of his own: he put the slip on the mobsters and caught the next train out of town.[85]

The new champion was a busy man, defending his belt fifteen times in the first seven months of 1937 alone. Lewis had soon defeated all comers and was forced to seek bouts against heavyweights to stay active. He also sought the higher purses for which heavyweights contested and harbored some hopes of fighting for the heavyweight title. During 1937 and 1938, Lewis took on heavyweights and tried to raise his weight to the upper 180s.[86] In 1938 Greenlee arranged a fight with Two-Ton Tony Galento which brought advance ticket sales in six figures. When Galento contracted pneumonia prior to the match, Gus incurred heavy losses.

The reigning champ in the heavyweight division during the late 1930s was Joe Louis, and while a bout with the Brown Bomber meant a good payday, it also meant going into the ring against one of boxing's toughest customers. A black man had never fought another black man for the heavyweight title, but Greenlee was able to arrange the fight, possibly because of his ties with Louis and his backers, John Roxborough and Julian Black, who also had been involved in the numbers racket. A few months after the Lewis-Olin fight, at which Louis had been present, Gus approached them with a proposal to back a team in the Negro National League. "I loved the idea," Joe Louis recalled in his autobiography. "If it hadn't been for boxing, I would have loved to have been a baseball player. . . . I already had my friends working the Brown Bomber Softball Team and that was eating up money. Roxborough felt the League was a great cause, but a new team just was too costly." While unwilling to join Greenlee in baseball, Louis was able to force boxing promoter Mike Jacobs to arrange a January 27, 1939, championship bout with John Henry Lewis in Madison Square Garden. It was Louis's fifth title defense. "Now I felt good. Here I was, a black man, going to fight another black man, and us blacks are on the money side this time."[87]

Lewis and his Pittsburgh fans took the impending title bout seriously, but Charles Greenlee testified that Gus saw it more as a chance for John Henry to earn the best payday of his career, not the championship. In his pre–training camp routine of calisthenics, swimming, and handball at the Centre Avenue YMCA, Lewis was cheered on by black supporters, hundreds of whom traveled to New York City for the fight. *Courier* editor Robert Vann, Woogie Harris, Sonnyman Jackson, Jew McPherson, and Teddy Horne were among those at ringside. Despite all the prefight bravado that Lewis was much quicker than the champ, few had rejoinders to those predicting doom once Louis's mighty fists connected. Besides, John Henry was stepping up in weight and giving away almost twenty poiunds to the champ. By the night of the fight there was more talk about how many rounds the challenger would last than whether or not he could win. The oddsmakers set the line on the fight at a prohibitive 7–1, leaving little doubt that they and most bettors saw little chance for an upset.

The fight took place amid tragic circumstances. Gus's younger brother Jack was killed the day before the bout when his coupe crashed head-on with a truck as he was driving to Pittsburgh to make arrangements to take the midnight train to New York City for the fight. Jack Greenlee, co-captain of the Howard University football team in 1935, had come to Pittsburgh just the summer before to set up a medical practice. There is little doubt that as Gus stood in John Henry's corner his thoughts were far away. Lewis and young Jack Greenlee had become close friends, and the news was withheld from the fighter until after the bout, which proved to be anticlimactic. Louis came out of his corner and caught John Henry with a left hook to the chin that sent him to the canvas. Two more knockdowns convinced Art Donovan, the third man in the ring that night, to stop the fight at 2:29 of the first round.[88]

Lewis bowed out of the fight game soon after his defeat. He had been bothered by an eye injury suffered early in his career, and his vision was deteriorating. Doctors warned him that he could continue to fight only at great risk. When he went overseas to fight the British light-heavyweight champ, the British Boxing Commission refused to license the bout, and after a similar roadblock in Michigan, the National Boxing Association lifted his crown. Greenlee argued that the NBA's action had been "instigated by someone on the inside" who was anxious to see the light-heavyweight title up for grabs. "Titles are won and lost in the ring," he protested.[89] But he also admitted that, "Rather than have anything happen to John, I'd be in favor of him hanging up his gloves, and I'd be willing to work for him and provide for him the rest of my life. That's how much I think of him." Unable to find a state commission that would sanction a fight, Lewis had little choice but to leave the ring. In 100 fights he had been declared the winner 87 times, 39 of them by KOs, and had lost only 8, with 5 draws. His title shot against Joe Louis was the only time he was knocked out.[90]

With Lewis no longer in his stable, Greenlee soon tired of the fight game and turned to other interests. The ring in his backyard was dismantled and the fighters scattered to other cities and other occupations.

6 The Decline of Black Sport

Cum Posey and the Grays: A Temporary Reprieve

When Gus Greenlee entered black professional baseball in 1932, the biggest loser was Cum Posey, whose Homestead Grays lost both players and fans to Greenlee's Pittsburgh Crawfords. As fall brought the 1932 season to an end, Rollo Wilson, Posey's boyhood friend from the Monongahela River valley, wrote:

Always a fighter, and with the will to win, Posey has just about finished the most disastrous year of his baseball career. He made enemies of men who had once been his best friends; he saw himself become the mighty somnambulist of a vanished dream when his personal league [the East-West League] crashed about his head. He lost his grip on a profitable territory. He saw his club raided by the same ruthless methods which he had employed against other owners in the history years. And he comes up, well I don't know whether he is smiling, but he comes up anyhow. He is still "Cum" Posey, stormy petrel of sport, shrewd, resourceful, selfish, with an eye to the main chance for—"Cum" Posey.[1]

Wilson's diagnosis was correct—Cum Posey was down, but he remained too committed to black baseball to stay there for long. The Grays not only weathered the storm but bounced back to become the most dominant team in black baseball from 1937 until their demise in the late 1940s.

John L. Clark, the sportswriter who championed the Crawfords during Gus Greenlee's five-year struggle with the Grays, became Posey's confidant in later years as they traveled together for the Elks' Athletic Division. Clark wrote after Posey's death that the Gray's owner had never doubted he would win his baseball war with Greenlee because Gus simply did not understand the economics of the game.[2] Gus probably would have agreed, pointing out that turning a profit was not his primary aim, nor was it even a particularly necessary one, given his numbers revenue. But Posey depended on baseball for his livelihood and he lacked Greenlee's capital reserves. With the 1933 season drawing to a close, Posey didn't even have the money to pay off his players. If numbers money could fuel his rival's forays, he reasoned, it could bail him out as well. Thus, Posey turned to Homestead's principal numbers banker, Rufus ("Sonnyman") Jackson, and tried to convince him to invest in the club. Jackson declined at first, but the allure of becoming part-owner of one of black baseball's most famous outfits and Posey's persistence eventually led him to enter the sporting world.[3]

Sonnyman Jackson was a lot like Gus Greenlee. Both were enterprising young men from the South who had come to Pittsburgh during the World War I–era migrations. Both enjoyed sport, especially boxing. Both entered the numbers game while it was still in its infancy in the late 1920s and operated poolrooms and nightclubs in their respective towns. And both were known for lending a helping hand.

Jackson's principal source of income was the numbers business, but the Sky Rocket Cafe, with its upstairs Peacock Room Nightclub, and the jukeboxes he rented out in Allegheny and Westmoreland counties nicely supplemented his numbers earnings. The popularity of the latter, a collection of several hundred Seeburgs and Wurlitzers, encouraged Jackson to open a mail-order record shop in Homestead. The Sky Rocket, a post-Prohibition nightclub, was a center for interracial socializing and provided the best live entertainment in Homestead. A number of the Homestead Grays' players could usually be found there after a game.

Although Posey persuaded Jackson to buy into the financially ailing Grays, he retained primary control over the club's affairs. However, Jackson, who enjoyed the sporting scene and would travel across the country just to see Joe Louis or Henry Armstrong fight, soon began to take an active part in the Grays' operations. He went on the road with the club, was listed as treasurer when it was incorporated in 1934, and when Cum Posey was elected NNL secretary in 1937, Jackson was voted to the league's board of trustees.[4]

The Grays still had the support of Homestead, which toasted the 1933 ball club with a reception and dance at the Manhattan Hall, hosted by sportsman Jew McPherson and attended by

Burgess Jack Cavanaugh and the leading lights of black Home-stead.[5] They retained some of their top pitchers and team leader Vic Harris, but Gus Greenlee's raids deprived the team of Ted Page, Oscar Charleston, and Josh Gibson. On the field their play deteriorated and the club managed only a .500 record against NNL clubs after they rejoined the league in 1935. In 1936 they fell into the second division, occupying the basement during the first half of the season. They turned things around in 1937, however, and once they made it back to the top they stayed there. A major reason for their resurgence was the return of Josh Gibson after a five-year sojourn with the Crawfords and a brief stay in the Dominican Republic. Batting behind Gibson and giving the Grays an awesome right-left combination was Buck Leonard. He and Gibson were often called the Gehrig and Ruth of black baseball.

Walter F. ("Buck") Leonard, born in Rocky Mount, North Carolina, was twenty-five before he began his professional base-ball career, but it was capped by selection to the Baseball Hall of Fame. In 1934 he joined the Grays and remained with them until the end. Leonard, a left-handed first baseman, hit for both power and a high average. One of the better-paid athletes in black baseball, he continued his career after the Grays collapsed by playing in Mexico, until he retired at the age of forty-eight in 1955. He participated in the Grays' second coming with Gibson, Vic Harris, Pittsburgh's Sam Bankhead and Euthumm Napier, Jerry Benjamin, Roy Partlow, and eventually Cool Papa Bell. From their 1937 NNL championship season until 1948, the Grays won league honors every year but two, and in several of these seasons they also won the Negro Leagues' World Series by defeating the winner of the Negro American League in post-season play. No other club in black baseball ever put together a record quite like theirs. The Grays became such a balanced squad from the late 1930s on that when Josh Gibson went south to Mexico for the 1940 and 1941 seasons, they won without him.

At the top of their game, the Grays nevertheless could not turn a profit. The disastrous second dip in the economy in late 1937 and early 1938 battered them so badly at the gate that they considered moving out of Pittsburgh. During the summer of 1939, co-owner Jackson informed the press that the team might rent Griffith Stadium in Washington, D.C., as their home grounds for the 1940 season.[6] The announcement caused great consternation among sports fans. Jesse ("Sonny") Davis argued in the *Courier:* "It is the duty of every colored baseball fan of Pittsburgh to give the Homestead Grays his whole-hearted support. . . . The Grays belong to this city. It is a great team and a credit to our community. Let us, as a race, give this great team our full measure of appreciation and support. It is our duty. . . ." Perhaps Posey and Jackson were listening, for the team decided not to relocate but simply to expand.[7]

Beginning in late 1939 and continuing through World War II, the Grays played out of both Homestead and Pittsburgh: Saturdays they were at Forbes Field, Sundays at Griffith Stadium, the home of the Washington Senators. Drawing on the capital city's large black population, the Grays outdid themselves at the gate. At a banquet honoring the team for winning the 1941 NNL pennant, Jackson announced that for the first time in eight years the Grays had wound up in the black.[8] The amount of profit is difficult to determine, partly because of the nebulous connection between Jackson's numbers income and the ball club's financial records. In 1942 the team drew 170,000 paid admissions to Griffith Stadium; and being a far superior club to the Washington Senators, who were perennial cellar dwellers in the American League, many white as well as black fans helped the Grays to draw 25,000–30,000 spectators to an attractive league hook-up.[9]

During World War II, black baseball attained a new plateau of prosperity. The relatively high take-home pay of workers boosted by overtime, Office of Price Administration restrictions on travel, and limited recreational alternatives created a larger than usual pool of potential fans. Black baseball played to over three million fans in 1942, making it, as Cum Posey argued, the largest black enterprise in the world except for the insurance companies.[10]

If the war years brought the Grays unprecedented financial success, they also witnessed renewed challenges to the team's hold over their players and the Pittsburgh territory. The first threat came from the armed services, which drafted a handful of players and scared several others, including player-manager Vic Harris, into defense plant jobs.[11] A second challenge came from the Mexican League, which lured Josh Gibson and pitchers Roy Partlow and Terris McDuffie south of the border for a season or two.

In July 1943 the appearance of Mexican Consul A. J. Guina at Forbes Field led to a scuffle and Sonnyman Jackson's arrest. Guina had gone to the ballpark to talk to the Grays' Howard Easterling and Sam Bankhead, who had agreed to terms with Mexican ball clubs. The Mexican Embassy in Washington had handled all the necessary immigration matters, and the government had sent representatives to the border to meet the two men and escort them to Mexico City, but the players never showed up. Guina had come to find out why; he also planned to offer contracts to Josh Gibson and Buck Leonard. When he got to the park, he made the mistake of asking Jackson where he could find Easterling and Bankhead. Hearing Guina's accent and suspicious of anyone inquiring about his players, Jackson asked Guina if he was Mexican. The startled Guina, not realizing who Jackson was, explained that he was a representative of the Mexican government, at which point he was forcefully ejected from the ballpark. Jackson was arrested for his part in the altercation, and he later declared, "I don't care if they send Pancho Villa, they're not going to get my ballplayers."[12]

Gus Greenlee Returns to Black Baseball

A far more serious threat to the Homestead Grays came from an old foe, Gus Greenlee, who decided it was time to reenter the world of black baseball. After losing Greenlee Field, light-heavyweight champ John Lewis, and his brother Jack, it certainly did seem, as one journalist put it, that Dame Misfortune had decided to camp overtime on Gus's doorstep. But the man "who brought promotion of Negro sports out of the yokel class and placed it in the bigger time" was not an easy man to keep down.[13] In April 1940, little more than a year after he had resigned both the presidency of the NNL and the Crawfords, Gus confessed to Wendell Smith, "I'd like to get back in baseball because I know I can make a go of it in Pittsburgh. . . . I will build my team back up again by starting out with some of these youngsters around here."[14] Pointing out that his old club had evolved from a bunch of youths playing ball for the Crawford Bath House, Greenlee argued that the "kids could do it again." Infused with the spirit of spring training, he called for ballplayers to contact him to try out for a reorganized Pittsburgh Crawfords team. Little came of his efforts that spring, but in subsequent years he applied to both the NNL and the NAL for league franchises.[15]

Greenlee attended NNL meetings and wrote repeatedly to the NAL requesting a franchise for a revived Pittsburgh Crawfords. His many appeals were rejected, mostly because Cum Posey did not want a rival competing for fans and players in the Pittsburgh area. Greenlee realized during the summer of 1944 that no matter how persuasive his pitch, neither league was going to offer him admission, and he thus vowed to "expose the deplorable conditions of organized Negro baseball and wipe out the men who are ruining it." With his resurrected Crawfords playing semipro ball, Greenlee began raiding Negro League ball clubs, plucking players off the rosters of the Homestead Grays, the Chicago American Giants, and the Baltimore Black Sox. He arrived in Chicago on the eve of the 1944 East-West Classic and allegedly met with a number of the all-stars, urging them to demand a higher cut for their participation in the game. When the Eastern squad subsequently told the game's promoters that they would play only if paid $200 each, league officials blamed Greenlee for fomenting dissent.[16]

If his appearance in Chicago caused a stir, Greenlee's maneuvering over the winter months threw the Negro Leagues into a panic. A struggle began, with control over black baseball the prize. Denied a franchise, Gus built a rival league instead: the United States League (USL), which operated in 1945 and 1946 with franchises in Pittsburgh, Brooklyn, Chicago, Boston, Detroit, Cleveland, Philadelphia, and Toledo, although not all at the same time. Headquartered over the Crawford Grill, the USL listed attorney John Shackleford as its president and Gus Greenlee as vice-president; however, Gus was the force behind the league's formation and its actual operation. The USL lasted but two seasons, with the Crawfords taking honors the second year with a 64–20 record.

There was a strong USL–Pittsburgh connection. Not only were the Crawfords based in Pittsburgh, but many of the league's players were from the city, too. Beltzhoover's Ralph Mellix managed the Brooklyn Brown Dodgers, and Gabe Patterson, Willie Pope, Howard Kimbo, and Eudie Napier were among a score of black Pittsburghers on the rosters of USL teams. Bobby Williams, who had managed Greenlee's Crawfords in 1932 and then had settled in Pittsburgh, again took over the manager's job for the Crawfords.[17]

The Integration of the Major Leagues

While Gus Greenlee was the league's progenitor, its unlikely godfather was Branch Wesley Rickey, then part-owner and general manager of the Brooklyn Dodgers. Rickey had traveled from a devoutly Methodist household on a small farm in southern Ohio to the front offices of the St. Louis Browns in 1913 after brief stays in the majors, the ranks of college coaching, and the legal profession. A few years later he went across town to join forces with the St. Louis Cardinals. In 1919 he bought half-interest in the Fort Smith, Arkansas, minor league club and started the Cardinals on their way, building a baseball empire that linked thirty-two clubs and almost 700 players in baseball's first farm system. Rickey acquired a reputation as white baseball's most innovative executive and probably its shrewdest one, too. Few players looked forward to sitting across the table from him at contract negotiation time.[18]

In 1942 Rickey became the chief executive of the Brooklyn Dodgers, accepting a quarter-ownership in the team as compensation. Three years later, in early May 1945, he called a press conference at which he publicly committed himself and the Dodger organization to Gus Greenlee's United States League. Expressing an interest in the welfare of black baseball, Rickey declared to the packed room that "there does not exist in a true sense such a thing as organized Negro baseball."[19] The USL, he argued, could fill the void. Pledging support for Greenlee's venture, Rickey offered the league permission to play in Ebbetts Field and any of the twenty-two parks controlled by the Brooklyn Dodgers farm system.[20] His open disavowal of the NNL and NAL put them on notice that the USL was out to take their play away. Indeed, Newark Eagles' owner Effa Manley, who attended Rickey's press conference, proceeded to pepper him with questions about his sudden interest in black baseball. Manley and the Negro League owners were not the only ones who were upset. Clark Griffith, owner of the Washington Senators, made a considerable sum by leasing his ballpark to the Homestead Grays. He challenged Rickey's right to "set himself up as the czar of Negro baseball," a refrain echoed by the black press, which distrusted Rickey as simply another white man moving in on black baseball.[21]

Six months later, on October 29, 1945, Rickey announced that the Brooklyn Dodgers earlier had signed Jackie Robinson to a contract and had sent him to their Montreal Royals farm club. The baseball world was stunned. Robinson, a young infielder with the Kansas City Monarchs, was the first black man to play organized ball with whites since a color line had been drawn through baseball in the 1890s. Rickey himself would occupy a place in black American history next to that of the Great Emancipator.

Branch Rickey did little to discourage his newfound image as the white man who had integrated baseball. Not long after signing Robinson, he told a *Look* magazine editor, "I cannot face my God much longer knowing that His black creatures are held separate and distinct from His white creatures in the game that has given me all my own."[22] He often described the vow he had made, as baseball coach at Ohio Wesleyan, to his team's black catcher, who had been refused accommodations at a South Bend hotel: he promised that if he could ever do anything about baseball's color line, he would.[23]

Keeping that promise was not the only thing behind Rickey's actions. Clearly, he wanted to integrate the major leagues but in a way that would offer the Brooklyn Dodgers first crack at the enormous pool of black talent previously off-limits to white organized ball. In January 1943, soon after taking over the

Dodgers' helm, Rickey addressed its board of directors, arguing that the team was aging and that they should engage in an extensive scouting program to enlist a large number of young players to revamp the team. Most teams had allowed their operations to shrink during the war years, but Rickey proposed a bold, expansive program that would allow the Dodgers to reign as National League champions in the late 1940s and early 1950s. He closed his address to the board by stating that he wanted to scout black baseball players as part of his plans. When George McLaughlin, chairman of the board and president of the Brooklyn Trust Company, which owned a controlling interest in the team, agreed, Rickey began to work toward the eventual integration of organized ball.[24]

His participation in the USL thus should be seen in this context. Rickey spent over $35,000 during the next few seasons scouting black talent, including future stars Roy Campanella and Don Newcombe, as a few trusted associates appraised potential recruits. It was during this time that Greenlee and Rickey met and began to discuss the possibilities of breaking the color line. Gus argued that blacks could play major league ball and pointed out the possible advantages to the club that first signed them: they would not only gain access to considerable talent but to large numbers of paying black customers. In Rickey, who had already committed himself to a course of action that would result in integration, Greenlee found a willing listener.[25]

Rickey's participation in the USL screened his true motives from other owners who were subsequently taken by surprise and left behind in the ensuing scramble for black talent. His connections with the USL gave him access to black players and recognition in the black community. By sponsoring a rival league, Rickey had furthered divisions among the owners of black ball clubs. While the USL hardly lasted two seasons, its very existence detracted from both the NNL and the NAL and cost them players and gate receipts. By denying the legitimacy of the Negro Leagues, Rickey also laid the groundwork for what became a policy of signing black players from Negro League teams without compensating the teams for them. Lastly, the USL attracted fairly wide press coverage, which helped foster an atmosphere more conducive to bringing blacks into the majors.[26]

When the United States League folded, Greenlee and other team backers were able to absorb the financial losses. But the league had upset the already tenuous control that the Negro Leagues exerted over black baseball and left them vulnerable to the onslaught that followed the crossing of the color line. Gus Greenlee's last venture in baseball was a fiscal failure, but it served as a prelude to the integration of the national pastime.

The End of an Era in Black Sport

The death knell of black baseball was sounding. Gus Greenlee's reentry into the game had kindled another patronage fight with Cum Posey's Homestead Grays. Unlike their first battle in the early 1930s, Posey won this one but lost fans and players in the process. Furthermore, the Negro League teams as a whole suffered attendance losses and a decline in credibility as they juggled schedules in an attempt to combat USL competition.[27] The Grays fell to third place in the NNL in 1946 and into the second division the following year. Although they rebounded to win the NNL championship in 1948, they, like the rest of organized black ball, were on the ropes.

On Thursday, March 28, 1946, black baseball lost its most perspicacious leader, as Cum Posey succumbed to a lingering illness at the age of fifty-three. "In his death," John L. Clark wrote, "the race lost one of its most dynamic citizens, baseball lost its best mind, [and] Homestead lost its most loyal booster."[28] Thousands of friends of both races paid tribute as Posey's body lay in state, a final salute, sportswriter Ches Washington wrote, to "the sagacious sportsman who made the Homestead Grays as magic a name in the baseball world as Joe Louis in the fistic firmament."[29] Homestead declared a school holiday on the day of his funeral; and the basketball squad wired his widow, Ethel Posey, on the eve of their state championship game that they would try to "win this one for Cum."[30] City leaders and local and national sports figures joined in a chorus of praise. At the funeral, Pittsburgh Mayor David L. Lawrence, Allegheny County Commissioner John Kane, and other local politicians sat with the leaders of black Pittsburgh, Homestead's entire school board, Pittsburgh Steeler owner Art Rooney, scores of athletes,

Gus Greenlee, NAL President J. B. Martin, and hundreds of black Pittsburghers. The ten pallbearers were mostly Posey's old friends and fellow athletes, black and white, and his twenty-three honorary pallbearers included Rooney and Josh Gibson.[31]

Later that summer the Grays clashed with the Baltimore Elite Giants in a game dedicated to Cum Posey. A large portion of the gate was used to establish the Cum Posey Scholarship Fund, to help western Pennsylvania scholar-athletes attend college. The Frogs Club attended en masse to pay homage to their deceased fraternal brother, and during the seventh inning stretch the audience stood in silent tribute to the man who had meant so much to black sport both in Pittsburgh and the nation.[32]

A few years later, Posey's native Homestead paid him one last honor, naming their new athletic facility the Cumberland W. Posey Memorial Field House. Dedication ceremonies were conducted at half-time of a football game between Homestead and Braddock, a mill town on the Monongahela River. The keynote address that night was "Democracy in Action." Black and white players lined up on both sides of the line of scrimmage.[33]

On January 20, 1947, only weeks after celebrating his thirty-fifth birthday, Josh Gibson died. An athlete dying young has always evoked a sense of tragedy, but Gibson's untimely death was especially poignant. He had been in physical decline for several seasons: his knees had long given him trouble, but every catcher expects that; excessive drinking and what might have been hypertension hurt him even more, however, and there also were allegations of hard drug use.[34] While playing for Santurce in Puerto Rico during the winter of 1945–46, Gibson was temporarily committed to a sanatorium after being found dazed and confused on the streets of San Juan. His weight dropped considerably over the next year and by January 1947 he was suffering from an acute case of bronchitis. A severe headache caused him to take to his bed on January 19. He died after midnight, probably as a result of a stroke. What effect the signing of Jackie Robinson and a number of other NNL players in 1945 and 1946 had on him is impossible to tell. While happy to see the color line crossed, Gibson must have felt bitterness at being passed over by the white major leagues. He had been black baseball's premier hitter for over a decade, but it is likely he was considered too old to be brought into organized ball.

Lacking both their helmsman and their best hitter, the Grays began to flounder. After Posey's death, Sonnyman Jackson took over most of the administrative tasks and Ethel Posey became the club's co-owner. When Jackson died in 1949, Ethel Posey and Helen Jackson operated the club together for a few months. But Helen, who had also taken over the management of her husband's record shop, jukebox business, and the Sky Rocket Cafe, soon persuaded Ethel to turn over their interest in the Grays to Seward ("See") Posey.

See Posey never fully emerged from his brother's shadow. As a youth he had played for the Homestead Grays and the Monticello and Loendi basketball teams, all of which his brother managed. During Gus Greenlee's first go-round with the Crawfords, See Posey served as the team's booking agent, and from 1937 until 1949 he was business manager and traveling secretary for the Grays. He ran the club in its last two seasons, but it was a losing proposition. The team he fielded was a weak reflection of the Grays' earlier squads, and in 1950, after losing an estimated $30,000 over the previous two years, See Posey announced the dissolution of the Homestead Grays. He died the following summer.[35]

Even if Cum Posey and Josh Gibson had lived, it is unlikely that the Grays could have survived much beyond 1950. The integration of the major leagues in April 1947 had plunged black baseball into an immediate crisis. The Grays were not the only victims. The Newark Eagles and the New York Black Yankees called it quits in 1948, and the NNL itself ceased operations at the end of that season. While a handful of clubs reverted to barnstorming and semipro ball, and the NAL continued into the 1950s, black baseball was soon history.

After the 1950 season Pittsburgh was without a black professional ball club. Rumors circulated that winter that the Crawfords were to re-form, perhaps picking up the pieces of the disbanded Grays, but nothing came of it.[36] Gus Greenlee retreated from black sport to the friendlier confines of the Crawford Grill, which he made into one of the top-grossing night spots in town. In 1948, at a banquet at the Loendi Club, the Business and Professional Association of Pittsburgh honored him as the outstanding local businessman of the year, citing his role in promoting better race relations and advancing the civic and economic status of blacks in Pittsburgh. But while the Grill was going strong, Gus ran into difficulty elsewhere. White numbers men carved pieces out of his operation and the federal government took him to court over unpaid income taxes. It is difficult to determine if Greenlee was forced out of the numbers game, voluntarily surrendered his territory to other blacks, or remained in the game until the end. Extensive discussions with his confidants and both active and retired numbers men have resulted in conflicting testimony. At any rate, Greenlee found himself in increasing financial trouble, and when a fire destroyed the Crawford Grill in 1951, it was rebuilt at a new location under new ownership. A parking lot for the city's largest indoor sports arena was eventually built where the original Grill stood. In early July 1952, Big Red died.[37]

The Sandlot's Demise

Black Pittsburgh sport, which possessed an elan rivaling that of any black community in the 1930s and 1940s, declined precipitously in the 1950s. As autonomous, black-controlled sport, it largely disappeared. Black Pittsburgh's loss was part of two interrelated trends revamping American sport: the first witnessed the general absorption of black athletes into the mainstream of American sport; the second saw a wholesale restructuring of sport as its professional and commercial components overwhelmed its more community-based elements. While these changes propelled black athletes to the forefront in subsequent years, the black community lost control over its sporting life in the process. The sandlots and the Negro Leagues disintegrated during the 1950s as American sport underwent a radical shakedown. For the Negro Leagues, these changes meant extinction; for sandlot, minor league ball, and club boxing, survival came only after massive self-liquidation.

By the end of the 1950s the Negro National League was a

corpse and the Negro American League was about to become one. The black sandlots, which annually had fielded a score of football and baseball teams in Pittsburgh from the 1920s on, were almost empty. The city's wider sandlot arena, which encompassed over 400 baseball and 100 football teams each season in the 1920s and 1930s, had also contracted. Minor league ball, whose 59 leagues played to over 41 million paying fans in 1949, had shrunk to 21 leagues playing before 12 million fans a decade later.[38] And local boxing clubs, which had nurtured generations of fighters and could be found in most inner-city neighborhoods, were about to go down for the count. No single assassin can be held accountable for the demise of the more community-oriented sectors of American sport, but a combination of integration, television, the surge in influence of professional/commercial sport, and changing community patterns was more than enough to restructure American sport.

When on October 29, 1945, it was announced that Jackie Robinson had signed a contract with the Dodgers' top farm club, the Montreal Royals, the *Pittsburgh Courier* argued that Robinson carried "the hopes, aspirations and ambitions of thirteen million black Americans heaped on his broad, sturdy shoulders."[39] The Negro Leagues, however, died with the integration of baseball. Organized ball first took their players, then their fans, and finally the attention of the black press after Robinson joined its ranks. The NNL perished within a few seasons, while the barely viable NAL played with fewer teams each year and was reduced to a burlesque style of ball to attract fans.

In taking the Negro Leagues' most talented players, organized white baseball often simply signed the players to contracts and refused to compensate the previous owners. Sometimes a black team received a small sum for a player worth five or ten times that amount, but protests could hardly be voiced too loudly without appearing to be against the integration of major league ball. Cum Posey and Sonnyman Jackson cried "thief and robber" when the Dodgers signed the Grays' ace hurler, John Wright, to a 1946 contract with the Montreal Royals. "We have invested a lot of money in Wright and Montreal should offer us some kind of financial compensation," Posey declared; Branch Rickey offered him nothing.[40] Effa Manley echoed Posey's sentiments as her Newark Eagles lost Larry Doby, Monte Irvin, and Don Newcombe.

Black players obviously could earn more in organized ball than in the foundering Negro Leagues, and, more important, playing major league ball had become the goal of many talented black athletes. Most veterans signed with major league teams but never made it out of the minors. Even there, however, they were usually better compensated that they would have been if they had remained with a black team. The Negro Leagues continued to turn out talented young players like Willie Mays, Hank Aaron, and Ernie Banks, only to see them sign on with major league clubs. As the 1950s progressed, the best young black players never even appeared in the Negro Leagues, entering instead the conduit to major league ball with their first contracts.

Losing their best players hurt at the gate, too, but even if the black teams had retained their top talent, they couldn't have held on to the black fans who wanted to see blacks in major league action. The Newark Eagles, 1946 NNL champions and winners of a dramatic seven-game Negro World Series against the Kansas City Monarchs that fall, entered the 1947 season with confidence. In the early part of the campaign they drew large crowds, barnstorming their way through the South and some border states. But when they played in Washington, D.C., Philadelphia, and New York, they soon discovered that the East had become Jackie Robinson country.

As the *Courier* put it, "Jackie's nimble, Jackie's quick, Jackie makes the turnstiles click."[41] Indeed, black fans turned out in record numbers whenever Robinson and the Dodgers were in town, deserting black teams in the process. With Robinson in the line-up, the Dodgers set National League attendance records at home and on the road during the 1947 season. To an extent, they became black America's team. In New York, black attendance at Ebbets Field increased 400 percent that season.[42] In Pittsburgh, a local black businessman organized a bloc of 500 fans to attend Robinson's first game at Forbes Field. "Anyone with the least bit of racial pride should join us and show Mr.

Rickey we are grateful," Sam Jackson explained. He added that
the demonstration of support for the Dodgers was directed at the
Pirates' general manager, too. "When he sees us out there at the
park, he may realize how much money he is missing by refusing
to sign Negro players to the Pirates."[43]

The Newark Eagles had drawn over 120,000 fans in 1946 but
managed only a little more than 57,000 in 1947 and 35,000 in
1948, losing $47,000 in the latter two seasons alone.[44] What
was true for the Eagles was true for most of the other NNL clubs.
The NAL, based in the Midwest, did not feel the crunch as
severely, although the East-West Classic, which had regularly
drawn 45,000–50,000 fans, had only half that many in 1949
and again in 1950. Buck Leonard summed it up: once black
players appeared in major league uniforms, "we couldn't draw
flies."[45]

Accompanying the loss of black players and the desertion of
their fans was the abandonment of the Negro Leagues' cause by
the black press, on whom they had depended for the coverage
that made it possible for black fans to follow black teams. Even
though most black newspapers were weeklies, they provided
their readers with at least some sense of continuity vital to
maintaining interest in a team during the long baseball season.
When black players entered the major leagues, however, the focus
of black press coverage shifted dramatically. The *Courier* and
other black papers chronicled Jackie Robinson's every move and
printed the statistics of black players in organized ball in
boldface type; coverage of the Negro League games declined
considerably. Symbolic of this shift of interest was the story in
the *Pittsburgh Courier* on October 16, 1948, informing black
Pittsburgh that the Homestead Grays had won what turned out
to be their final Negro World Series. The article, two paragraphs
long, was virtually hidden among a cluster of stories about
blacks in the major leagues.[46]

Integration also affected other levels of black sport, as black
colleges and sandlot teams found themselves in competition
with white colleges and teams for black players and fans. The
more skilled among the black athletes gravitated to predominantly white teams, and as they began to star in the Big 10, the

PAC 8, and other major conferences, black fans changed their allegiances accordingly.

The Integration of Pittsburgh Sport

The Pirates and the Steelers always had a following in black Pittsburgh, but until the 1960s they could hardly consider themselves black Pittsburgh's teams. The black community was more involved with the Grays, the Crawfords, and sandlot teams in general, whose games they attended in greater numbers than those of the Pirates and the Steelers. The *Courier* usually mentioned the Pirates and the Steelers only in conjunction with black athletes or racial matters. But the demise of the Negro Leagues and sandlot ball left the Pirates and the Steelers just about the only games in town. Black attendance increased at Pirate games following Jackie Robinson's arrival and the initial appearances of black players in Pirate uniforms. *Courier* coverage increased, too. Most telling of all, black Pittsburghers began following and talking about the Pirates in ways that showed they finally thought of them as their team. That represented a swing of historic proportions. Integration, the decline of a sandlot alternative, and the remarkable record of blacks in Pittsburgh's pro sports meant the Pirates and the Steelers could finally claim to truly be Pittsburgh's team.[47]

The Pirates

Pittsburgh's major league baseball team was slow to integrate, despite the efforts of the *Courier,* the hiring of Branch Rickey as the Pirates' general manager in 1951, and the team's dismal record on the field in the early 1950s. From the 1920s through the 1940s the Pirates rented Forbes Field to the Grays and the Crawfords, but that was the extent of their relationship with local black teams. Franchise owners Barney Dreyfuss and Bill Benswanger considered Cum Posey their friend and welcomed black patrons to their park, but neither man moved to add a black player to the squad. Black sportwriters, players, and fans fantasized about a match between the Pirates and a top black team, but the Pirates were either reluctant to risk defeat or unwilling to share the spotlight. Such a game probably would have drawn well and vastly improved black baseball's stature, but like the rest of organized white ball, the Pirates showed little interest in helping black baseball.

The Pirate owners were painfully aware of the talent to be had beyond the racial boundary that divided black and white ball, but they made no attempt to tap it. Instead, they sat in their box seats and wondered what it would be like to have Martin Dihigo, Cool Papa Bell, or Smokey Joe Williams in their line-up. In 1933 William Benswanger wrote the *Courier*: "I have seen any number of [Negro League] games and was impressed with the ability of some of the players. Such men as Charleston, Gibson, Washington, Scales and Cannady and other appeared to be of highest calibre and WORTHY OF THE HIGHEST IN BASEBALL."[48] THE *Courier* noted his comments with satisfaction but frequently chided the team for not integrating its ranks. When the Pirates were slumping, a not infrequent occurrence in Benswanger's tenure, the *Courier* delighted in suggesting they sign Josh Gibson and company.[49]

After Cum Posey was elected secretary-treasurer of the NNL in 1938, he and Ches Washington sounded out Benswanger on the racial question. "I've seen lots of colored clubs play," Benswanger told them. "In fact, I watched almost every game involving colored teams at Forbes Field for many years. I've seen several players who appear to be just as good as many of our men in organized ball." Benswanger agreed that the day would come when blacks would be admitted to the major leagues, and he assured them, "If the question of admitting colored ball players into organized ball becomes an issue, I would be heartily in favor of it. I think that colored people should have an opportunity in baseball just as they have an opportunity in anything else."[50]

Benswanger did not volunteer to lead the way, however, and the *Courier* maintained pressure on him and the rest of white baseball by keeping the issue before its readers. In 1939 it interviewed players and coaches from each of the National League teams, one of their motives being to rebut the assertion commonly leveled by defenders of the color line that white players were against integration. The *Courier* interviews indicated otherwise. The final story in the series dealt with the opinions of eight Pittsburgh coaches and players, most of whom had played against blacks, either on the sandlots or in the California winter leagues, in the Caribbean, or on barnstorming tours. These men overwhelmingly endorsed the quality of their black opponents and each named a handful he thought were of major league caliber. Pirates' Manager Pie Traynor stated, "If given permission, I would certainly use a Negro player who had the ability." But he neither sought nor was granted permission to do so.[51]

Three years later, in August 1942, Benswanger became the center of a controversy when he reportedly agreed to conduct tryouts for three black players. He subsequently reneged on his offer when an article appeared in the *Daily Worker,* the Communist party newspaper, naming the three players. Benswanger angrily told the *Courier,* "The sports editor of the *Daily Worker* put words in my mouth. He called me and asked me what my stand was on the question of Negro players in the major leagues. I told him I was all for it." But, Benswanger protested, he had not stipulated any particular players nor agreed definitely to a tryout. The *Courier* reported that Benswanger was "still willing and ready to give a Negro player a chance on the Pirate team," but he would not let the *Daily Worker* name the players, preferring the *Courier's* recommendations. Benswanger suggested that the paper submit four names for a late-summer tryout. The *Courier* went to work, scrutinizing a list of 200 black players.[52]

Sensing an unprecedented coup, the paper praised Benswanger effusively as "a man who has the courage of his convictions . . . the greatest liberal in baseball history."[53] But the tryouts were never conducted. Benswanger later claimed that Cum Posey had persuaded him to call them off, arguing that integration would kill the Negro Leagues.[54] The *Courier's* praise soon turned to scorn, and when Benswanger, commenting on the integration of baseball in 1950, implied that he had tried to break the color line years before Branch Rickey finally had, sportswriter Wendell Smith called him "an unmitigated storyteller" and "baseball's #1 phony."[55]

The sale of the Pirates in 1946 to a four-man syndicate ultimately headed by real estate magnate John Galbreath was welcomed by black Pittsburgh as a possible step toward integration. Bing Crosby's seat on the new board was especially well received because of the actor's participation in movies and records with black entertainers.[56] But when the Pirates moved slowly in racial matters, the new ownership's honeymoon with hopeful black fans ended quickly and the *Courier's* criticisms resumed. The management argued that they would eventually bring a black player up through their farm system, but they could not convince black sportswriters that their search for talent was sincere.[57]

Blacks finally entered the Pittsburgh farm system in the early 1950s. The club could not help but notice that the National League teams winning pennants in those days were using blacks. Moreover, with Branch Rickey as general manager from 1951 to 1955, the team was being led by the man who had first breached the color line. Why it took Rickey three years to insert a black player in the line-up is difficult to ascertain. Perhaps he was waiting for someone who met certain of his standards. His first choice, at any rate, was less than successful.

On April 13, 1954, a black man in a Pirate's uniform, second baseman Curt Roberts, slashed a ball into the gap in Forbes Field and wound up on third in his first major league at-bat.[58] The twenty-four-year-old handled his second-base position competently but hit only .232 that year. His main nemesis was the curve ball, but off-the-field racial pressures could not have helped. Roberts hung on with the Pirates but played in only six games in 1955 and thirty-one in 1956 before being released. The *Courier* demanded to know, "Who 'Killed' Curt Roberts?": "Who's to blame? Is it Bobby Bragan [the manager]? Joe Brown [the general manager]? Branch Rickey Jr.? Who cut the hog that finally resulted in Curt Roberts, Pirate infielder, being sold down the river while the team was taking its dive on the toboggan? There are thousands of Pittsburgh fans who just can't keep from mumbling, 'Who killed Curt Roberts?' "[59]

While many agreed Roberts was not given much of a chance, his dismissal did not mean a return to segregation by the Pirates, for Roberts clearly lost his job to a better hitter. The club brought up two young black men from the Caribbean for the 1955 season: Roman Mejias of Rio Damuji, Cuba, played parts of six seasons with the Pirates; and joining him in the outfield was a lithe twenty-year-old from Carolina, Puerto Rico, by the name of Roberto Clemente.

When the Pirates finally climbed out of the cellar in the late 1950s and brought the championship banner back to Forbes Field in 1960, they did it with a mostly white team; only Clemente, Gene Baker, and Joe Christopher were black. But the next Pittsburgh championship team reflected the emergence of blacks on the squad. The 1971 Pirates won the World Series in seven games, becoming only the sixth club to ever come back from a two-games-to-none deficit. They did it with an international line-up featuring players from Panama, Cuba, Venezuela, Puerto Rico, and the United States, and a team that was over 40 percent black. The team leader, Clemente, made the series his showcase to the world.

Roberto Clemente had endured both racial hostility and relative neglect throughout his first fifteen years in the major leagues. He slowly won over the fans, however, and they came to see his flamboyance not as showboating but as a natural expression of his verve. In the 1971 series Clemente batted .414, hitting safely in all seven games; on the field he played like a man possessed. Footage of him snaring a fly in right field, whirling, and throwing out a runner at third appears in more than a few series highlight films.

The baseball world finally took note of Clemente after the 1971 series, but he was to play only one more season. In 1972, when an earthquake devastated Managua, Nicaragua, Clemente organized relief efforts in Puerto Rico. After discovering that Nicaraguan dictator Anastasio Somoza was plundering the relief supplies, Clemente decided to fly to Nicaragua to personally oversee their distribution. He left in a small plane on December 31, 1972. The aircraft plunged into the Caribbean soon after take-off, and Clemente's body was never recovered. Pittsburgh was in shock; Puerto Rico was in mourning.

Ironically, Clemente achieved two breakthroughs in what was his last season of play. Pittsburgh finally recognized his special qualities as a player and packed recently constructed Three Rivers Stadium for a fan appreciation night for him. And on the closing day of the season, Clemente joined that very select group of players who had tallied 3,000 hits in their careers. In his last at-bat he connected for a double and stood proudly on second base as the fans rose to cheer his 3,000th, and final, hit. Pittsburgh's recognition of Clemente illustrated not only the changed attitudes of black Pittsburghers toward the Pirates but also that many, perhaps most, white fans were capable of unabashedly cheering for a black man as their representative. More than a few white Pittsburghers cried on hearing of Clemente's death.[60]

The Steelers

When Art Rooney's Pittsburgh Steelers made it to football's promised land in the 1970s, they did so with an abundance of black talent. Rooney's first sandlot team, the Hope-Harveys, included a black player from the Northside, Rudy Cole; when Rooney formed the Steelers, he signed another black, Ray Kemp. Kemp had grown up in Cecil, a small coalmining town west of Pittsburgh, playing both soccer and football in the mostly immigrant community. A walk-on at Duquesne University, Kemp won a football scholarship and played on the team between 1929 and 1932. Rooney recruited Kemp for his J. P. Rooneys, a semipro team named after his brother, an aspiring politician who had starred at the University of Pittsburgh before playing ball for Art. In 1933 the team was renamed the Pirates (and eventually renamed the Steelers) and entered the National Football League.[61]

Ray Kemp played parts of two seasons for Rooney, but after he was released the Steelers became an all-white squad for the better part of the next two decades. There was no official, public policy banning blacks from the NFL, but during the 1930s the league nonetheless became an all-white enclave. The *Courier* tried to make the Steelers aware of players who could have made the grade, but to no avail. Wendell Smith highlighted the exploits of Herb Trawick, a Schenley High graduate who wound up playing pro ball in Canada, where he was named the Canadian League's outstanding lineman in 1946. "How about it, Dr. Sutherland?" Smith asked the Steeler coach; he got no reply.[62]

The Steelers remained without black players until the league as a whole began to integrate following the challenge posed by the rival All-American Football Conference after World War II. By the time of the two leagues' merger in 1950 segregation became a thing of the past in football. The number of black players remained relatively small, though, until another league jeopardized the NFL's hegemony in the 1960s. The American Football League posed a serious threat because of its television network backing and its effective use of black players. By the time these two leagues merged for the 1966 season, black players had arrived center-stage in pro football.

Black players like Alcorn A&M running back Jack Spinks and Pitt quarterback Henry Ford played briefly with the Steelers in the 1950s, and black all-pros John Henry Johnson and Gene ("Big Daddy") Lipscomb starred in the 1960s, but the Steelers remained a mediocre club. Their dramatic turnaround in the 1970s, however, was in large part the result of their successful scouting of the small black colleges that produced Frank Lewis, John Stallworth, Mel Blount, Ernie Holmes, L. C. Greenwood, and Dwight White, and their drafting of players like Joe Greene, Franco Harris, and Lynn Swann from integrated universities.

Basketball

The integration of Pittsburgh sport did not necessarily reflect greater integration in Pittsburgh. Neighborhoods and schools were becoming more segregated in the 1950s despite break-throughs in sport. There was one sport, however, over which the black community retained greater control. During the 1950s basketball provided both a transition from the black sandlots to integrated scholastic and pro sport and a harbinger of its preeminence as the city game in the 1960s. Basketball's heyday in black Pittsburgh occurred prior to the depression, when Cum Posey's Monticellos and his Loendi team put the city's game on a par with that of any urban locale. But during the 1930s and 1940s, when the New York Renaissance and then the Harlem Globetrotters dominated black basketball, Pittsburgh offered only a handful of semipro squads that no longer were nationally competitive. The game was more an off-season interlude between football and baseball than anything else. The *Courier,* the YMCA, and black social clubs sponsored teams but not as money-making ventures.

What basketball could offer black youth became more apparent during the early 1950s when local athletes began to parley their skills into college scholarships and then professional careers. The man who led the way was Westinghouse High School's Charles Cooper, an All-American at Duquesne University who broke into the ranks of the NBA in 1950 as the league's first black player. "Cooper was an inspiration to us," Homewood's Ed Fleming recalled more than thirty years later.[63] At that time city basketball was still largely dominated by white players. Fleming and Maurice Stokes, co-captains of Westinghouse's 1951 city championship team, were the only two black starters on the squad. But both received scholarships, Fleming to Niagara University and Stokes to St. Francis. Moreover, Duquesne, then a national basketball powerhouse, had black stars Sihugo Green and Jim Tucker on the roster. All four of these players joined Cooper in the pros. Stokes, his white college teammate Jack Twyman, who had played high school ball for Pittsburgh Central Catholic, and Fleming were the Rochester Royal's top three draft choices in 1955.

Fleming played five years of pro ball, with Rochester and then the Minneapolis Lakers, but each summer found him back in Pittsburgh playing sandlot basketball. When he and Stokes were in high school they had played at Homewood Park each summer in a never-ending series of pick-up games in which the winners kept the court to be challenged by the next five players. Despite its sewer grates and obstructing poles and walls, "it was the best there was at that time."[64] When Mellon Park, on the border of East Liberty, Squirrel Hill, and Shadyside, opened, Stokes and Fleming began making the trek from Homewood each day. "It was a long walk for us to get there but when we did, it was pure basketball against the best the city could offer."[65]

Mellon Park was both newer and larger and became the mecca for the city's top high school, college, and professional players in the 1950s and 1960s. From early morning until evening, fifty or more players battled in games of ten buckets. "The asphalt got so hot you'd have to take your shoes off," Fleming remembered, but "guys came to play ball and that was it. There were never any problems. It was one heck of an experience." The ratio of black to white players was about two to one, and games were rarely marred by racial tension.[66]

Fleming recalls the competition getting better each summer that he was back from college and then the pros. The earlier

generation of professional ballplayers was later joined by Connie
Hawkins, John Brisker, Kenny Durrett, and Maurice Lucas.
Pittsburgh Pirate shortstop Dick Groat, a Swissvale native, often
brought a team of players over. University of Pennsylvania star
and Rhodes scholar John Wideman, one of Pittsburgh's finest
contemporary writers, also played there, as did *Courier* writer
Bill Nunn, Jr., and a host of local collegiate and high school
players. "They played," Fleming recalled "for the sheer love of the
game."

The presence of a growing number of black college and pro
players undoubtedly lent basketball greater credibility in black
Pittsburgh, as did the increasing national exposure blacks were
gaining in the game during the 1950s. Fleming recounted the
days when he and Maurice Stokes would borrow Chuck
Cooper's Olds 98 convertible to drive over to Mellon Park for a
game. "The chance to play with guys who had made it in the
pros during the summers at Mellon Park—to sit and talk with
them—was important," he said. That and the accessibility of
gyms and outdoor courts, as well as the relative inexpensiveness
of playing basketball, Fleming reasoned, help to explain its rise
as the city game in black Pittsburgh during the 1960s.

In 1954 Fifth Avenue won the city championship with four
black players in the starting line-up. The high school for much of
the Hill, Fifth Avenue had a mostly black student body and
fielded all-black teams by the late 1950s. Its championship teams
in 1961 and 1962 started five black players, including standouts
"Flippy" Reynolds and Aldon Lawson. Fifth Avenue and Schenley, another Hill high school, vied for the city title over the next
decade. Schenley's 1965, 1966, and 1967 championship squads
featured future pro Kenny Durrett and Josh Gibson's grandson
Pete. Schenley returned to form in 1970 with Jeep Kelley, Ricky
Coleman, and Maurice Lucas. In 1971 the trio led the team to
the state championship.

During the 1960s, however, the emphasis shifted from sandlot
basketball to summer league play. A number of suburban districts organized summer league competition and Carl Kohlman
started the Ozanam League in the city. These leagues institu-
tionalized the Mellon Park approach for high school and, in later
years, college players. A fairly active set of winter and summer

leagues ensures that those who desire to play basketball long after their scholastic or pro careers are over can do so. Basketball, in some ways, is the last of the sandlot sports still evident in Pittsburgh.[67]

The integration of major college and professional sport was only part of the demise of the sandlots and the Negro Leagues. It primarily signaled the end of black control over black athletes and teams. An even larger factor in the decline of community-based sport was the ascendancy of television.[68]

Sport and the One-Eyed Monster

Minor league baseball felt the impact of television most directly, shrinking from fifty-nine to twenty-one leagues within the decade of the 1950s. Not only the size of minor league ball changed but its locus of control did, too. For most of the century minor league baseball had been a community affair, linked to organized baseball through territorial and player control agreements but largely oriented toward local audiences and local ownership. By the 1960s most of the surviving clubs were part of major league farm systems, with policy and personnel decisions being made by the parent organizations.

Minor league baseball had never been primarily geared toward profits. A study of minor league teams in 1950 revealed that almost two-thirds operated at a loss.[69] A survey of 2,287 officers and directors of minor league teams the following year found that only 291 of them, less than 13 percent, made their living from baseball; the rest included small businessmen, attorneys, farmers, doctors, and housewives. These "public-spirited people . . . who are interested in building their town," Colorado Senator and Western League President Edwin Johnson offered, "take their losses and they take them cheerfully, and they are glad to do it because it is all done in the interests of the community."[70] "Our minor-league clubs," George Trautman, president of the National Association of Professional Baseball Leagues (NAPBBL; i.e., the minors), added, "for the most part, are the result of community effort and pride. They are not profitmaking organizations."[71]

Community involvement in minor league teams had more in

common with sandlot and semipro baseball than with major league ball. When television undercut the minors' attendance in the early 1950s, a core of townspeople often rallied behind their teams. A Buffalo, N.Y., club sold 182,000 shares at one dollar a share to over 2,600 local shareholders, rescuing the franchise from bankruptcy. Similar efforts were mounted in Wilson, N.C., Columbus, Ohio, and Rochester, N.Y.[72]

But these teams were exceptions to the television-induced decimation of minor league ball in the 1950s. Organized baseball (i.e., the two major leagues and the NAPBBL) recognized as early as the 1930s that broadcasting could seriously affect its product's marketability, and in 1936 Commissioner Kenesaw Mountain Landis ruled that clubs could not broadcast in another team's territory. A decade later, rule 1(d) prevented a major league team from broadcasting its game by radio or television in a minor league club's territory without the latter's consent. Organized baseball felt that radio and, increasingly, television would keep fans from going to the games and tried to circumvent the threat. In 1949, rule 1(d) was amended to exclude broadcasts only during the hours of a minor league team's games. But in 1951, after warnings from the antitrust division of the Justice Department, the rule was repealed and no new rule offered in its stead. The impact on minor league baseball was devastating.[73]

Attendance plummeted, with the drop most severe at the B, C, and D levels of the minors.[74] Even Class A International League stalwarts Jersey City and Newark succumbed, in their cases to broadcasts from New York. Scores of teams and leagues across the land did likewise. National League President Ford Frick dolefully remarked that allowing a Yankee game to come into a town like Keokuk, Iowa, when its own club was playing is like "forcing us to eat our own young."[75] Hartford, Conn., saw its team's attendance drop from 109,000 in 1952 to 36,000 a year later; Albany, N.Y., from 198,000 to 98,000.[76] "People," minor league president Trautman told Congress in 1958, "are having their baseball appetites satisfied by being what I call 21-inch alumni."[77]

Charley ("Brute") Kramer ran a minor league team in Oil City, Pa., in 1950. His independent team was winning the pennant against the major league farm teams in his league. "We're playing the Butler Yankees, a good club, one night but there's only about 400 people in my ball park. I got madder'n hell. I took my car and went down to the main part of town, parked my car and walked for about an hour. And everybody on the front porch had the Pirates game on. That's when I knew that the game was over."[78]

Minor league ball was not alone in its adverse reaction to television. The sandlots, too, lost out as their fans stayed home to watch televised games. Gil Gordon, whose Corsairs were one of black Pittsburgh's last sandlot elevens, simply pointed to his television set when asked what killed sandlot ball in Pittsburgh. His sentiments were echoed by a score of former sandlotters in the city. The president of the American Baseball Congress wrote Emanuel Celler, chairman of the House Subcommittee on the Study of Monopoly Power, in 1951 that "widespread broadcasting has reduced gate receipts on amateur baseball to a point where many teams can no longer afford to make up the necessary differences to maintain themselves. It is our belief that the widespread televising in the Greater New York area has driven as many as 40 percent of the rural teams from amateur baseball because of declining receipts, small as those receipts originally were. . . ."[79]

Television had a similar impact on boxing, almost totally wiping out local prizefighting in the postwar decade by inundating the market. After televised boxing caught on in 1946, fights were broadcast in some regions almost every night of the week. Between then and the demise of the "Friday Night Fight of the Week" in 1964, the fight game went from a business supported by live gates at some 300 small fight clubs and a score of larger arenas to an industry almost totally dependent on television for its audience and its financial support. While some fighters prospered, many found their careers prematurely ended. As Chris Dundee explained, "There always had to be a loser, and you couldn't bring back a loser because the sponsors wouldn't take him."[80] More important, the local boxing clubs where young fighters could develop their skills and mature lost their paying fans. Between 1952 and 1959 over 250 of the nation's 300 small fight clubs folded. Madison Square Garden, boxing's best-known forum, went from an average of 10,000–12,000 fans for a Friday night card in 1948 to barely 1,200 a decade later. When boxing returned to form in the Muhammad Ali era, it did so largely as a televised and closed-circuit broadcasting phenomenon.

National Collegiate Athletic Association (NCAA) football and major league baseball also reacted negatively at first to widespread television broadcasting. As the number of television sets in American homes went from 1 million in 1948 to 14 million in 1951, total attendance at NCAA football games dropped from 19.1 to 17.5 million, sending the NCAA into a panic. The University of Chicago's National Opinion Research Center concluded that controlled broadcasting of games cut attendance by over 26 percent, while unlimited television would lead to a drop of 40 percent. College ball did not regain its 1948 level of attendance until 1960.[81] Hardest hit were the smaller schools, of which over seventy dropped the sport in the first half of the 1950s.[82]

Major league baseball's first involvement with television was almost its last. Overall attendance fell from a 1948 high of about 21 million to 14.3 million in 1953, and some teams came perilously close to disaster as a result of having their home games televised. The Cleveland Indians saw home attendance fall by 67 percent between 1948 and 1956; the Boston Braves from 1,455,000 in 1948 to 281,278 in 1952, a drop of 81 percent.[83] But both major league baseball and the NCAA, unlike the minor leagues and the sandlots, overcame their initial troubles with television. Each, in fact, came to depend on broadcast revenues for an increasing share of its income.

Television has since irrevocably altered the economics of professional sport. *Sports Illustrated* writer William Johnson noted in 1970 that "TV made it all a new game."[84] In 1982, television and radio accounted for an estimated 58 percent of the NFL's revenues, 30 percent of major league baseball's, and 27 percent of the NBA's.[85] The NFL, whose 1982 negotiations with the three major networks led to a five-year, $1.9 billion pact distributed equally among the league's teams, has most effectively harnessed the economic power of television, while baseball is poised on the brink of long-term commitments to cable and pay-TV.

The enormous revenues that broadcasting pumped into the game were part of the reason that community-based sport withered while pro and college ball prospered. The NFL, which had seen thirty of forty-two franchises perish in its first three decades, attained unprecedented prosperity during the mid-1950s, mainly due to its newly found broadcast revenues.[86] Between 1952 and 1957 baseball's broadcast earnings increased by 70 percent as the number of television sets in the United States increased from 18 to 47 million.[87] During the 1960s these revenues climbed even higher. Rights to NCAA college football leaped from $3,125,000 to $12,000,000, combined network payments to major league baseball from $3,250,000 to $16,000,000, and pro football revenues from $7,600,000 in 1963 to $34,700,000 in 1969.[88] The figures have spiraled even higher with each renegotiation. Minnesota Twins president Calvin Griffith declared, "TV is a matter of life and death, that's all. We couldn't operate without it." *Sports Illustrated*'s Johnson captured the television-sport nexus when he wrote that during the 1960s, ". . . sport in America has come to be the stepchild of television and, in a sense, handmaiden to the vicissitudes of Madison Avenue."[89] But television was not the only reason that pro and college sport gained such a dominant position on the nation's sporting landscape.

The Hegemony of Major League Baseball

The major leagues, which had successfully repelled challenges by the Federal League early in the century and then Mexican baseball after World War II, sought and gained sway over baseball throughout the entire western hemisphere. They destroyed the Negro Leagues, and when rule 1(d) was abrogated they did not attempt to shelter the minors from the effects of the broadcast of major league games. Rather, the clubs rushed pell-mell into hundreds of broadcast agreements, saturating the baseball market and drastically reducing the size of minor league ball. At the same time the major leagues restructured their working relations with minor league clubs.

The goal was to increase control over minor league clubs by incorporating them and their players into major league farm systems. Through a draft of minor league players and new working agreements between minor and major league clubs, the latter enlarged the size of the player pools they controlled to an average of 400–500 players per team during the 1950s. The major leagues drove independently owned minor league teams out of existence in the process. In 1952, independents (i. e., minor league clubs locally owned and without a working agreement with a major league club) comprised 143 of 326 minor league teams; by 1956 they made up only 39 of the 197 surviving clubs, a drop from 43.8 percent to 19.8 percent.[90] "The interests of the independent owner," Dallas Baseball Club president R. W. Burnett told Congress in 1953, "is in conflict with and directly opposed to the interests of the major league chain operator. . . . The present deplorable plight of minor league ball did not 'just happen.' There are minor causes or problems . . . but in my opinion, the major causes of the unfavorable and deteriorating condition in which minor league baseball finds itself are directly traceable to . . . the determination of the major league clubs to dominate the game. . . ."[91]

Others reiterated Burnett's charges. *Milwaukee Journal* sports editor R. G. Lynch called for an end to the monopoly of sixteen major league owners who were "ruining baseball below the major league level."[92] The majors, he declared, had converted minor league teams into vassal states. The crux of the problem was that a major league team ran its farm teams for the benefit of the parent club, with little or no regard for the local community's allegiance to its minor league team. Player personnel shifts, often a mid-season decision, wreaked havoc with "civic pride, public confidence and . . . interest," Lynch charged, in addition to destroying the club's on-the-field chances. "And from my observation it is a completely self-serving operation. They are not operating the minor leagues for the good of baseball or for the good of competition in the minors. They are operating only to produce baseball players for themselves."[93] The president of the Central League warned that major league teams simply pulled their farm teams out of a town when they lost money. "I know this much, that they will not stay in a town unless they are making money. They will not stay like an independent fellow will and lose his money year after year."[94] The decline of independent minor league teams, virtually complete by the 1970s, meant the demise of the more community-oriented sector of minor league ball. Many communities lost their teams in the process.

A further aspect of major league ball's increased influence was the conclusion of working agreements with organized baseball in several Caribbean basin countries that effectively brought them under the majors' sway. Cuba, Mexico, Venezuela, Colombia, Puerto Rico, Panama, and the Dominican Republic were ultimately brought into the fold.[95] The working agreements, which controlled player movement between each country and the majors, made these foreign leagues more or less high-level minor league appendages of the majors. The new relationship coincided with the integration of major league ball and allowed the majors to more fully exploit the storehouse of Caribbean baseball talent without risking competition for players from these leagues.[96]

The NFL, the NBA, and the NCAA also solidified their positions in the 1950s. The NFL and the NBA were able to transform college ball into a farm system and in the 1960s successfully co-opted the challenges posed by the American Football League and the American Basketball Association. NCAA football, basketball, and baseball cut deeply into semipro sport as college-bound athletes decided not to risk compromising their amateur status through semipro or sandlot competition. While these bastions of organized sport prospered, sandlot and lesser-capitalized levels of sport faded.[97]

Rising Costs and Restructured Communities

Sandlot ball survives today only in a greatly reduced form. Many of those who ran teams in the 1940s and 1950s cited increasing costs and declining support as the immediate reasons for its downfall. "It made it tough," Terrace Village co-founder Jack Hopkins remembered. "The cost of doing it," his partner Harold Tinker agreed, "had a whole lot to do with its going downhill." "Equipment, transportation, medical insurance started skyrocketing," Pittsburgh Corsairs owner Gil Gordon explained. "There was no money to be made . . . and all the teams started dropping off."[98] Of the "several reasons why these teams have quit playing," *Courier* columnist Earl Johnson wrote in 1953, "the chief ones are a lack of funds and a lack of playing fields. Umpires, transportation and equipment are prohibitive to the average sandlot team."[99]

These sandlot organizers and their fellow activists blamed other factors, too. Several spoke in terms of changing communities and cultural patterns. "After World War II . . . a lot of people had good jobs and on the average, everybody's financial status and everybody's outlook on life was changed," Gil Gordon offered. "You lived in an alley before. After the Second World War, you could move onto the front street. And being in the service, fellas that had never been away from home got out in the world and learned more. You were in a cocoon before. They got in the service . . . and it changed their outlook." Furthermore, "a trend started of people moving to outlying areas . . . to the suburbs." Gordon's Corsairs, like so many other sandlot clubs, had been a close-knit group. "Here on the Northside, everybody had grown up together. This fella was going out with this other fella's sister and so on. You ate together and slept at each other's house. . . . Everybody more or less knew each other. . . . You partied together and jitterbugged together. . . . But then fellas started getting married off and having children, growing up, drifting apart."[100] Many moved away from the Northside and the team was finished.

Dr. James Stewart, who played on Homewood's sandlots before the war, also thought that "the communities dissolving" had much to do with sandlot's decline. "I remember when I came back from the war. I used to drive around and look for a ballfield because that would tell me where something was going on. If you couldn't find one, you'd know there was nothing holding [the community] together." He found far fewer than he had just a decade earlier.[101]

Chuck Klausing grew up in the Monongahela River valley and played semipro ball there after World War II. When he was football coach at Braddock High during the 1950s his integrated teams were the scourge of the valley. Klausing, head football coach at Carnegie-Mellon University before joining the Pitt staff in 1986, recalls the importance of sandlot ball during his youth.

Travel was difficult then. To go see the Pirates play was a streetcar
ride and no one had cars. But every Sunday afternoon our local
baseball team was our pride. And the plant baseball teams played
almost every night of the week. . . . During my era, we had no TV and
we enjoyed seeing a sandlot baseball game in the summer, a high school
or sandlot football game in the fall and an independent basketball
game in the winter. . . . It's my sense that until maybe even the '60s, it's
the sandlot and the high school teams that the people really care about,
much more so than the Pirates and the Steelers.[102]

Both black and white Pittsburghers were a part of these changing postwar community patterns. Although the black population
in Pittsburgh increased from 86,000 to over 100,000 between
1950 and 1960, Pittsburgh as a whole lost people, declining
from 677,000 to 604,000. Many whites were moving to suburban communities, often fleeing increasingly black inner city
neighborhoods. The Lower Hill, meanwhile, fell victim to re-
development. It was virtually leveled in the 1950s to erect a high-
rent, high-rise apartment building and the Civic Arena, a domed
sporting center. The end of the Lower Hill pushed black families
further up the Hill and into Homewood-Brushton, making each
neighborhood blacker. Homewood-Brushton, which had made
greater gains in terms of homeownership, occupational stability,
and neighborhood development than other black areas, had
trouble incorporating this influx.[103]

The automobile, a wider range of recreational options, and
people leaving their old communities all contributed to sandlot's
demise. Many teams had a life cycle of their own, and when
most of their players had reached an age of advancing respon-
sibilities and declining abilities, they folded. Few new teams were
there to replace them. In Pittsburgh, only a handful of sandlot
football and baseball clubs remained active into the 1980s.

The sporting impulse did not die as much as rechannel itself
elsewhere. High school, college, and organized youth programs
such as the Little League replaced the outlet sandlot offered to
earlier youth. In 1962 there were an estimated 99,500 baseball
teams across the country enrolled in Little League, Babe Ruth,
Pony League, American Legion, American Baseball Congress,
and high school and college programs.[104] Older brothers,

friends, and fathers often switched to slow-pitch softball, a tame substitute for baseball but one played by over 3,000 teams with 35,000–45,000 players annually in Allegheny County during the 1980s.[105] On the other hand, while a handful of semipro football teams have survived in the Northeast, mostly members of the 200-team Minor Professional Football Association, no effective replacement for sandlot football has developed.[106]

Black Sport: Past, Present, and Future

What have these changes meant for sport and the black community? Over the last thirty years racial barriers have crumbled, freeing blacks to compete in professional and collegiate sport. The quality of play, as a result, improved. And as a sandlot and semipro presence all but disappeared, pro and college ball filled the vacuum, gaining wider exposure and greater revenues. The professional athlete began to reap unheralded financial rewards from his or her work. But what of the athlete outside the professional pale?

These changes ushered in a new epoch for the black athlete in which rewards comparable to those achieved by his or her white counterparts were attainable. But the black community lost control over its sporting life at the same time. From the late 1920s through the 1940s, the forces that organized the sporting life of black Pittsburgh were largely from within its own ranks. Most sandlot as well as the two Negro League teams there were organized and directed by blacks. White financial support was often important but rarely essential to sandlot clubs like the Garfield Eagles, Terrace Village, and the 18th Ward, or to professional outfits like the Grays and Crawfords. Yet autonomous black sport is now largely a thing of the past, surviving at black colleges, in a few community-controlled sporting centers, and on what remains of the street life.[107] Long gone are the Negro Leagues and the scores of black-owned and organized sandlot and semipro teams which were the core of black Pittsburgh sport in the first half of the century. While there are currently more black athletes in the major professional sports, there are no more black owners and fewer black coaches. Black America might have left its stylistic imprint on professional football, basketball, and baseball, but decision making in these sports lies elsewhere.

With those losses, the distance between the public and its games has widened. The minors, the Negro Leagues, and es- pecially the sandlots were intermediate levels of sport linking the professional game with those played by children on the streets, empty lots, and ball fields of their neighborhoods. Earlier in the century players easily moved back and forth between sandlot and professional ball, for the differences in level of skills required and rewards offered were not that great. But that has changed. No longer does a player like Honus Wagner begin and end his career on the sandlots. A prospective professional follows a more fixed career trajectory, and few succeed in circumventing it.

These changes have affected not only the players but the fans, too. The athlete is no longer a member of the community but part of a well-paid caste whose life-style and expectations have little in common with most fans. The bond between fan and player has changed from the intimacy of rooting for friends, workmates, and neighbors on a sandlot club to supporting professionals with whom most fans have little or no contact outside the ballpark. The gap has grown even wider with the mediating influence of television.

Further casualties of these changes have been the athletes themselves. With the almost total disappearance of sandlot foot- ball and the collapse of the minors and sandlot baseball, fewer opportunities remain for men to continue playing ball after high school and college. The decrease in playing opportunities is most graphic in professional baseball, which employs only about 30 percent as many players as it did in the early 1950s.[108] But the loss of a sandlot outlet has been more keenly felt, denying men the chance to keep playing the games of their youth as they advance in age.[109] Most playing opportunities are concentrated in high schools, colleges, and youth leagues. The man in his twenties or older who wants to continue playing cannot follow in the footsteps of the sandlotters of earlier decades who often played into their forties and, sometimes, like Ralph Mellix, into the twilight of their lives.

These athletes lost control over their teams, too, as the self-

organized sandlot club à la the Eagles or early Crawfords became a historical oddity. And with the increasing specialization
of sport, the opportunity to partake of a varied athletic career has
dwindled. The age of the all-around athlete has passed. Youths
are encouraged to concentrate on one sport, and often a particular position, at an early age. Career athletic decisions are
made at an earlier age. In 1982, *Sports Illustrated* lamented the
graduation of the last three-sport college letterman in America.

Despite these changes, sport has continued to capture the
fancy of black America. In some ways the events of the last three
decades have only further magnified the stature of the athlete in
the black community. The dream of sport as the way out of the
ghetto remains a potent force, despite the overwhelming odds
against such a journey. Indeed, the currency of the notion that
sport is an effective ladder for social mobility has had tragic
consequences for recent generations of black youth.

It is ironic that sport is seen by so many in the black community as primarily a means of raising oneself out of the ghetto,
for sport held a handful of different and ultimately more important meanings to black America in earlier years. Sport became
such an important element of black consciousness because it
fulfilled vital social and community functions and served as a
political arena, too, in which black struggles for recognition and
equality were symbolically waged, not just because it offered to a
few the ticket out.

It is often argued that sport erases the consciousness of everyday reality, allowing a brief moment of transcendence for participants and spectators. But during most of this century sport in
black America has rarely been able to separate itself from racial
realities—from restrictive color lines, racial discrimination in its
multiple forms, and the quest for white hopes. Consequently,
sport in the black community has been indelibly stamped by the
dimensions of race in America.

Through symbols and struggles over the access to recreation
and the right to play, however, sport played a central role in the
recomposition of American black consciousness on both a local
and national level following the migrations of the World War I
years. In the 1920s, 1930s, and 1940s, sport offered black
Americans a cultural counterpoint to their collective lot, one

that promoted internal cohesion in the black community by bringing together both the older residents and the migrants in the context of a changing black consciousness. Moreover, it helped the newly scattered black community gain a sense of itself as a national community.

Joe Louis was the best-known black American sporting symbol, and what he accomplished in the ring, Jesse Owens, Ralph Metcalfe, and Eddie Tolan did in Olympic competition; Fritz Pollard, Paul Robeson, and Kenny Washington matched on the gridirons; and a host of other black athletes strived for on basketball courts and baseball diamonds. There were hundreds, even thousands, of these men, and occasionally women, who stood out in the sporting landscape. And for every black athlete who attained a national or international reputation, there were a hundred more who achieved a comparable status in their neighborhood or city. In Homewood it might have been Joe Ware, in Garfield Rink Davis, and on the Hill Harold Tinker or Johnny Moore. They were to their neighbors, workmates, and fellow citizens what men like Joe Louis and Josh Gibson were to the national black community—figures of emulation and respect whose actions lent the community a greater sense of its own competence and unity.

Black sport was more than recreation or a means of socializing. It was a focus of concern in which considerable energy, emotion, and thought were invested. Black Pittsburgh read and talked about their teams and watched them closely when they performed. Almost everyone knew at least a few members of the sporting fraternity as friends, family, neighbors, or workmates. As a result, how they fared was of vital importance.

The sandlot teams were among the most visible and well-organized neighborhood-based ventures in black Pittsburgh. They provided their neighborhoods with sporting events in season and a never-ending series of fundraising affairs throughout the year. The Garfield Eagles' annual Broad Street Fair, the 18th Ward smokers at Weil Hall, and Terrace Village's Fourth of July festivities brought their respective black neighborhoods together in celebration of their athletic prowess and community solidarity. Black Garfield identified with its Eagles, backing them with coins and cheers and basking in the reflection of both their gridiron and off-the-field successes. It was the same in Beltzhoover and Terrace Village, as these sandlot teams furnished their neighborhoods with a focus that comingled fun and pride.

The core of sport activists who organized and maintained these teams were also often the center of their neighborhoods' political life. The Eagles' main backer, Buck Phillips, was commonly referred to as the "Mayor" of Garfield, and several team members remained active in community-based organizing around neighborhood services and utilities long after the team had folded. Ralph Mellix and Willis Moody mobilized Beltzhoover around recreational issues and into a black 18th Ward voting bloc. Terrace Village's leaders recognized the connections between the ward organization and sandlot ball, too, and exchanged their politicking for the organization's support of community sport and recreation. Nor were the owners of the Homestead Grays and the Pittsburgh Crawfords indifferent to the body politic. Cum Posey was black Homestead's most prominent politician, a long-time member of the school board and an indefatigable advocate for his constituents. Gus Greenlee worked within the Republican party, primarily to protect his racket-related businesses but also to provide the Third Ward Voter's League with cash and leadership.[110]

Sport not only affirmed an impressive array of athletic skills and administrative talents, it showcased the black community's potential to win in interracial competition. Team members took special pride in proving their ability against white sandlot opponents, while the Grays and Crawfords demonstrated black excellence against white semipro and pro competition. Most veteran sandlotters were reluctant to project too overt an importance onto these victories, but they allowed that they had filled them with an abiding satisfaction.[111] Sport offered black Pittsburgh a bridge to the white community in other ways, too. For some outlying white towns, games with the Eagles, Crawfords, or Pittsburgh Corsairs were the only times blacks ever set foot there. Team leaders like Ray Irvin, Harold Tinker, and Gil Gordon recognized that on these occasions they were their race's ambassadors.[112] Black-owned clubs like the Crawfords or Grays, or fighters like Joe Louis or John Henry Lewis, were practically the only black-controlled businesses with large white clienteles. And despite laws in some states barring interracial competition into the late 1950s, and color lines which blocked black participation in certain collegiate and professional leagues, the cumulative impact of interracial competition was profound. Hundreds of thousands, maybe even millions, of whites competed against blacks in sport, especially on the sandlots. For many, sport was their primary source of interracial contact; for some, that contact changed long-held prejudices. Witnessing black equality in one aspect of life was not entirely lost on these white competitors.

When a team like the Homestead Grays barnstormed through predominantly white rural areas of Pennsylvania and Ohio, they were frequently feted by their hosts. In coalmining towns the miners took the afternoon off to field a team against the visiting black professionals. When Joe Louis or Sugar Ray Robinson fought, or Jesse Owens or John Woodruff ran in the Olympics, they often had whites cheering for them. It is difficult to evaluate the effects of these interracial sporting contacts, but in the opinion of many involved in them they promoted better race relations. While sport was not the only area of interracial contact in these decades, it was exceptional in that it presupposed conditions of equality on the playing fields. Although these conditions of fairness were often violated, there was, nonetheless, the feeling that the rules applied evenly to black and white alike. This was frequently not the case in housing, work, or politics.

Ironically, sport's visibility in the black community increased while black control over black sport crumbled. Integration combined with the decline of community-based sport to propel black athletes into mostly white leagues and schools. There, these athletes received greater publicity and remuneration. Television and the attention of the press further heightened their prominence. Where once black youth looked to the local sandlot or Negro League star, they now dreamed of heroes in the majors, the NFL, and the NBA.

In black Pittsburgh the sandlot era of Joe ("Showboat") Ware and Gabe Patterson was over by the 1960s. The aura surrounding Josh Gibson and Buck Leonard had vanished, too. The new heroes were men like Westinghouse's Chuck Cooper, who with Sweetwater Clifton first integrated the NBA; and later the Hill's Larry Brown, who galloped to stardom in the NFL. They, along with Cookie Gilchrist, Maurice Lucas, and a score of local blacks who successfully competed on college teams and in the pros, replaced earlier generations of black Pittsburgh athletes as the focus of black Pittsburgh sport.[113] Their achievements in white-oriented sport reinforced the tendency among black youth to try to follow sport as the path out of black Pittsburgh despite the unlikelihood of their making it. The Jeep Kelleys and Ricky Colemans are all too easily forgotten.[114]

The racial and social foundations on which contemporary images of black sport rest, however, are radically different than those on which the sandlots and the Negro Leagues were built. While sport undoubtedly has still more roles to play in the unfolding of black history, it is not likely to simply repeat the roles of the past. A sense of the past, however, might help the black community extricate itself from the sporting dilemmas of the present.

Notes

1 Sport in Black Pittsburgh, 1900–1930

1. John Bodnar, Roger Simon, and Michael P. Weber, *Lives of Their Own: Blacks, Italians, and Poles in Pittsburgh, 1900–1960* (Urbana: University of Illinois Press, 1982), pp. 78, 82, 131–33.

2. Ibid., pp. 188–96.

3. Ibid., pp. 187, 265.

4. Elsie Witchen, "Tuberculosis and the Negro in Pittsburgh: A Report of the Negro Health Survey" (Pittsburgh: Tuberculosis League of Pittsburgh, 1934), p. 2; Alonzo Moran, "Distribution of the Negro Population in Pittsburgh: 1910–30" (M.A. thesis, University of Pittsburgh, 1933), p. 10, cites Bureau of Census Press Release 3/21/32 on "State of Birth of the National Population"; U.S. Bureau of the Census, *Negroes in the United States: 1900–1932* (Washington, D.C., 1935), pp. 6, 14, 24–25. Much of this rural-to-urban migration was to southern cities, and many other migrants stopped over in southern urban areas for a few weeks or a few years before heading north. While Pittsburgh was not a major route for the migration and had a lower rate of black population growth than Chicago and Detroit, for example, the net effect was to create a sizable black community.

5. Witchen, "Tuberculosis," p. 2; John Nicely Rathnell, "Status of Pittsburgh Negroes in Regard to Origin, Length of Residence, and Economic Aspects of their Lives" (M.A. thesis, University of Pittsburgh, 1935), p. 22; *Social Science Research Bulletin* 1 (no. 5, 1933): 2.

6. Andrew Buni, *Robert L. Vann of the* Pittsburgh Courier: *Politics and Black Journalism* (Pittsburgh: University of Pittsburgh Press, 1974), p. 23, cites Charles Dahlinger, *Pittsburgh and Sketch of Its Early Social Life* (New York, 1916).

7. Witchen, "Tuberculosis," pp. 2–3; Joe T. Darden, *Afro-Americans in Pittsburgh: The Residential Segregation of a People* (Lexington, Mass.: Lexington Books, D. C. Heath and Co., 1973), pp. 6–7.

8. Darden, *Residential Segregation,* pp. 6–7; interviews with Bill Harris, 7/29/80, Pittsburgh; Bus Christian, 2/20/81, Pittsburgh; Wyatt Turner, 12/29/80, Pittsburgh.

9. Rathnell, "Status," p. 32; Bodnar et al., *Lives,* pp. 71–72.

10. Buni, *Vann,* p. 32, cites Ernest Price McKinney, "These Colored United States, Pennsylvania: A Tale of Two Cities," *Messenger* (May 1932): 692.

11. Peter Gottlieb, "Making Their Own Way: Southern Blacks' Migration to Pittsburgh, 1916–30" (Ph.D. thesis, University of Pittsburgh, 1977), p. 256.

12. Miriam Rosenbloom, "An Outline of the Negro in the Pittsburgh Area" (M.A. thesis, University of Pittsburgh, 1945), p. 29.

13. Gottlieb, "Making," p. 261; Bodnar et al., *Lives*, pp. 60–66, cites research confirming that northern-born blacks held a higher percentage of white-collar, skilled, and semiskilled jobs than southern migrants.

14. J. Ernest Wright, "Negro in Pittsburgh" (WPA Writers' Project, 1940), pp. 13, 24. I used a typed copy of this in C. Rollo Turner's possession.

15. Ibid., p. 11.

16. Buni, *Vann*, p. 32, also cites Wright, "Negro," pp. 9–12.

17. For an excellent presentation of this argument, see Gottlieb, "Making," pp. 109–10.

18. Bodnar et al., *Lives*, p. 188.

19. Buni, *Vann*, pp. 61–62; Witchen, "Tuberculosis," pp. 64–65; Ira DeA. Reid, "Social Conditions of the Negro in the Hill District of Pittsburgh" (General Committee on the Hill Survey, 1930), p. 38.

20. Witchen, "Tuberculosis," pp. 8–9; Reid, "Social Conditions," p. 12. The percentage of black deaths per 1,000 population in Pittsburgh was from two to fourteen points higher than the percentage of white deaths per 1,000 every year between 1910 and 1928. In 1933, for example, the rate of deaths for blacks was 22.5 per 1,000 as compared to 12.5 per 1,000 for whites. In 1933 the black population of Pittsburgh (8.2 percent of the total population, according to the 1930 U.S. census) accounted for 14 percent of all deaths, 15 percent of all infant deaths, 24 percent of all deaths from pneumonia, and 35 percent of all deaths from tuberculosis.

21. Buni, *Vann*, pp. 25, 69–71, 109.

22. Reid, "Social Conditions," pp. 52–55; Buni, *Vann*, pp. 24–27; William Y. Bell, "Commercial Recreation Facilities among Negroes in the Hill District" (M.A. thesis, University of Pittsburgh, 1938), p. 10. According to Wright, "Negro," chap. 1, p. 2, about one-third of black workers in Pittsburgh in 1930 were working as laborers in the steel and glass industries, the building trades, or other manufacturing and industrial activity; one-half were domestics or engaged in personal service; one-sixth were in trade or transportation; and one-fifteenth were involved in white-collar or professional work.

23. Wright, "Negro," chap. 1, p. 4.

24. Ibid., p. 14. An Urban League member contended, "The absence of a solidly Negro community in Pittsburgh reduces very materially the power of the Negro population to compel retail dealers to employ Negro clerks in Negro residential districts and to secure Negro political representation as in some Northern cities." A. G. Moran and F. F. Stephan, "The Negro Population and Negro Families in Pittsburgh and Allegheny County," *Social Research Bulletin* 1 (Apr. 20, 1933): 4.

25. See Cary Goodman, *Choosing Sides* (New York: Schocken Books, 1979), for a case study of the clash between the organized play movement and street life.

26. Philip Klein, *A Social Study of Pittsburgh* (New York: Columbia University Press, 1938), p. 281; Buni, *Vann*, p. 29; M. R. Goldman, "The Hill District as I Knew It," *Western Pennsylvania Historical Magazine* 51 (July 1968): 285.

27. Bell, "Commercial Facilities," pp. 30–31, 67–68; Ruby E. Ovid, "Rec-

reational Facilities for the Negro in Manchester" (M.S. thesis, University of Pittsburgh, 1952); Hilda Kaplan and Selma Levy, "Recreational Facilities for the Negro in East Liberty District with Special Emphasis on Tracts 7G, 12D and 12E" (M.S. thesis, University of Pittsburgh, 1945), pp. 14–32; Geraldine Hermalin and Ruth L. Levin, "Recreational Resources for the Negro" (M.S. thesis, University of Pittsburgh, 1945), p. 53.

28. *Pittsburgh Courier*, 7/5/41, sec. 2, p. 3.

29. Goodman, *Choosing Sides*, p. 15.

30. The local black press credited the Urban League's John Clark for its existence. Reid, "Social Conditions," pp. 71–75; *Pittsburgh American*, 9/8/22.

31. *Pittsburgh Courier*, 4/24/54, p. 27.

32. Reid, "Social Conditions," p. 72.

33. Ibid., pp. 76–78; *Pittsburgh Courier*, 5/5/51, p. 17; 2/2/52, p. 18; 3/29/52, p. 28.

34. Klein, *Social Study*, p. 865.

35. Ibid., pp. 283–84; Buni, *Vann*, pp. 49, 338, cites YMCA, "Annual Concerted Operating Budget Canvas," Oct. 15, 1928, in the possession of Percival L. Prattis, Pittsburgh.

36. It is also safe to say that when the YMCA athletes were from the professional and middle-class ranks of the black community, they received more recognition in the black press for their play. Reid, "Social Conditions," pp. 15–17, 75, 107; *Pittsburgh Courier*, 1/27/34, sec. 2, p. 5; 2/3/34, sec. 2, p. 5; 2/10/34, sec. 2, p. 4; 3/10/34, sec. 2, p. 5; 3/17/34, sec. 2, p. 5; 3/24/34, sec. 2, p. 5; 1/14/39, p. 17; 11/18/39, p. 16; 2/15/41, p. 18; 4/7/45, p. 17; 12/18/54, p. 24.

37. Reid, "Social Conditions," pp. 14–17, 75.

38. Klein, *Social Study*, p. 282.

39. Reid, "Social Conditions," pp. 75–79.

40. *Pittsburgh Courier*, 5/5/51, p. 17; 2/2/52, p. 19; 3/29/52, p. 28.

41. Reid, "Social Conditions," pp. 95–105; *Pittsburgh Courier*, 12/20/41, p. 17; 6/9/45, p. 14.

42. Reid, "Social Conditions," p. 13.

43. David Montgomery, "The New Unionism and the Transformation of Workers' Consciousness in America: 1909–1922," *Journal of Social History* (Summer 1974): 511. This piece is an excellent analysis of the labor upsurge.

44. New American Movement reprint of 1932 *Time* magazine advertisement.

45. Montgomery, "New Unionism," p. 514, quoting Leon C. Marshall, "The War Labor Program and Its Administration," *Journal of Political Economy* 26 (May 1918): 429.

46. Montgomery, "New Unionism," p. 515; *Monthly Labor Review* 17 (Dec. 1923): 82–85.

47. L. C. Gardner, "Community Athletic Recreation for Employees and Their Families" (Carnegie Steel Co., Munhall, Pa., typeset, n.d.), found in the back room of the Munhall Carnegie Library. Gardner was superintendent of the plant in the early twentieth century. All Gardner statements are from this eight-page essay.

48. *Monthly Labor Review* 24 (May 1927): 867–82.

49. George Halas, with Gwen Morgan and Arthur Veysey, *Halas by Halas: The Autobiography of George Halas* (New York: McGraw-Hill, 1977), pp. 54–76.

50. *Monthly Labor Review* 24 (May 1927): 874.

51. Klein, *Social Study*, pp. 60–63; interview with Russell Weiskircher, 9/28/79, Boston, Pa.

52. Homestead Album Project, interviews with George Miller, Mel Rutter, Anna Mae and Russell Lindberg, Archives of Industrial Society, Hillman Library, University of Pittsburgh, 1976; *Homestead Daily Messenger,* 12/22/29, 10/9/30, 9/17/40, 4/23/76; *Pittsburgh Sun-Telegraph,* 8/11/58; from typed copy, Catherine Butler to Mr. Hogan, 3/10/43, Carnegie Munhall Library.

53. Gottlieb, "Making," p. 250.

54. Klein, *Social Study,* p. 60.

55. *Pittsburgh Courier,* 2/26/27, sec. 2, p. 4; 12/18/26, sec. 2, p. 6.

56. Ibid., 9/8/23, sec. 2, p. 4; 1/14/39, p. 16; 3/25/39, p. 17; 4/1/39, p. 15; 5/15/39, p. 15; 6/3/39, p. 16; 6/10/39, p. 15; 7/26/41, p. 16; 7/8/50, p. 31. These are the primary sources for the discussion of the Edgar Thomson team.

57. Interview with Harold Tinker, 6/19/80, Pittsburgh.

58. Interview with Charlie Hughes, 2/1/81, Pittsburgh.

59. Interview with Walt Hughes, 1/9/81, Pittsburgh.

60. Interview with Willis Moody, 1/6/81, Pittsburgh.

61. Robert Hughey, in *Pittsburgh Courier,* 4/15/39, p. 15.

62. Betty Ann Weiskopf, "A Directory of Some of the Organizations to Which People in the Hill District of Pittsburgh Belong: 1943" (M.S. thesis, University of Pittsburgh, 1943), p. 43.

63. *Pittsburgh Courier,* 8/8/25, p. 12; 1/2/26, sec. 2, p. 2; 7/17/26, p. 14; 1/1/27, sec. 2, p. 6.

64. Ibid., 7/21/28.

65. Ibid., 12/18/26, sec. 2, p. 6.

66. For company sports, see interviews with Harold Tinker, 6/19/80, and Willis Moody, 1/6/81; *Pittsburgh Courier,* 1/1/27, sec. 2, p. 6; 1/15/17, sec. 2, p. 6; 2/26/27, sec. 2, p. 4; 5/28/27, sec. 2, p. 5.

67. *Pittsburgh Courier,* 3/1/41, sec. 2, p. 2; 5/24/72.

68. Klein, *Social Study,* pp. 62–63.

69. Ibid., p. 63; Bob Hughes, "How Many Are Playing?" *Pittsburgh Press,* 4/15/31.

70. Klein, *Social Study,* p. 63.

71. George Weinstein, in *Coronet* (Apr. 1951): 56–59. This study found over 18,000 U.S. industrial and business firms sponsoring some form of recreation or sport for their workers. The author argued that industry had learned during World War II that such programs could reduce absenteeism and increase productivity.

72. Gardner, "Community Recreation."

73. Current examples of this in Pittsburgh are the Connie Hawkins and

Ozanam summer basketball leagues.

74. *Pittsburgh Courier*, 3/22/41, p. 16.

75. Countless interviews confirmed this: for example, Bill Harris, 7/29/80; Fred Clark, 12/29/80; Bus Christian, 2/20/81; Wyatt Turner, 12/29/80; Jack Parker and Joe Ware, 7/15/80.

2 Sandlot Ball

1. George Trautman, president of the National Association of Professional Baseball Leagues (i.e., the minors), explained in 1957 what he meant by organized baseball: "Organized baseball consists of the two major leagues and . . . the minor leagues. It makes claim to but one consideration in the over-all picture of baseball in America. It proudly asserts that by the verdict of the people after seventy-five years, it has been designated as the guardian of the game. . . ." In "Study of Monopoly Power," hearings before the Subcommittee on Study of Monopoly Power, Committee of the Judiciary, House of Representatives, 82nd Cong., 1st Sess., ser. 1, pt. 6: "Organized Baseball" (United States Government Printing Office, Washington, D.C., 1957), pp. 169–70 (hereafter cited as "Organized Baseball").

2. Frederick Lieb, *The Pittsburgh Pirates* (New York: Van Rees Par, 1948), pp. 4–16. When professional baseball players revolted in 1889 and formed the Brotherhood League, a brief venture into a player-controlled cooperative league, almost the entire Pittsburgh club went over to the Brotherhood League franchise established in Pittsburgh. The fans who preferred the pro game went with them, forsaking the already largely spurned owners of the National League franchise.

3. For many examples, see Lawrence Ritter, *The Glory of Their Times* (New York: Macmillan, 1966), and Donald Honig, *Baseball When the Grass Was Real* (New York: Coward, McCann and Geogegan, 1975).

4. When the Pirates left Forbes Field for Three Rivers Stadium in 1970, the statue was moved, too.

5. Lieb, *Pirates,* pp. 50–51; Robert Objoski, *Bush League: A History of Minor League Baseball* (New York: Macmillan, 1975), p. 11; Ritter, *Glory,* p. 179; ed. Joseph Reichler, *The Baseball Encyclopedia* (New York: Macmillan, 1979), pp. 1478–79; *Pittsburgh Press,* 6/16/81, p. C-4.

6. See, for example, Montgomery, "New Unionism"; "American Labor in the 1940's," *Radical America* (July–Aug. 1975); James Green, *The World of the Worker: Labor in Twentieth-Century America* (New York: Hill and Wang, 1980).

7. Donald Gropman, *Say It Ain't So, Joe: The Story of Shoeless Joe Jackson* (Boston: Little, Brown and Co., 1979), pp. 6–7, 148. Shoeless Joe Jackson, whose remarkable exploits will be forever overshadowed by the 1919 Black Sox scandal, went to work at a Bethlehem Steel subsidiary in Wilmington, Delaware, following the "work or fight" decree and played in Charley Schwab's Bethlehem Steel League alongside other major leaguers. Jackson had played on mill teams as a teenager in Brandon Mills, South Carolina, where the textile

owners sponsored teams to reduce alienation with cotton mill and mill town life. But the Bethlehem Steel League and similar operations were on a more highly capitalized basis.

8. Harvey Keck, in *Pittsburgh Post-Gazette*, 3/2/43; Harold Seymour, *Baseball: The Golden Years* (New York: Oxford University Press, 1971), vol. 2, pp. 249–51.

9. Bob Hughes, in *Pittsburgh Press*, 4/5/31.

10. "How Uncle Sam Has Created an Army of Athletes," *Scientific American*, 2/8/19, pp. 114–15.

11. For an account of the divisions within American society during World War I, see Gabriel Kolko, *Main Currents in Modern American History* (New York: Harper and Row, 1976); Joyce Kornbluh, *Rebel Voices: An IWW Anthology* (Ann Arbor: University of Michigan Press, 1972); Jeremy Brecher, *Strike!* (San Francisco: Straight Arrow Books, 1972).

12. *Pittsburgh Press*, 4/11/26.

13. "Sandlotters' Baseball Guide 1927," *Pittsburgh Post*, found in the "Sandlot File," National Baseball Library, Cooperstown, N.Y.

14. *Pittsburgh Press*, 4/5/31.

15. *Pittsburgh Courier*, 7/10/43, p. 19; Steven Riess, "Professional Baseball and American Culture in the Progressive Era: Myths and Realities, with Special Emphasis on Atlanta, Chicago and New York" (Ph.D. thesis, University of Chicago, 1979). Riess discusses the factors attracting blacks and immigrant workers to attend sandlot and semipro games rather than trek to Forbes Field and other major league parks.

Black Pittsburgh's sporting life prior to the migration was largely limited to a few neighborhood baseball teams and the private social clubs of its relatively small elite. The Blue Ribbons from Homestead, which evolved into the Homestead Grays, and the Keystones, which briefly tried to make a go of it as a professional squad, were two of the city's earliest black teams, with histories dating back to the turn of the century. On July 4, 1910, as Jack Johnson took on Jim Jeffries in Reno in a heavyweight championship bout, three other neighborhood clubs tangled in a championship of their own making in the city's Strip district. Lawrenceville's Silver Leaf Giants, the Hill's Iron City Giants, and Homewood's Frick Giants later pooled their talents to create the Clay Giants. These basically working-class teams were sometimes joined by squads representing the Loendi Club and the Delany Rifles Athletic Club. The Loendis and the Delany Rifles, however, were more inclined to play basketball and football than baseball. Their members were drawn from black Pittsburgh's professional and mercantile classes.

16. Interview with Bill Harris, 7/29/80, Pittsburgh.

17. The McKelvey and Watt schools were the most recently constructed facilities on the Hill in 1925 and the only two there to score above the school board's minimum educational efficiency rating cutoff.

18. Reid, "Social Conditions," pp. 82–86.

19. Interview with Bill Harris, 7/29/80.

20. *Pittsburgh Courier*, 1/9/26, p. 3.

21. *Pittsburgh American,* 9/8/22, 8/9/29, clippings in the possession of Zerbie Dorsey.

22. *Pittsburgh Courier,* 1/23/26, p. 3; 5/15/26, p. 13.

23. Ibid., 5/15/26; 5/22/26, p. 13.

24. This photograph appeared in ibid., 10/20/73.

25. Ibid., 6/11/27, sec. 2, p. 5; 7/2/27, sec. 2, p. 4; 7/30/27, sec. 2, p. 4.

26. Ibid., 9/17/27, sec. 2, p. 6.

27. Interviews with Bill Harris, 7/29/80, and Harold Tinker, 6/19/80, Pittsburgh.

28. Interview with Harold Tinker, 6/19/80.

29. No cumulative records are available, but I would estimate that the Crawfords won about 80 percent of their games in these seasons, based on my reading of the *Pittsburgh Courier.*

30. Interview with Harold Tinker, 6/19/80.

31. In the spring of 1981, I asked my sport history class at the University of Pittsburgh to conduct interviews with former sandlotters. Although I had never mentioned Tinker to the class, two of the students heard stories about him and his outstanding play from the white subjects of their interviews.

32. Interview with Charlie Hughes, 2/1/81, Pittsburgh.

33. Interview with Harold Tinker, 6/19/80.

34. William Brashler, *Josh Gibson: A Life in the Negro Leagues* (New York: Harper and Row, 1978), is the source of some of this biographical information.

35. Interview with Harold Tinker, 6/19/80.

36. Ibid.

37. Interview with Wyatt Turner, 12/29/80, Pittsburgh.

38. Interview with Harold Tinker, 6/19/80.

39. Ibid.

40. *Pittsburgh Courier,* 2/23/29, sec. 2, p. 5.

41. Ibid., 7/12/30, p. 5; 7/19/30, p. 4; 7/25/30, p. 4.

42. Interview with Harold Tinker, 6/19/80.

43. Interview with Bill Harris, 7/29/80.

44. *Pittsburgh Courier,* 8/24/29, sec. 2, p. 4.

45. Ibid., 7/15/30, sec. 2, p. 5. Another columnist lamented that fans sat in the grandstands and spent their loose change with the hot-dog vendor and peanut man but failed to chip in a dime for the team. Ibid., 6/6/30, sec. 2, p. 4.

46. Interview with Harold Tinker, 6/19/80.

47. Ibid.

48. Charlie Kelly, in *Pittsburgh Post-Gazette,* 6/8/81, p. 6; Rosenbloom, "Outline of Negro History, p. 29; Jacqueline Wolfe, "The Changing Patterns of Residence of the Negro in Pittsburgh, Pennsylvania with Emphasis on the Period 1930–60" (M.A. thesis, University of Pittsburgh, 1964), pp. 76–85.

49. In one form or another, the team continued into the 1960s.

50. Interview with Willis Moody, 1/6/81, Pittsburgh.

51. Ibid.

52. His father, George Hall, was a founder of the Loendi Club. Born in the

Hill, Sell Hall excelled in high school athletics and played for the Clay Giants and the Homestead Grays before forming his own team. He promoted basketball and dance shows at the Labor Temple and the Pythian Temple and ran a florist shop and a print shop. He died in 1951 at the age of sixty-two. *Pittsburgh Courier*, 2/24/51, p. 1.

53. During the early 1920s the Grays were made up mostly of local ballplayers. The chief exceptions were on the pitching staff, where Posey sometimes imported a hurler like Smokey Joe Williams or occasionally borrowed a sandlot pitcher like Ralph Mellix for a game. Playing virtually every day of the week and often engaging in two or three contests a day required depth at pitching. The Grays were the top sandlot attraction in the tri-state area and frequently outdrew their major league competitors, the Pittsburgh Pirates. As their popularity increased and their record improved, the Grays spent more and more time on the road, barnstorming through small towns and mining communities for weeks at a time.

54. Bill Nunn, Jr., "Change of Pace," *Pittsburgh Courier*, 1/28/50, p. 22.

55. Interviews with Ralph Mellix, 6/6/80, 6/11/80, Pittsburgh.

56. Interview with Wyatt Turner, 12/29/80.

57. *Pittsburgh Courier*, 9/8/45, p. 16.

58. Bill Nunn, Jr. "Change of Pace," ibid., 4/28/51, p. 16.

59. Interview with Willis Moody, 1/6/81.

60. Interview with Ralph Mellix, 6/6/80.

61. See, e.g., *Pittsburgh Courier*, 4/8/39, p. 15; 10/18/52, p. 28; 11/15/52, p. 27; 11/14/53, p. 28.

62. 18th Ward program, 1952, 1953, 1954, in the possession of Ralph Mellix.

63. The brainchild of baseball magnate Branch Rickey and Pittsburgh's Gus Greenlee, the U.S. League developed during the 1940s as a short-lived alternative to the Negro National League, from which Greenlee had severed all ties. The league never got off its shaky financial underpinnings and was only a footnote to black baseball history by the time the major leagues were integrated in 1947. Rickey's intentions, never easy to decipher, were probably to develop a pool of black baseball talent he could quickly exploit once the color line in the major leagues came down. Interviews with Ralph Mellix, 6/6/80, and Willis Moody, 1/6/81; *Pittsburgh Courier*, 3/23/46, p. 28; 3/21/53, p. 27.

64. Interview with Ralph Mellix, 6/6/80.

65. Undated newspaper clipping in a Ralph Mellix scrapbook.

66. Interview with Joe Ware, 7/15/80, Pittsburgh.

67. Interviews with Ralph Mellix, 6/6/80, Willis Moody, 1/6/81, and Wyatt Turner, 12/29/80.

68. Interview with Willis Moody, 1/6/81.

3 More Sandlot Ball

1. Bodnar et al., *Lives*, p. 187.

2. Ibid., pp. 79–82.

3. Buni, *Vann*, pp. 174–202.

4. Bodnar et al., *Lives*, pp. 185–86; Robert L. Ruck, "The Origins of the Seniority System in Steel" (M.A. thesis, University of Pittsburgh, 1977), chap. 5.

5. *Pittsburgh Post-Gazette*, 6/15/81.

6. Bodnar et al., *Lives*, p. 224.

7. Ibid., pp. 176, 214–16, 226.

8. From "Beat Yesterday," 1952 Terrace Village program, Harold Tinker's personal scrapbooks.

9. Interviews with Jack Hopkins, 1/5/81, and Ocey Swain, 9/14/81, Pittsburgh.

10. Interview with Harold Tinker, 6/19/80, Pittsburgh.

11. *Pittsburgh Courier*, 3/31/51, p. 17.

12. Interview with Harold Tinker, 6/19/80.

13. Interviews with Jack Hopkins, 1/5/81, and Harold Tinker, 6/19/80.

14. Interview with Jack Hopkins, 1/5/81.

15. Ibid.

16. Ibid.

17. Interviews with Billy Caye, 1/31/81, and Joe Studnicki, 1/7/81, Pittsburgh.

18. Interview with Harold Tinker, 6/19/80.

19. Ibid.

20. Ibid.

21. Frank Matthews, in *Pittsburgh Post-Gazette*, 1/29/73, p. 9.

22. See undated news clippings in David B. Roberts file, Pennsylvania Room, Carnegie Library, Pittsburgh.

23. *Pittsburgh Courier*, 5/3/58, p. 6; 5/24/58, p. 3.

24. Earl Johnson, "The Sport Whirl," *Pittsburgh Courier*, 3/1/52, p. 19; also 2/26/55, p. 3; 2/12/55, p. 21; 2/26/52, p. 28; 9/8/51, p. 17.

25. Interview with Harold Tinker, 6/19/80; *Pittsburgh Courier*, 6/6/51, p. 5; 6/28/52, p. 27; 7/4/53, p. 27; 6/14/58, p. 19; 6/27/59, p. 21.

26. Interviews with Gabe Patterson, 7/12/80, Larnell Goodman, 7/12/80, and Ray Irvin, 12/12/80, Pittsburgh.

27. Interviews with James Dorsey, Jr., and Zerbie Dorsey, 3/30/81, Pittsburgh. Zerbie Dorsey played with the Delany Rifles' women's basketball team, the Della Robias. Delany, born in Virginia in 1812, came to Pittsburgh in 1831, where he established a school for blacks and later an abolitionist newspaper. He started the *Northern Star* with Frederick Douglass, graduated from Harvard Medical School, and practiced medicine in Pittsburgh, where he became a leading national black figure in the 1850s. The Rifles reflected Delany's stature and his military history. Delany was one of the first black commissioned officers in the Civil War. Interview with C. Rollo Turner, 9/11/81, Pittsburgh.

28. This description is based primarily on interviews with former Garfield Eagles, including Joe and Gertrude Barranti, 12/15/80; Walt Hughes, 1/9/81; Ray Irvin, 12/12/80; Vernon and Catherine Phillips, 1/2/81; Benny Jackson,

12/16/80; Fred Clark, 12/29/80; Gabe Patterson, 7/12/80; and Larnell Good-man, 7/12/80, all in Pittsburgh.

29. Interview with Ray Irvin, 12/12/80; Wolfe, "Changing Pattern of Negro Residence," pp. 76–85.

30. In later years, Lewis was athletic director of the Kay Club and coach of its baseball team.

31. The description of the early years of the Garfield Eagles is based on an interview with Ray Irvin, 12/12/80.

32. Wendell Smith, "Time Out," *Pittsburgh Courier*, 10/7/39, p. 15.

33. Interview with Gabe Patterson, 7/12/80.

34. Interview with Ray Irvin, 12/12/80.

35. Interview with Gabe Patterson, 7/12/80.

36. It should be noted, as several former Eagles stressed, that the riot was an exception to an otherwise good racial atmosphere.

37. Robert Hughey, *Pittsburgh Courier*, 10/18/41, p. 17.

38. Blacks had few opportunities to play ball and organize teams until after the Civil War. This lack of a playing tradition meant that blacks' knowledge of the game was behind that of white players for several decades. Knowledge of the sport has long been a vital part of the game.

39. Bob Smizik, *Pittsburgh Press*, 6/18/81, p. C-3.

40. Interview with Joe Studnicki, 1/7/81.

41. "Organized Baseball," p. 452.

42. For a fuller discussion of sport and class, see Frances G. Couvares, *The Remaking of Pittsburgh: Class and Culture in an Industrializing City, 1877–1919*, (Albany: SUNY Press, 1984), chaps. 3, 8.

4 Professional Black Sport and Cum Posey

1. See John A. Lucas and Ronald D. Smith, *Saga of American Sport* (Philadelphia: Lea and Febiger, 1978), p. 268, for a discussion of Molyneux's career.

2. The phrase "the world the slaves made" is the subtitle of Eugene Genovese's *Roll, Jordan, Roll* (New York: Pantheon Books, 1972) and suggests the ability of the slaves to create a measure of control over certain aspects of their own lives within the slave system.

3. Robert Peterson, *Only the Ball Was White* (Englewood Cliffs, N.J.: Prentice-Hall, 1970), pp. 34–40. Teams like the Acme Colored Giants and the Page Fence Giants were owned by white businessmen, while the Cuban Giants and the Lincoln Giants, two of early black baseball's most successful teams, were backed by whites who were well versed in sports promotion. Ibid., pp. 49–82. See also Donn Rogosin, *Invisible Men: Life in Baseball's Negro Leagues* (New York: Atheneum, 1983), which is an excellent addition to the scholarship of black baseball.

4. *Pittsburgh Courier*, 9/24/33, sec. 2, p. 4.

5. At the bottom of Wilson's list is a team that, as much as any squad, helped to establish black baseball in America. The Kansas City Monarchs started as a multiracial ball club, the All Nations Club, the creation of a white Kansas City

man, J. L. Wilkinson. He placed whites, American-born blacks, and Latinos on the field alongside a Japanese, a Hawaiian, and an American Indian, demonstrating that a diverse mix of races could not only play superior ball but travel and cooperate off the field, too.

In 1920 Wilkinson decided to break up the All Nations and form an all-black club, the Kansas City Monarchs, which he and his white partner, Tom Baird, placed in a new black league they helped Rube Foster to organize. The Monarchs regularly fielded one of black baseball's finest teams, and if there was a league play-off or black world series between the Negro National and Negro American leagues, they were more often than not a part of it.

Wilkinson was regarded as a man who genuinely cared for his players. The *Courier*'s Wendell Smith expressed the sentiments of many people when he wrote,

> One of those who has made a definite contribution [to black baseball] . . . is J. L. Wilkinson, the silver-thatched soft-spoken owner of the fabulous Kansas City Monarchs. Wilkinson has been in Negro baseball for more than twenty years, and during that time he has not only invested his money, but his very heart and soul. He has stayed in the game through storm and strife because he has loved it, not because he had to. There is no owner in the country—white or Negro—who has operated more honestly, sincerely or painstakingly. His baseball history is an epic as thrilling and fascinating as any sports story ever written. (*Pittsburgh Courier*, 6/9/45, p. 16)

6. The Homestead Grays rented Forbes Field directly from the Pittsburgh Pirates and were thus an exception.

7. Michael Crosby, "Yesterday," *Sports Illustrated*, 6/15/81; *Pittsburgh Courier*, 10/3/30, sec. 2, p. 4.

8. He sold the team in 1962 but served as chairman of the NBA Rules Committee and as its chief schedule-maker until his death in the late 1970s. When the National Baseball Hall of Fame made a belated effort to secure recognition for players from the Negro Leagues, the commissioner of baseball, Bowie Kuhn, asked Gottlieb to serve on the selection committee. Art Rust, *Get That Nigger Off the Field* (New York: Delacorte Press, 1976), pp. 50–56; John Holway, *Voices from the Great Black Baseball Leagues* (New York: Dodd, Mead and Co., 1975), pp. 81–82, 321.

9. *Pittsburgh Courier*, 2/8/47, p. 10.

10. Ibid., 8/12/33, sec. 2, p. 5.

11. Ibid., 3/9/40, p. 17; 8/31/40, p.16; 7/5/41, p. 16; Holway, *Voices*, p. 282–83.

12. *Pittsburgh Courier*, 4/4/42, p. 16.

13. Wendell Smith, in ibid., 5/16/42, p. 17. The Clowns were one of Saperstein's more dubious attractions. Just who owned them was in dispute; no one wanted to claim that distinction, and Syd Pollock, for one, attempted to shed the mantle of responsibility. In the late 1920s and the 1930s Pollock barnstormed the Havana Red Sox, a team allegedly composed of Cuban ballplayers, through the East and Midwest. By the 1940s his entourage was renamed the Havana Cubans, and they were joined by a new attraction, the Ethiopian Clowns. Black sportswriter Wendell Smith denounced Pollock, a theater man-

ager from Tarrytown, N.Y., for his "Awful Clowns": "This aggregation travels around the country capitalizing on slap-stick comedy and the kind of nonsense which many white people like to believe is typical and characteristic of all Negroes. Mr. Pollock's Clowns paint their faces and put on a show before every game. Mr. Pollock, of course, would have us believe that the exhibition his team puts on is good enough for Broadway. But those of us who know about it believe it belongs on one of those Mississippi show-boats, and not to be flaunted on baseball diamonds throughout the country" (ibid.). Cum Posey granted that Syd Pollock was a "nice fellow" but objected to his "capitalizing on the downfall of the only empire which really belonged to the Negro race" (*Pittsburgh Courier*, "Posey's Points," 7/5/41, p. 16).

14. Ibid., 5/16/42, p. 16.
15. Ibid., 5/30/42, p. 16.
16. Ibid., 11/9/40, p. 18; 10/31/42, p. 17.
17. Peterson, *Ball*, p. 103.
18. John Holway, "Rube Foster: Father of the Black Game," *Sporting News*, July 1981.
19. Peterson, *Ball*, pp. 63–64, 82, 107–44.
20. *Pittsburgh Courier*, 6/13/25, p. 1; Wright, "Negro," chap. 11, p. 12.
21. One of his charges was John McClean, later the burgess of Homestead and clerk of courts for Allegheny County. Posey and Dr. McClean became not only steadfast friends but life-long allies in the often murky world of borough politics.
22. *Pittsburgh Courier*, 1/20/34, sec. 2, p. 4.
23. Ibid.
24. Ibid.
25. Ibid., 12/19/42, p. 17.
26. A frequent compromise meant that dribbling and shooting regulations were changed at the half, allowing each team to play part of the game under its own rules.
27. Ibid., 1/23/43, p. 17.
28. Ibid., 12/19/42, p. 17; 1/20/34, sec. 2, p. 4; 1/29/39, p. 17; Ocania Chalk, *Black College Sport* (New York: Dodd, Mead and Co., 1976), pp. 80–82.
29. *Pittsburgh Courier*, 3/21/30, sec. 2, p. 5; 2/31/55, sec. 2, p. 5; 2/9/52, p. 1; 8/27/55, p. 17; 3/7/53, sec. 2, p. 4.
30. When he returned to Homestead he played for the Homestead–Carnegie Steel Company team in the United States Steel League.
31. Ibid., 3/11/33, p. 4.
32. Ibid., 4/6/46, p. 23.
33. Ibid., 7/7/23, p. 6; 4/5/24, p. 10; 8/9/24, sec. 2, p. 6; 6/13/25, p. 12.
34. Peterson, *Ball*, p. 131.
35. *Pittsburgh Courier*, 11/14/25, p. 12; 8/21/26, p. 14.
36. Ibid., 9/25/26, p. 14.
31. Ibid., 7/4/25, p. 12.
38. Ibid., 1/16/26, p. 12.

39. Ibid., 8/22/25, sec. 2, p. 7.
40. Interviews with Ralph Mellix, 6/10/80, 6/11/80, Pittsburgh.
41. *Pittsburgh Courier*, 8/25/23, p. 1; 9/1/23, p. 1.
42. The teams were the Gimbel Browns, the Monarchs, the North Side Elks, the Garfield ABCs, the Duquesne Lights, and the Woodmen. Ibid., 5/10/30, sec. 2, p. 5.
43. Ibid., 1/8/27, sec. 2, p. 6.
44. Ibid., 1/29/27, sec. 2, p. 4.
45. Ibid., 3/21/30, sec. 2, p. 5.
46. Peterson, *Ball*, pp. 92–93.

5 Gus Greenlee, Black Pittsburgh's "Mr. Big"

1. *Pittsburgh Post-Gazette*, 10/10/32.
2. Interview with Dr. Charles Greenlee, 6/18/80, Pittsburgh.
3. *Pittsburgh Courier*, 7/12/52, p. 1.
4. Ibid., 3/28/25, p. 1.
5. Ibid., 11/18/24, p. 3; 3/28/25, p. 1.
6. Ibid., 11/28/25, p. 2.
7. Ibid., 3/27/26, p. 3.
8. Ibid., 1/7/33, p. 3.
9. At one point Gus ran three different Crawford Grills, but Grill #1 on Wylie Avenue on the Lower Hill was the most popular.
10. Ibid., 11/29/41, p. 16; 12/6/41, p. 16.
11. Interview with Charles Greenlee, 6/18/80.
12. William Brashler, *The Don: The Life and Death of Sam Giancana* (New York: Harper and Row, 1977), pp. 81–88; Francis A. J. Ianni, *A Family Business* (New York: Russell Sage Foundation, 1972), p. 67; Francis A. J. Ianni, *Black Mafia: Ethnic Succession in Organized Crime* (New York: Simon and Schuster, 1974), p. 111.
13. Mark Haller, "The Changing Structure of American Gambling in the Twentieth Century," *Journal of Social Issues* 35 (no. 3, 1979): 87–114.
14. Brashler, *Don*, pp. 81–83.
15. Ivan Light, "Numbers Gambling among Blacks: A Financial Institution," *American Sociological Review* 42 (Dec. 1977): 892–904; Haller, "American Gambling," p. 93; Ianni, *Black Mafia*, p. 93.
16. Ianni, *Black Mafia*, pp. 110–11; Haller, "American Gambling," pp. 94–95; Jervis Anderson, "That Was New York (Harlem—Part III)," *New Yorker* (July 13, 1981): 72.
17. Ben Hayllar, "All about the Numbers," *Pittsburgh* 2 (Oct. 1972): 39; William Rimmel, in *Pittsburgh Post-Gazette*, 1/3/81; *Pittsburgh Press*, 2/10/36; *Bulletin Index*, 2/20/36. Countless interviews and conversations about Pittsburgh confirm this view.
18. Interview with Charles Greenlee, 6/18/80.
19. Interview with Ralph Koger, 7/8/80, Pittsburgh.

20. Interview with Clarence Clark, 8/2/80, Pittsburgh.

21. This story was confirmed by several unidentified black men in their late seventies in discussions at the Crawford Grill, 6/27/80.

22. Interview with Clarence Clark, 8/2/80.

23. *Pittsburgh Courier* 1/7/33, p. 1.

24. *Pittsburgh Press,* 1/30/36.

25. *Bulletin Index,* 2/20/36; *Pittsburgh Courier,* 7/14/28, p. 1; 7/21/28, p. 9.

26. For a recounting of the 8-0-5 disaster, see *Pittsburgh Post,* 2/13/36.

27. Ibid.

28. Interview with Sam Solomon, 1/29/81, Pittsburgh.

29. Interviews with Clarence Clark, 8/20/80; Charles Greenlee, 6/18/80; Ralph Koger, 7/8/80; Sam Solomon, 1/29/81; Teenie Harris, 2/23/81, Pittsburgh.

30. The best source of this is Haller, "American Gambling." The black numbers operators generally lost money as a result.

31. *Pittsburgh Press,* 7/30/32.

32. Benjamin Hayllar, Jr., "The Accommodation: The History and Rhetoric of the Rackets—Political Alliance in Pittsburgh" (Ph.D. thesis, University of Pittsburgh, 1977).

33. The heavy turnout in black parts of New York City for the 1964 elections, for example, was in large part a result of the efforts of the numbers community. As Fred Cook reported in "The Black Mafia Moves into the Numbers Racket," *New York Times Magazine,* Apr. 4, 1971, p. 108:

The community people who were strongly anti-Goldwater got together and decided to offer a special inducement. All the numbers boys were in on it. They agreed to give a $1 free play on the numbers to those who would register to vote. The controllers and runners sent cars to drive voters to the polls on Election Day; and if a woman had children at home and couldn't leave them, one of the numbers boys sat with the kids while she was driven in the Cadillac down to the polling place. I don't think the city politicians ever really understood why the Harlem vote was so heavy that year and nobody told them.

34. *Pittsburgh Post,* 9/21/26, p. 1.

35. *Pittsburgh Post-Gazette,* 2/13/26, 8/17/32.

36. Ibid. If 5,000 seems a high figure, estimates as high as 100,000 exist for the total employed by the numbers in New York City in 1971. Cook, "Black Mafia," p. 26. James Lolton, identified as a New York City official on an NBC special report entitled "Gambling" (12/27/80, David Brinkley and Lloyd Dobbins), estimated there were 400,000 part-time employees in New York, making the numbers the fourth largest employer in the state.

38. Hayllar, "Accommodation," p. 117; interviews with James Rooney, 3/1/82, Pittsburgh; Clarence Clark, 8/2/80.

39. Interview with Nick Raddick, 7/11/80, Pittsburgh. Confirmation of Rooney's involvement in the rackets: interviews with Sam Solomon, 1/29/81; Archie Litman, 7/15/82; Jack Parker, 6/28/80; Joe Ware, 7/15/80. Art Rooney, however, denies any involvement in racket-related activity: "I never was in the

numbers business in my life. Never had anything to do with it." He does, however, acknowledge that, "Maybe they [numbers men and racketeers] contributed to the campaign and all that, but they had absolutely no other connection." Interview with Art Rooney, 7/30/80, Pittsburgh.

40. Ibid.

41. Interviews with Gabe Patterson, 7/12/80; Joe Ware, 6/28/80, Pittsburgh.

42. This distinction was suggested by Ralph Koger, 7/8/80.

43. Interview with Walter Rainey, 2/12/80, Pittsburgh.

44. Interviews with Clarence Clark, 8/2/80; Joe Ware, 6/28/80; Jack Parker, 7/15/80; Charles Greenlee, 6/18/80; Ralph Koger, 7/8/80.

45. Interview with Joe Ware, 6/28/80.

46. Interview with Charles Greenlee, 6/18/80.

47. Interview with Clarence Clark, 8/2/80.

48. Interview with Gabe Patterson, 7/12/80.

49. Interview with Charlie Hughes, 2/1/81.

50. *1938 Yearbook of the National Semi-pro Baseball Congress*, "Sandlot Files," National Baseball Library; interview with Bill Harris, 6/19/80.

51. Interview with Clarence Clark, 8/20/80.

52. *Pittsburgh Courier*, 6/13/30, sec. 2, p. 4.

53. Ibid., 4/14/34, sec. 2, p. 5.

54. Interview with Bill Harris, 6/19/80.

55. *Pittsburgh Courier*, 6/20/31, sec. 2, p. 4.

56. Interview with Harold Tinker, 6/19/80.

57. Ibid.

58. Ibid.

59. *Pittsburgh Courier*, 2/27/32, sec. 2, p. 4.

60. Ibid.; 4/6/45, p. 23.

61. Interviews with Ralph Koger, 7/8/80; Charles Greenlee, 6/18/80; Clarence Clark, 8/20/80; *Pittsburgh Courier*, 4/15/39, p. 17.

62. He persuaded the president of the company, which had been hard hit by the depression, to become president of his Bedford Land and Improvement Company.

63. *Pittsburgh Courier*, 7/9/32, sec. 2, p. 4.

64. Ibid., 4/9/32, sec. 2, p. 5; 5/7/32, sec. 2, p. 4; 5/21/32, sec. 2, p. 4; 7/30/32, sec. 2, p. 4; 7/9/32, sec. 2, p. 4.

65. Greenlee Field, according to John L. Clark, could seat about 7,000 fans for baseball. *Pittsburgh Courier*, 12/10/38; 9/17/32, sec. 2, p. 4; 10/1/32, sec. 2, p. 4; 11/19/32, sec. 1, p. 1; 12/3/32, sec. 2, p. 4; 9/17/32, sec. 2, p. 5; 4/15/33, sec. 2, p. 4.

66. Figures are from an exhibit on black baseball in Three Rivers Hall of Fame and *Pittsburgh Courier*, 3/13/37, p. 16. The Crawfords played over 100 games to reach the 200,000 attendance mark. Ibid., 2/22/41, p. 17; 5/9/36, sec. 2, p. 4.

67. Interview with Charles Greenlee, 6/18/80.

68. *Pittsburgh Courier*, 6/5/35, p. 17.

69. Ibid., 4/15/39, p. 17, reprints Povich's column from the *Washington Star*, 4/6/39.
70. Undated column by Jim Murray in files of National Baseball Library.
71. *Pittsburgh Courier*, 6/15/37, p. 17.
72. Interviews with Winston Llenas, Pedro Garcia, Octavio Acosta, Tomas Silverio, and Manny Mota in Santo Domingo, Santiago, and San Pedro de Macoris, Dominican Republic, January 18–30, 1984. Peterson, *Ball*, pp. 135–37; Brashler, *Gibson*, pp. 105–11. Interviews with Ted Page, Buck Leonard, Chet Brewer, Ray Dandridge, and Effa Manley, all June 24, 1980, Ashland, Ky.
73. *Pittsburgh Courier*, 3/27/37, p. 16.
74. Ibid., 4/18/37, p. 18.
75. Ibid., 12/10/38, p. 17.
76. Ibid.
77. Ibid.
78. Ibid., 3/25/39, p. 17.
79. Ibid., 4/8/39, p. 15.
80. Ibid., 4/22/39, p. 17.
81. Interview with Charles Greenlee, 6/18/80.
82. *Pittsburgh Courier*, 7/17/39, p. 17; 12/11/37, p. 16.
83. Ibid., 10/26/35, sec. 2, p. 4.
84. Ibid., 11/9/35, sec. 2, p. 4.
85. Ibid., 5/27/49, p. 21.
86. Ibid., 4/3/37, sec. 2, p. 6.
87. Joe Louis, with Art and Edna Rust, *Joe Louis: My Life* (New York: Harcourt Brace Jovanovich, 1978) pp. 29–32, 79, 146–47.
88. *Pittsburgh Courier*, 12/31/38, p. 15; 1/28/39, p. 1; 1/14/39, p. 15.
89. Ibid., 6/24/39, p. 15; 5/13/39, p. 17.
90. Ibid., 5/13/39, p. 17.

6 The Decline of Black Sport

1. *Pittsburgh Courier*, 10/1/32, sec. 2, p. 4.
2. Ibid., 4/6/46, sec. 2, p. 1.
3. Joe Ware and Jack Parker thought that Jackson came to Posey's rescue partially at the urging of Gus Greenlee and Woogie Harris, with whom Jackson maintained cordial friendships; Greenlee, they thought, had wanted to best Posey on the ball field, not run him out of business. I could not, however, corroborate this argument.
4. Interviews with Helen Jackson, 7/30/80; Cos Blount, 7/30/80, Pittsburgh; *Pittsburgh Courier*, 10/10/36; sec. 2, p. 4; 2/7/42, p. 17; 1/25/47, p. 16.
5. Ibid., 4/8/32, sec. 2, p. 4.
6. Ibid., 7/8/39, p. 17.
7. Ibid., 7/29/39, p. 15.
8. Ibid., 10/4/41, p. 17.
9. Ibid., 4/29/50, p. 25.

10. Ibid., p. 20.

11. Ibid., 6/3/44, p. 17.

12. Ibid., 7/17/43, p. 18; 7/31/43, p. 18.

13. Randy Dixon, in ibid., 2/4/39, p. 16.

14. Wendell Smith, in ibid., 4/27/40, p. 14.

15. Ibid., 4/27/40, p. 14.

16. Ibid.

17. Ibid., 4/7/45, p. 17; 4/21/45, p. 17; 9/14/46, p. 27.

18. Seymour, *Baseball,* vol. 2, pp. 414–15. The development of a farm system meant that the St. Louis Cardinal organization controlled considerably more baseball talent than its competitors. This vast player pool allowed Branch Rickey and the St. Louis front office to keep the Cardinals in the forefront year after year, make a profit by selling minor leaguers to other teams, and hold player salaries down by pointing out to their regulars that they were not irreplaceable.

19. *Pittsburgh Courier,* 5/12/45, p. 17.

20. Ibid., 3/17/51, p. 17.

21. Ibid., 5/19/45, p. 16.

22. Tim Cohane, "A Branch Grows in Brooklyn," *Look,* Mar. 19, 1946, p. 16, quoted in Lee Lowenfish, "Sport, Race and the Baseball Business: The Jackie Robinson Story Revisited," *Arena Review* 2 (no. 2, Spring 1978): 2.

23. Peterson, *Ball,* p. 186.

24. Lowenfish, "Robinson," p. 3; Peterson, *Ball,* p. 185–86.

25. Wendell Smith, who claims he was a confidant to both Rickey and Greenlee in these matters, discussed their relationship in the *Pittsburgh Courier,* 7/19/52, p. 24.

26. A good analysis of Rickey's motives can be found in Lowenfish, "Robinson." A recent addition to the Robinson story is Jules Tygiel, *Baseball's Great Experiment: Jackie Robinson and His Legacy* (New York: Oxford University Press, 1983).

27. *New York Amsterdam News,* 10/5/46, clipping in the National Baseball Library files.

28. *Pittsburgh Courier,* 4/6/46, p. 23.

29. Ches Washington, in ibid., p. 27.

30. Ibid.

31. Ibid., p. 1.

32. Ibid., 8/3/46, p. 26.

33. Ibid., 9/24/49, p. 23.

34. Brashler, *Gibson,* p. 135.

35. *Pittsburgh Courier,* 9/1/51, p. 1; interview with Helen Jackson, 7/30/80.

36. *Pittsburgh Courier,* 12/9/50, p. 22.

37. Ibid., 7/12/51, p. 1.

38. Objoski, *Bush League,* p. 27.

39. *Pitttsburgh Courier,* 12/29/45, p. 1.

40. Ibid., 3/2/46, p. 1.

41. Ibid., 6/31/47.

42. See Lowenfish, "Robinson," p. 9.

43. *Pittsburgh Courier*, 7/20/47, p. 25.

44. Interview with Effa Manley, 6/24/80, Ashland, Ky. See also Effa Manley and Leon H. Hardwick, *Negro Baseball Before Integration* (Chicago: Adams Press, 1976), pp. 93–101.

45. Holway, *Voices*, p. 271.

46. *Pittsburgh Courier*, 10/16/48, p. 11.

47. There are no records of black attendance at Pirate and Steeler games (or, for that matter, at pro sports in general). It was the recollection of most people I talked with that black Pittsburghers were more likely to see Negro League and black sandlot games than the Pirates or the Steelers in the years before major league baseball was integrated. Many also thought that black attendance increased considerably when Robinson and the Dodgers, and then other black athletes, started playing in Pittsburgh. As to the evidence to support my argument that the Pirates and the Steelers became black Pittsburgh's teams, I confess that it is mostly my observations and conclusions after talking with many black Pittsburghers over the past twenty-five years.

48. Ibid., 8/26/33, p. 5.

49. Ibid., 10/14/39, p. 17.

50. Ibid., 2/12/38, p. 17.

51. Ibid., 9/2/39, p. 16.

52. Ibid., 8/1/42, p. 1.

53. Ibid., 8/28/42, p. 17.

54. Interview with Eleanor Benswanger, 6/11/80, Pittsburgh; *Pittsburgh Courier*, 4/28/45, p. 16.

55. *Pittsburgh Courier*, 1/28/50, p. 21.

56. Ibid., 3/17/46, p. 27.

57. Ibid., 3/25/50, p. 24.

58. Ibid., 4/17/54, p. 27. Another black player, pitcher Lino Dinoso, reported to spring training that season but was sent to the minors before opening day. Dinoso, a left-handed Puerto Rican hurler, had previously played in the Negro American League.

59. Ibid., 7/31/56, p. 3.

60. Reichler, *Baseball Encyclopedia*, p. 819.

61. Interview with Ray Kemp, 7/17/81, Pittsburgh.

62. *Pittsburgh Courier*, 12/7/46, p. 26.

63. Interview with Ed Fleming, 12/19/84, Wilkinsburg, Pa.

64. Ibid.

65. Ibid.

66. Ibid.; interviews with Carl Kohlman, 12/4/84, and George Cupples, 12/21/84, Pittsburgh.

67. Interview with George Cupples, 12/21/84.

68. Black control continues today, mostly at black colleges and in public schools where blacks comprise a large portion of the student body. In the latter, however, coaches and administrators are often white.

69. Subcommittee Hearings on Interstate and Foreign Commerce, "Broadcasting and Televising Baseball Games," U.S. Senate, 83rd Cong., 1st sess., May 1953, U.S. Government Printing Office, Washington, D.C., p. 3.

70. "Organized Baseball," p. 383.

71. Antitrust Subcommittee, "Organized Team Sports," House of Representatives, 85th Cong., 1st sess., U.S. Government Printing Office, Washington, D.C., June–August 1957, p. 190.

72. Ibid., p. 194. For example, the Red Wings of the International League had been the focus of baseball in Rochester since the turn of the century. A St. Louis Cardinal farm club since 1928, the Red Wings were on the chopping block in 1956 following a drop in attendance to 180,000. Rochester residents mobilized to prevent their team's demise, forming Rochester Community Baseball, Inc., which bought the club from the Cardinals. The organization was made up of over 8,000 local fans who, with no expectation of dividends or capital gains, bought stock in this public corporation in order to keep their team in town. The quasi-public ownership was a success, and in 1971 attendance was up to 463,000. Objoski, *Bush League,* pp. 124–32.

73. "Broadcasting and Televising Baseball Games," pp. 11–18.

74. Minor league ball then was divided among four levels, A, B, C, and D, in descending order of skill.

75. Ibid., p. 23.

76. Ibid., p. 38.

77. Subcommittee on Antitrust and Monopoly, "Organized Professional Team Sports," U.S. Senate, 85th Cong., 2nd sess., U.S. Government Printing Office, Washington, D.C., July 1958, p. 209.

78. Interview with Charles Kramer, 2/6/81.

79. "Organized baseball,", p. 1473.

80. William O. Johnson, "TV Made It All a New Game," *Sports Illustrated,* Dec. 22, 1969, p. 101.

81. Philip Hochberg and Ira Horowitz, "Broadcasting and CATV: The Beauty and the Bane of Major College Football," *Law and Contemporary Problems* 38 (no. 1, Winter–Spring 1973): 115.

82. Robert Hill, "TV Money May Wreck College Athletics," *Sports Illustrated,* Jan. 10, 1955, pp. 52–53.

83. Johnson, "New Game," p. 102.

84. Ibid., p. 86.

85. Glen Waggoner, "Money Games," *Esquire,* June 1982, p. 53.

86. "Organized Team Sports," pp. 2574, 2630, 2718.

87. "Organized Professional Team Sports," p. 803.

88. Johnson, "New Game," p. 90.

89. Ibid., p. 88.

90. "Organized Professional Team Sports," p. 656.

91. "Broadcasting and Televising Baseball Games," p. 138.

92. Ibid., p. 800.

93. Ibid.

94. Ibid., p. 780.

95. Cuba, of course, left organized baseball's system after its revolution.

96. "Organized Professional Team Sports," pp. 1184–1257; "Organized Baseball," pp. 230–33.

97. To an increasing extent major league baseball has come to rely on the colleges for developing players in a fashion similar to pro football and basketball.

98. Interviews with Jack Hopkins, 1/6/81; Harold Tinker, 6/19/80; Gil Gordon, 12/31/80.

99. *Pittsburgh Courier,* 5/2/53, p. 27.

100. Interview with Gil Gordon, 12/31/80.

101. Interview with James Stewart, 5/28/80.

102. Interview with Charles Klausing, 2/4/81.

103. Bodnar et al., *Lives,* pp. 186, 231.

104. Undated press clipping in "Sandlot Files," National Baseball Library.

105. An increasing number of these teams are women's and girls' squads, a relatively recent development. *Pittsburgh Press,* 8/13/81.

106. *New York Times,* 1/19/81.

107. Basketball now dominates the sporting component of that street life.

108. This has been offset, to some extent, by the expansion of professional football and basketball. The total number of professional athletes in the United States, however, remains relatively small.

109. By this I mean football, basketball, and baseball, not softball.

110. Interviews with Ralph Mellix, 6/10/80, 6/11/80; Willis Moody, 1/6/81; Ocey Swain, 9/14/81; Jack Hopkins, 1/6/81; Harold Tinker, 6/19/80.

111. Interviews with Willis Moody, 1/6/81; Gabe Patterson, 7/12/80; Harold Tinker, 6/19/80; Bill Harris, 6/19/80; Larnell Goodman, 7/23/81.

112. Interviews with Gil Gordon, 12/31/80; Ray Irvin, 12/12/80; Harold Tinker, 6/19/80.

113. To some extent the largely segregated nature of Pittsburgh and Allegheny County schools kept some city and area teams largely black. Westinghouse's mostly black football teams dominated the city league, while Braddock reigned in the Monongahela valley. But these programs gradually lost their competitive edge over white schools in the 1960s and 1970s due to unequal enrollments and athletic budgets. They were, however, a complementary focus for black Pittsburgh sport.

114. Jeep Kelley and Ricky Coleman were Lucas's talented backcourt teammates on Schenley High School's 1971 state championship team. Jeep, who dropped out of two schools, and Ricky, who played college ball but failed a tryout with the Boston Celtics, never joined Lucas in the pros. In 1984 they were serving prison sentences after conviction for the possession and delivery of heroin.

Index

Easterling, Howard, 174
Eastern Colored League, 124, 134–35
East Liberty, 12, 13, 15, 58, 64–65, 77
East Liberty Scholastics, 94
East Liberty Stars, 40
East-West Classic, 120–21, 157, 175, 185
East-West League, 119, 136, 155, 170
Ebbetts Field, 177, 184
Edgar Thomson Steel Works clubs, 29–
30, 32, 36–37, 50–53
18th Ward, 4, 45, 62–76, 108–9, 112,
115, 204, 207–8
18th Ward Juniors, 72, 76
Elks, 102, 170
Ethiopian (Cincinnati) Clowns, 121–22
Evers, Johnny, 123

Falcons, 111
Federal League, 199
Fifth Avenue Braves, 85, 108
Fifth Avenue High School, 51, 80, 194
Fifth Ward, 13, 69, 88–89
Fleming, Ed, 193–94
Flinn, William, 147
Forbes Field, 41, 61–62, 83, 90, 133,
135, 173–74, 184, 186–87, 189–90
Ford, Henry, 85, 192
Foster, Andrew ("Rube"), 122–24, 130,
134
Foster, Willie, 132
Frick, Ford, 196
Frogs Club, 180
Fuchs, Billy, 87, 108–9

Galbreath, John, 188
Galento, Two-Ton Tony, 167
Gant, Norman, 85, 90
Garagiola, Joe, 159
Gardner, L. C., 24–25, 35
Garfield, 92–107, 114, 207–8
Garfield ABCs, 50, 60
Garfield Eagles, 4, 45, 51, 94–106, 112,
114, 204, 206–8
Garfield Eagles Social Club, 101–3, 105–
6
Garfield Merchants, 96
Garlick, Bus, 108
Gauffney, Dick, 142–43
Gibson, Josh, 20, 51, 53–55, 67, 74,
154–55, 158–59, 162, 172, 174, 180–
81, 187, 207, 209
Gibson, Josh, Jr., 90
Gibson, Pete, 194
Gilchrist, Cookie, 210
Gilmore, George, 127
Gimbel Brothers, 30–31, 53

Glick, Charlie, 82
Goodman, Cary, 17
Goodman, Larnell, 92–93, 105–6
Gordon, Gil, 197, 200–201
Goslin, Goose, 132
Gottlieb, Eddie, 117–20, 122, 162–63
Great Depression, 13, 33, 44, 77–78, 95
Greenlee, Dr. Charles, 138, 142, 158,
164–65, 168
Greenlee, Dr. Jack, 168
Greenlee, William A. ("Gus"), 5, 49, 99,
114, 117, 120, 122, 137–172, 174–76,
178–82, 208
Greenlee Field, 99, 137, 155–57, 163–64
Greenwood, L. C., 192
Griffin Stadium, 173
Griffith, Clark, 177, 199
Groat, Dick, 194
Grove, Lefty, 132
Guinea, A. J., 174

Hall, Harry, 48–49
Hall, Sellers, 64, 66, 74, 94, 126–27,
129, 134, 217–18n
Harlem, 14, 38, 141–42
Harlem Globetrotters, 120–21, 192
Harlem Stars, 118
Harris, Bill, 46–62, 113, 152–54
Harris, Earl, 46
Harris, Franco, 192
Harris, Mo, 129–30
Harris, Muscles, 98–99
Harris, Neal, 29, 50–51, 60
Harris, Teenie, 47–49, 145
Harris, Vic, 22, 62, 130, 172, 174
Harris, Woody, 20
Harris, Woogie, 50, 142–51, 168
Harrisburg Giants, 134
Hawkins, Connie, 194
Hays, Carlton, 143
Hemlock Athletic Club, 32
Herlong, Sid, 110
Herron, John, 29, 50
Highland Park Pool, 15
Hilldale Club, 118, 135–36, 155
Hill district, 9–13, 15–19, 37, 46–62, 64,
77–80, 88–90, 125, 137–65, 194, 203,
207–8
Hobson, Robert ("Doug"), 128
Holmes, Ernie, 192
Holstein, Caspar, 141
Holy Cross Athletic Club, 32
Holy Ghost College, 125
Homestead, 8, 11, 27–30, 32–34, 124–
36, 138, 151, 170–73
Homestead Grays, 4, 5, 29, 30, 45, 49,

A Note on the Author

ROB RUCK, a Pittsburgh-based writer and historian, is a graduate of Yale University and holds a Ph.D. from the University of Pittsburgh, where he is on the faculty of the Center for Latin American Studies and a fellow at the Social History Center. The author of *The Tropic of Baseball: Baseball in the Dominican Republic* and coauthor of *Steve Nelson: American Radical,* his work has also appeared in the *Washington Post,* the *Los Angeles Times,* and *Baseball History.* Since 1989 he has been collaborating with Molly Youngling on *Kings on the Hill: Baseball's Forgotten Men,* a documentary that resulted from this book.

Books in the Series Sport and Society

A Sporting Time: New York City and the Rise of Modern Athletics,
1820–70
Melvin L. Adelman

Sandlot Seasons: Sport in Black Pittsburgh
Rob Ruck

West Ham United: The Making of a Football Club
Charles Korr

Beyond the Ring: The Role of Boxing in American Society
Jeffrey T. Sammons

John L. Sullivan and His America
Michael T. Isenberg

Television and National Sport: The United States and Britain
Joan M. Chandler

The Creation of American Team Sports: Baseball and Cricket, 1838–72
George B. Kirsch

City Games: The Evolution of American Urban Society and
the Rise of Sports
Steven A. Riess

The Brawn Drain: Foreign Student-Athletes in American Universities
John Bale

The Business of Professional Sports
Edited by Paul D. Staudohar and James A. Mangan

Fritz Pollard: Pioneer in Racial Advancement
John M. Carroll

Go Big Red! The Story of a Nebraska Football Player
George Mills

Sport and Exercise Science: Essays in the History of Sports Medicine
Edited by Jack W. Berryman and Roberta J. Park

Minor League Baseball and Local Economic Development
Arthur T. Johnson

Harry Hooper: An American Baseball Life
Paul J. Zingg

Cowgirls of the Rodeo: Pioneer Professional Athletes
Mary Lou LeCompte

REPRINT EDITIONS

The Nazi Olympics
Richard D. Mandell

Sports in the Western World
Second Edition
William J. Baker